Elisabetta Marchetti Letta

Introduction by Roberto Paolo Ciardi

PONTORMO ROSSO FIORENTINO

SCALA/RIVERSIDE

CONTENTS

Translation: Anthony Brierley
Layout: Ilaria Casalino
Photographs: SCALA (M. Falsini and M. Sarri) except for: n.° 8 (M. Rabatti and S. Domingie); n.os 19, 20 (Izobrazitelnoye Iskusstvo); n.os 21-25 (reproduced by courtesy of the Trustees, The National Gallery, London); n.° 34 (Los Angeles County Museum of Art, Gift of Dr. and Mrs. Herbert T. Kalmus); n.° 84 (Collection of the J. Paul Getty Museum, Malibu); n.° 100 (Charles Potter Kling Fund, Courtesy, Museum of Fine Arts, Boston); n.° 102 (reproduced by courtesy of the Trustees, The Walker Art Gallery, Liverpool)
Produced by SCALA
Printed in Italy by Amilcare Pizzi S.p.A.-arti grafiche Cinisello Balsamo (Milan), 1994

Page 80. Pontormo
Study for a Boy with a Turban
Florence, Prints and Drawings Collection of the Uffizi, no. 449 F r

Introduction

The almost identical birth dates — barely three months apart in the unsettled Florentine spring of 1494 — are certainly not the only thing Pontormo and Rosso Fiorentino have in common. A series of coincidences and affinities, not all of which can be considered fortuitous, joins their two lives, giving substance to the interpretation that was advanced in the great historical syntheses of the beginning of the century. Earning a place in school textbooks and consequently rooted in popular culture, this sees the two Tuscan painters as, if not exactly Siamese twins, at least the Dioscuri of incipient Mannerism. The two artists are united by the fact of being pupils of Andrea del Sarto — Pontormo certainly, Rosso probably — and their resolute, though far from slavish reference to other great artistic models: the "world school" of the cartoon for the *Battle of Cascina* and Michelangelo in general, and then the works of Leonardo and Fra Bartolomeo, Jacopo and Andrea Sansovino, Masaccio and Donatello.

The parallels between their careers are striking, punctuated as they are by matching dates that mark a series of professional achievements, of links with patrons, and of often ambivalent relations with the artistic tendencies of an extremely cultivated and at the same time difficult Florentine artistic milieu: between 1514 and 1516 the works in the complex of Santissima Annunziata and the decorations in Florence to celebrate the visit of Pope Leo X; in 1518 the contemporaneous completion of the altarpieces for San Michele Visdomini and Ognissanti; in the early 1520s the probable execution of the *Madonna and Child with two saints and two putti*, now in the Uffizi, and the certain execution of the *Madonna and Child with two saints*, formerly in Villamagna.

That all this may lead to a rearrangement — and consequent reinterpretation — of two biographies within the parameters of two parallel lives is acceptable, provided that hasty conclusions about possible parallels in style, or even merely about similarities at a typological level are avoided. Indeed, it is precisely the dual courses of their respective careers that make it easier to identify different and sometimes opposing results.

Vasari had already realized this, emphasizing the differences by inserting the biographies of about thirty more or less contemporary artists between those of Pontormo and Rosso (in Lanzi, on the other hand, the two biographies were practically adjacent), and placing the Florentine artist further back than his contemporary Pontormo, almost on the threshold of the "modern Manner." Vasari's version is also different in tone, being more anecdotal and descriptive, but also more laudatory and heroic in tone in the case of Rosso, whose talent and inventiveness he greatly admires; in the case of Pontormo it is more precise and analytical, greater emphasis being placed on the artist's creative torment, his dissatisfaction with results that were perceived as limited, leading to an uncertainty, alienation and solitude that were not merely physical and social, but also intellectual and existential.

In spite of this, both accounts, even though they place the emphasis on content and on psychological considerations, and are therefore irremediably approximate from the present critical point of view, discern in the works a distinct divergence in results that were attained from the starting-point of common tendencies and similar experiences.

Scholars have recently stressed the fundamental importance of ideas drawn from sculpture in the work of the two artists, particularly 15th-century sculpture, in which it is possible to identify not only the source of numerous citations, but even the model for the development of analogous systems of working. The admitted equivalence of the two sister arts, so dear to Renaissance theorists, encouraging the interpretation of painting in terms of sculpture (and vice versa), authorized the appropriation of common elements of composition and their use in mirrorwise or back-to-front versions. This is at first sight more obvious with Rosso, whose relations with the sculptor Baccio Bandinelli and interest in the technique of relief, at least at the level of design, at the time of the stucco decoration of the gallery at Fontainebleau, are well-known. But that Pontormo was also particularly interested in sculpture is confirmed by Vasari, who, in reference to the lost frescoes in the choir of the Florentine church of San Lorenzo, insists on the fact that Pontormo had made "finished models of clay in full relief" for all the main figures of that vast composition, adhering therefore to an already tried and tested technical procedure that was destined to have considerable success in the future.

Both Rosso and Pontormo recognized Donatello as one of their main influence in this regard. In him, in fact, the vital sense of power and the expressive turmoil in the direct representation of gestures and feelings, do not shrink, where necessary, from the laying bare of forms, an aggressive treatment of space, quivering luministic effects and a harsh and brutal approach to design. In this his work responded to the expectations and to the sense of crisis that pervaded those years to a greater extent than did the controlled elegance and masterly refinement of other sculptural models.

This same source, however, was to play a very different role in the work of the two painters. In Rosso the representation of groups and details served as a support for a simplification of composition and as a justification for a deliberate, controlled archaism, given that in him — in this and in other cases of evident direct influence (Masaccio, Paolo Uccello) — the feedback of morphologies and types was intended as an artistic updating that broke with current figurative conventions. In Pontormo, on the other hand, the ideas drawn from Donatello — from the *Abraham* formerly in Giotto's bell-tower or from the *St Jerome* in Faenza for the *Pucci Altarpiece*, and from the *Beardless Prophet* or the *Habakkuk* for the panel in the Uffizi — served to make plain the relationship between body, with correlated facial markings, and emphatically underlined gesture. A comparison between the pairs of putti sitting on the steps of the throne in the altarpieces by Rosso and Pontormo, now in the Uffizi (one coming from the collection of Carlo de' Medici and the other from Ognissanti), is indicative: in the first case we have a sequence of open symbols for successive contrasts that are produced in the correspondance between gestures and bodies, where any mirrorwise repetition is carefully avoided; in the other we see a linking together of closed, compact forms, in a series of reciprocal modulations that reunites and fuses the variability of gestures in the unitariness of the postures.

That the choice of stylistically diverse options, derived though they may have been from Donatello's whole body of work, resulted, in general, in the two painters taking a different approach to the modes of representation and communication is a fact. It suffices to consider the role played in Pontormo's work by gestures and glances, which serve to enhance the intensity of the image and reconnect elements of the structures. Their lines of vision that extend beyond the spatial limit of the representation succeed in involving even the spectator. In Rosso, on the other hand, the drastic confinement of actions and gestures within the planes of vision that bind together the single characters or frame the compositions, and the cancelling of the transitive function of the glances that dissolve their emotional value, allude to a quite different consciousness of existence. Thus the contrasting demarcation of the connotations of postures, actions and expressions in two works executed at around the same time, the *Deposition* in Santa Felicita and the *Moses defending the Daughters of Jethro*, leads to opposing definitions of places, states and emotions, and indicates a divergence in artistic, and perhaps not only artistic, temperament.

For this reason, the not inconsiderable merit of the pages that follow, in which the clarity and style of the smoothly flowing text illuminate the refinement of the analytical interpretations, seems to me to be that of having followed the paths — which interweave and sometimes overlap — taken by the two great Mannerists. At the same time the stylistic distinction between the two different personalities is always clearly and critically presented against the exceptional background of Florence in the first half of the 16th century.

1. Pontormo
Madonna and Child with two saints, detail of the putti
Florence, Uffizi

2. Rosso Fiorentino
Madonna enthroned with four saints, detail of the putti
Florence, Uffizi

3, 4. Portraits of Pontormo and Rosso Fiorentino taken from the 1906 edition of Giorgio Vasari's 'Lives'

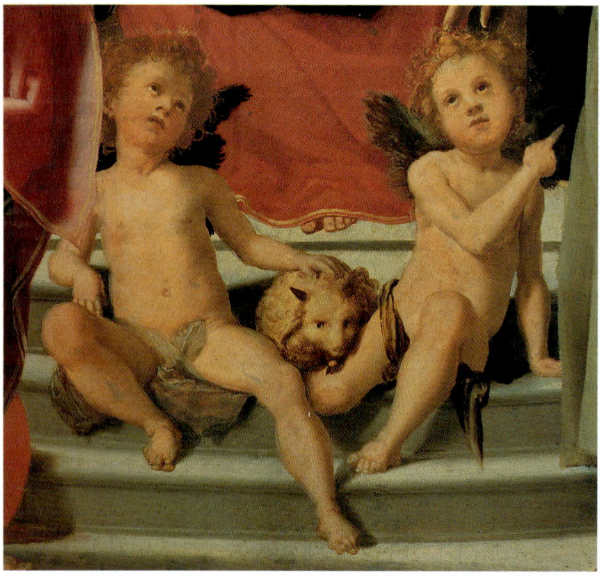

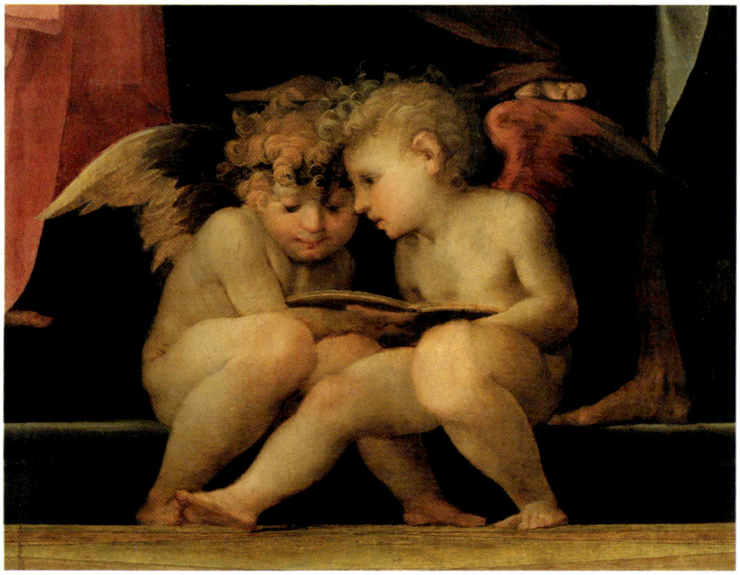

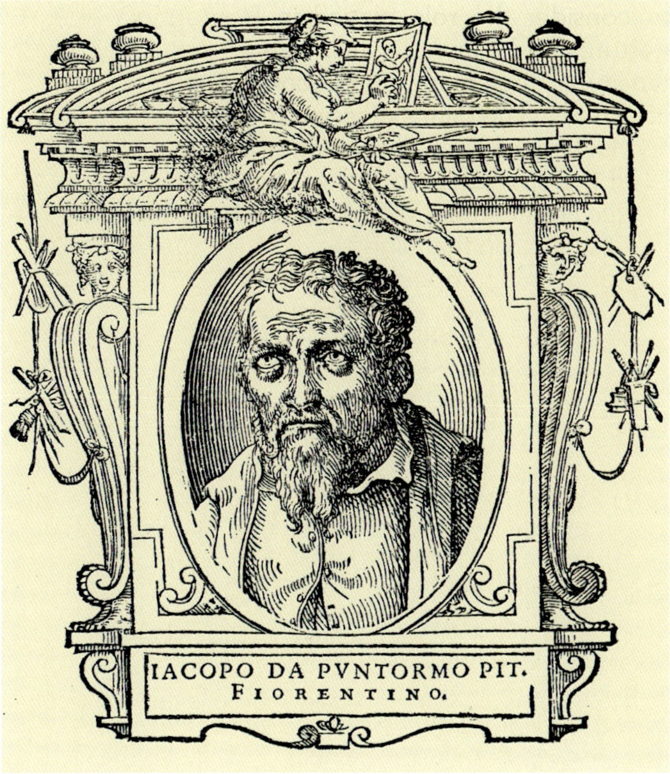

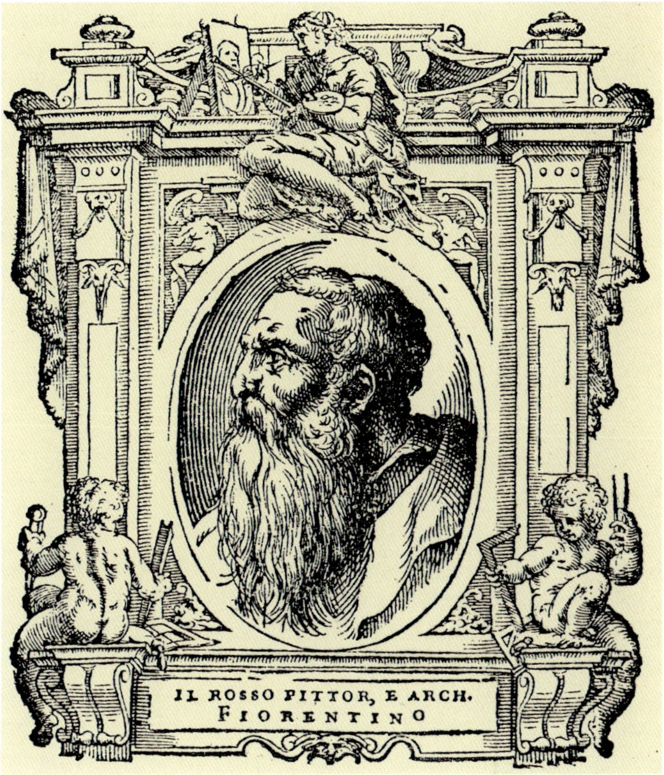

Pontormo and Rosso Fiorentino. The artists of "crisis"

The year in which Pontormo and Rosso Fiorentino were born, 1494, was a watershed dividing a period of stability from an age of political upheaval.

During the 15th century, great cultural and economic development took place within a fragile political structure, that of the regional states. While the great nation states of Europe were consolidating their power and revealing their expansionist aims, in Italy the difficult political equilibrium between the states was safeguarded by the shrewd diplomacy of Lorenzo il Magnifico.

Lorenzo died in 1492. Two years later, in 1494, Charles VIII of France entered Italy to claim the Kingdom of Naples. A period of turmoil ensued, during which the whole peninsula was caught up in the midst of conflicts between France and Spain. The hostilities ended only in 1559, with the peace of Cateau Cambrésis and the final inclusion of Italy in the sphere of Spanish rule.

This turbulent reality was reflected in Florence, the artistic homeland of Pontormo and Rosso Fiorentino. In 1494 the Medici family was exiled by Charles VIII and the Republic of Fra Gerolamo Savonarola was proclaimed. In 1512 Medici rule was re-established with the aid of the Spanish. In 1527, following the sack of Rome, the Florentines again proclaimed the Republic. The Medici dynasty established its rule in the city in 1530, again with the support of the Spanish, although this time in the form of a ducal state, thus giving political form to a profound change of climate.

Pontormo and Rosso Fiorentino grew up in this unsettled period in which destabilizing political developments were accompanied, in the figurative arts, by a profound crisis affecting the principles and rules of the Renaissance. In the very dissolution of formal and ideal harmony that had been reached during the watershed of those few years at the beginning of the 16th century lay the roots of that enduring phenomenon known as "Mannerism".

The name derives from the word "manner", which had already been used in 15th-century artistic literature to denote an artist's individual style, or the style of a given period. It is with Vasari, however, that this term acquired crucial significance. In the third part of the *Lives*, in fact, the author speaks of the *gran maniera* of his time, acknowledging its greatest exponents as Leonardo, Michelangelo and Raphael, artists who were at the apex of that upswing in Italian art that had begun with Cimabue and Giotto at the end of the 13th century. These three masters reached perfection in the representation of ideal beauty, attained through a selection of the best components of natural reality, demonstrating that in their works they surpassed the art of the ancients and nature itself. According to Vasari, all artists aspiring to the *bella maniera* could not but look to these three great models as an example.

In Vasari's work, therefore, "manner" had a positive meaning. Only later (17th/18th century) would the term, transformed into "Mannerism", assume a negative connotation. Artists labelled as Mannerists were those who no longer had nature as a model, according to the Renaissance ideal, but the "manner" of the three illustrious masters. Their work was harshly criticized as being an alteration of natural truth and a trite repetition of formulas. Only at the beginning of the present century was there a positive reappraisal of the anticlassical aspects of "Mannerism" and of the artists that represented it. As studies have advanced, it has been increasingly difficult to group together under this single term a series of phenomena that are diversified and often removed in time, phenomena that many have preferred to associate with the so-called "crisis" of the Renaissance.

The fundamental elements of this complex phase in Italian art, in which the basic principles of early 16th-century culture are questioned, can be found in the figurative style of Rosso and Pontormo, in their troubled and incessant dialogue with the great models of the mature Renaissance. Leonardo, Michelangelo and Raphael, departing from 15th-century figurative achievements, obtained undeniable results of extraordinary equilibrium in the representation of space, of nature, of the human figure anatomically described and plastically defined, and of the world of feelings. But in the last stages of their lives, they showed signs of restlessness and broke away from the classical rules of Renaissance art.

Reworking the formal tendencies of the three great models in a highly individual way, Rosso and Pontormo emphasized and in the end exasperated their most innovative aspects, completely subverting classical rules and developing a critical and modern artistic approach that led to the formulation of a new style, suited to expressing a new sensitivity. This is true not only in the pictorial works of the two artists, but also in their drawings, which are of an extremely high quality, placing their authors among the greatest interpreters of the prestigious Florentine tradition. The space crowded with figures in which northern European influences are clearly perceivable, the changing colours, wantonly free from any direct relationship with reality, and the tense, restless, visionary atmosphere are the most conspicuous aspects of their anticlassical painting. The most recent reappraisal of these characteristics on the part of both Italian and foreign critics has led to a complete redemption of the work of the two artists, thus freeing it from the accusation of being merely the formal imitation of models.

Before proceeding with the main analysis of the pictorial work of Pontormo and Rosso Fiorentino, here are their brief biographies containing some information on the environment in which they worked and the main events of their artistic careers.

Jacopo Carrucci, called Pontormo, was born in the small castle-town of Pontorme, near Empoli, on 24 May 1494, by the Florentine painter Bartolomeo Carrucci and Alessandra di Pasquale di Zanobi. According to Vasari, as a young man the artist frequented the workshops of various illustrious exponents of the Florentine figurative culture: Piero di Cosimo, Mariotto Albertinelli, Leonardo da Vinci and Andrea del Sarto. The teachings of the first two are discernible almost exclusively in the initial phase of the painter's activity, while Andrea del Sarto, who accepted Pontormo (as well as Rosso) in his workshop, accompanied his official debut in the Florentine artistic environment — Pontormo's participation in the decoration of Santissima Annunziata (1512-13). With Andrea del Sarto the painter would establish a relationship of dialectical emulation up to nearly the end of the second decade of the 16th century.

Although not figuring among the masters of Pontormo, Fra Bartolomeo was certainly another model in the artist's early years. The influence of Leonardo, and above all Michelangelo, would be constant and enduring.

Pontormo never strayed far from the city of Florence and its immediate surroundings, except for two presumed journeys to Rome. His main patrons, including several illustrious representatives of the Medici house, were all Florentine.

Of particular importance in the artist's progress towards a personal and fully independent style was his receptivity to northern European figurative culture, particularly noticeable in the panels for the Camera Borgherini (1515-18) and in the frescoes of *Christ's Passion* in the Carthusian monastery of Galluzzo (1523-25), together with the refined rustic reinterpretation of the classical story of *Vertumnus and Pomona* in the lunette of the salone in the Medicean villa of Poggio a Caiano (1519-21). The artist's formal research reached its peak in the decoration of the Cappella Capponi in Santa Felicita in Florence (1526-28), where the panel of the *Deposition* represents perhaps his highest achievement. This fine painting is embellished by a series of splendid portraits, the faces bearing contemplative, slightly melancholic, often impenetrable and sophisticated expressions. From the fourth decade of the century the artist closely followed the example of Michelangelo. This last stage in his activity would end tormentedly with his work on the lost frescoes of the church of San Lorenzo (1546-56), documented not only by the splendid preparatory drawings but also by the annotations in the *Diary* which Pontormo wrote during the last two years of his life. Pontormo died in 1556.

In contrast with Pontormo's fundamentally fixed and "Florence-centered" existence, the life of his contemporary was more restless and energetic. Giovanni Battista di Jacopo, called Rosso Fiorentino, very probably because of the colour of his hair, was born in the parish of San Michele Visdomini in Florence on 8 March 1494. The brief yet incisive personal portrait, which Vasari inserted at the beginning of the painter's biography, describes him as good-looking, endowed with great charm, polite and refined in behaviour, interested in music and literature, and skilled in the exercise of painting, whose whimsical and bizarre touches are emphasized by the biographer from Arezzo.

Rosso was firmly independent in spirit, conscious and at the same time protective towards his own originality from the time of his youth. Vasari wrote that the artist "wished to work at his art with very few masters, since he held certain opinions that were contrary to their styles". Leaving aside the brief period of apprenticeship which, according to Bronzino, he spent with Pontormo under the guidance of Andrea del Sarto, Rosso showed himself to be intolerant of the traditional practice of study in a master's workshop. This was due less to the painter's independent character, than to his firm resolve to establish a dialectical, rather than emulative, rapport with the figurative tradition. In this spirit he initially drew inspiration from the same models and masters as his contemporary Pontormo, first and foremost Michelangelo, whose cartoon for the *Battle of Cascina* was the only point of reference mentioned by Vasari in Rosso's artistic and cultural training. As well as the famous "world school", he observed the styles of Andrea del Sarto, the late works of Fra Bartolomeo and the contemporary sculptors Jacopo Sansovino and Baccio Bandinelli. Also identifiable are contacts with the eccentric Alonso Berruguete and in particular, at least as regards the artist's early period, with Franciabigio and Pontormo himself. With the latter two he executed his first important public commission, the fresco of the *Assumption of the Virgin* in the Chiostrino dei Voti of Santissima Annunziata (1513-14). In Rosso's work too there is the undeniable influence of northern European painting.

The daring innovations of the *Ognissanti Altarpiece*, the conclusive work in the artist's period of training, almost certainly led directly to the period he spent in Volterra. The remoteness from Florentine formality and the tranquillity offered by the provincial setting were better suited to the unprecedented figurative style proposed by Rosso after the end of the first decade of the 16th century. The extraordinary *Deposition* (1521), now in the Pinacoteca Comunale in Volterra, bears witness to the irreparable break with the harmonious equilibrium of Renaissance figurative culture.

Returning to Florence between the end of 1521 and the beginning of 1522, the artist executed his last Florentine commissions, the *Madonna enthroned and ten saints* for the Dei family (1522) and the *Marriage of the Virgin* (1523). In 1523 Rosso finally left his native city to go to Rome, where he decorated the chapel of the Cesi family in the church of Santa Maria della Pace and executed thirty-one drawings of mythological subjects, which were converted into prints by the engraver Jacopo Caraglio. Following the sack of Rome (1527), he was forced to leave the city and went to Perugia. From there he proceeded to Sansepolcro, Città di Castello, and Arezzo, where he met the young Vasari and exercised his indefatigable creative vein in the project for the decoration of the church of Madonna delle Lacrime. The most recent criticism tends to assign the canvas representing *Moses defending the Daughters of Jethro* (1523-24) to the end of the artist's second Florentine period. The painting is a supreme example of his reworking of Michelangiolesque plasticism, dynamically depicted in a violent unleashing of forces.

The work of Rosso is enriched by a series of charming portraits, notable particularly for the elegance of the poses and the expressions of the figures.

In 1530, after a brief sojourn in Venice at the home of Pietro Aretino, Rosso was called to France to the court of Francis I. Here the painter magisterially concluded his career with the decoration of the great gallery in the palace of Fontainebleau, where he executed fourteen scenes in fresco and supervised the realization of the stucco decoration framing them (1533-39). Rosso Fiorentino died on 14 November 1540.

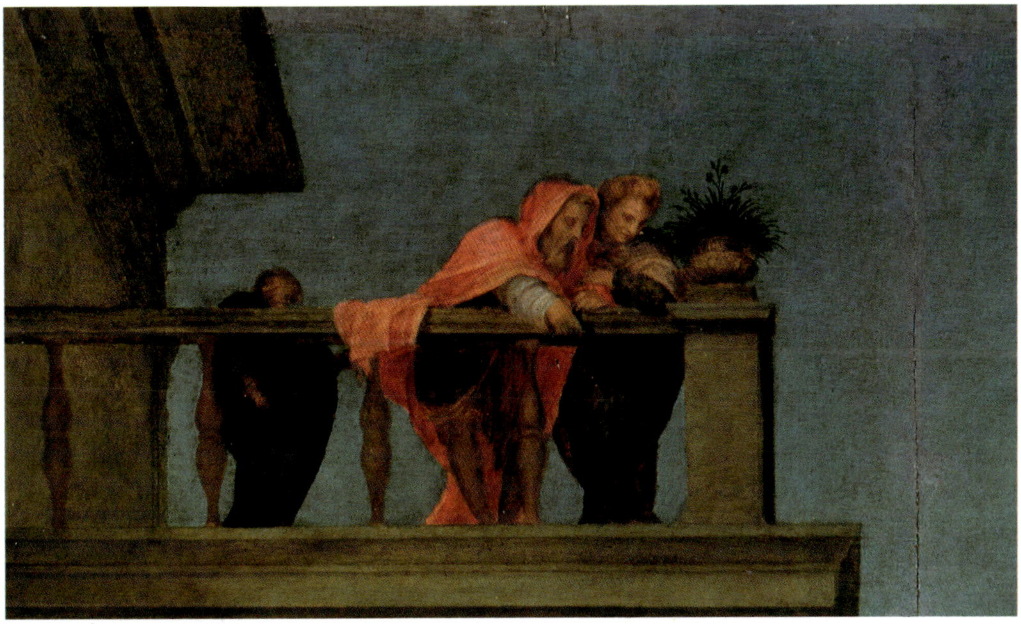

5. Andrea del Sarto Annunciation, detail of the figures on the balcony, probably the work of Pontormo, Florence, Galleria Palatina

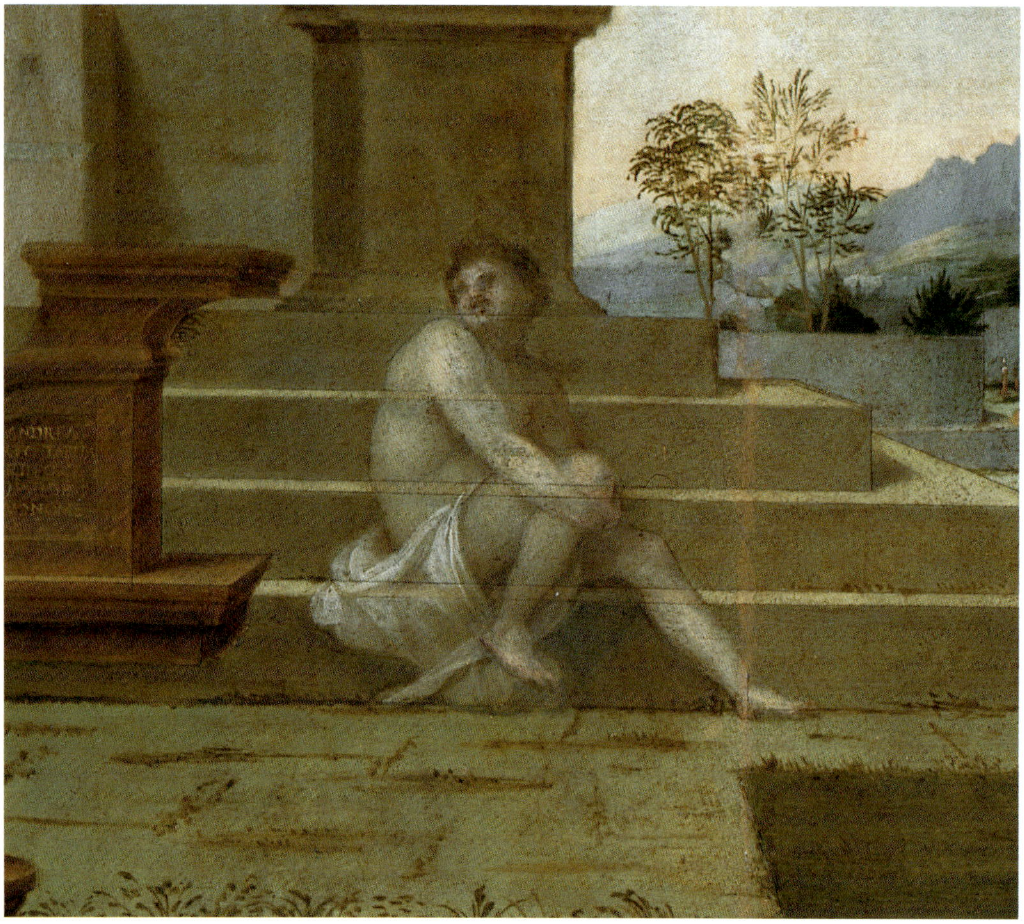

6. Andrea del Sarto
Annunciation, detail of the monochrome figure, probably the work of Pontormo
Florence, Galleria Palatina

A common start

In spite of the many praiseworthy contributions of contemporary critics, the work which (according to what Vasari says he learnt from Bronzino) marked the joint debut of the artistic activity of Pontormo and Rosso Fiorentino has still not been identified. According to one theory the young artists were both active in the workshop of Andrea del Sarto between the end of 1512 and the beginning of 1513. Under his direction they executed together the predella of the *Annunciation* which Andrea painted for the Agostinian friars of the church of San Gallo. After the siege of Florence (1529), in which the church was destroyed, the work with its surviving predella was transferred to San Jacopo tra' Fossi, where the predella appears to have been irreparably damaged or lost at the end of the 1550s during a flood of the Arno.

From Vasari's brief description at the beginning of the biography of Pontormo, we know that this work portrayed a dead Christ illuminated by torches held by two weeping angels. At the sides, in two tondos, were two figures of prophets which Vasari particularly admired.

As well as working with Rosso on the predella, Pontormo may have assisted Andrea del Sarto in the scene of the *Annunciation*, in which the small figures at the balcony of the imposing classical building in the background and the central figure in monochrome sitting on the stairs in line with the massive pilaster of the portico seem to be his work.

Working both together, therefore, and at the side of Andrea del Sarto on the decoration of Santissima Annunziata, Pontormo and Rosso Fiorentino made their official debut in the Florentine art world. The master had begun working there from the end of the first decade of the century, offering an excellent display of his painting "without errors", especially in the Chiostrino dei Voti.

The various phases of the activity of the two painters at Santissima Annunziata are documented in detail in the *Libro delle Ricordanze del Convento della Nunziata* (1510-59), in the *Notizie* compiled by Father Eliseo Biffoli from 1587, and especially in the *Libro del Camarlingo*, the register of payments compiled by the friar who held this office from the March of 1509 to the year 1516.

From the information contained therein it appears that on 19 September 1513 Rosso was entrusted with the realization of two coats of arms in the chamber of the superior-general of the Servite friars. Unfortunately nothing has survived of these first frescoes by Rosso, and very little is visible today of Pontormo's debut in the Annunziata. About a month after Rosso's first commission, on 7 October 1513, Pontormo received a first payment for the figures of *Faith* and *Charity*, painted in fresco around the marble coat of arms of Leo X at the entrance of the Annunziata. The fresco had originally been commissioned to Andrea di Cosimo Feltrini, who exercised numerous functions at the Annunziata especially in the field of the decorations, and who after having participated in the gilding of the papal coat of arms was reluctant to take on the pictorial work. In the scanty traces of it visible today, we can just distinguish the two female figures of the Virtues. The success of the work was considerable, to the extent that, according to Vasari, Andrea del Sarto, deeply impressed by the artistic talents of his young pupil, initially heaped praises upon him, although later expressed sentiments of profound envy and from that moment onwards "never again looked upon Jacopo favourably".

In spite of this, thanks to the grandiose achievements of their first works Pontormo and Rosso Fiorentino were involved in the realization of the decorative cycle of the "Scenes from the Life of the Virgin" in the Chiostrino dei Voti. Pontormo's *Visitation* (1514-16) and Rosso's *Assumption* (1513-14) complete the scenes of the *Birth of the Virgin* by Andrea del Sarto (1513-14) and the *Marriage of the Virgin* by Franciabigio (1513). The frescoes of the two young artists represent the moment of direct confrontation with the classical figurative tradition. Common to both artists, however, already in this youthful phase, was the desire to break away from it.

The first step away from tradition was the work of Rosso, who from the end of 1513 had started work on the *Assumption of the Virgin*. The division of the scene into two areas, one above the other, recalls the compositional idea of the *Last Judgement*, painted at the beginning of the century by Fra Bartolomeo for the Chiostro delle Ossa of the Hospital of Santa Maria Nuova and presently in the Museo di San Marco. The motif of the Virgin surrounded by the group of rejoicing angels, in whose anatomies it is possible to recognize the influence of Michelangelo, is also of Bartolomeesque inspiration. In the lower section the majestic emphasis of the figures recalls the people in the frescoed scenes of Andrea del Sarto. In addition to the obvious references to classical authority, the work is equally characterized by numerous innovative touches, particularly as

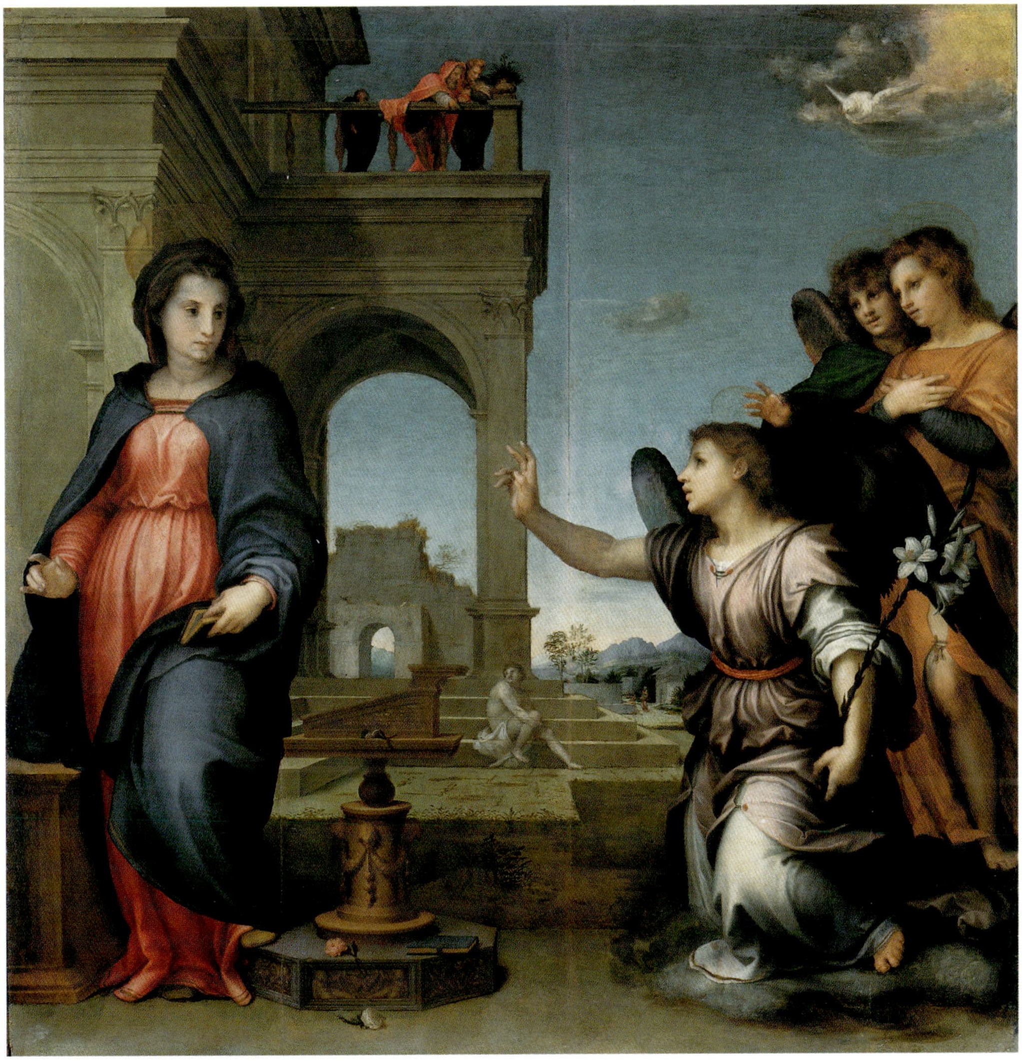

7. Andrea del Sarto Annunciation Florence, Galleria Palatina

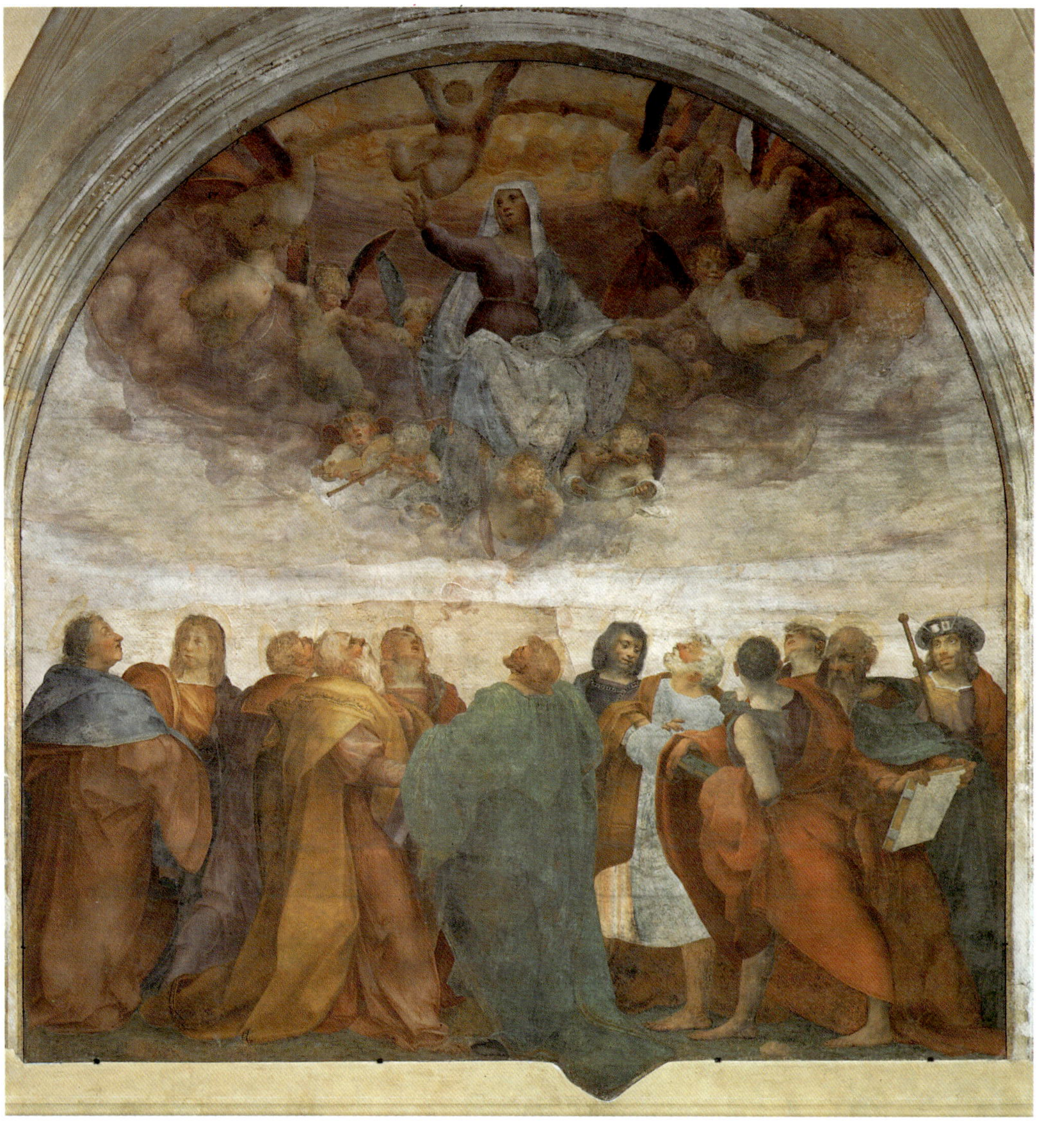

8. Rosso Fiorentino
Assumption of the Virgin
385x395 cm
Florence, Santissima Annunziata

9. Andrea del Sarto
Birth of the Virgin
Florence, Santissima Annunziata

10, 11. Pontormo
Visitation
392x337cm
Florence, Santissima Annunziata

12. Fra Bartolomeo
Mystical Marriage of St Catherine
Florence, Galleria dell'Accademia

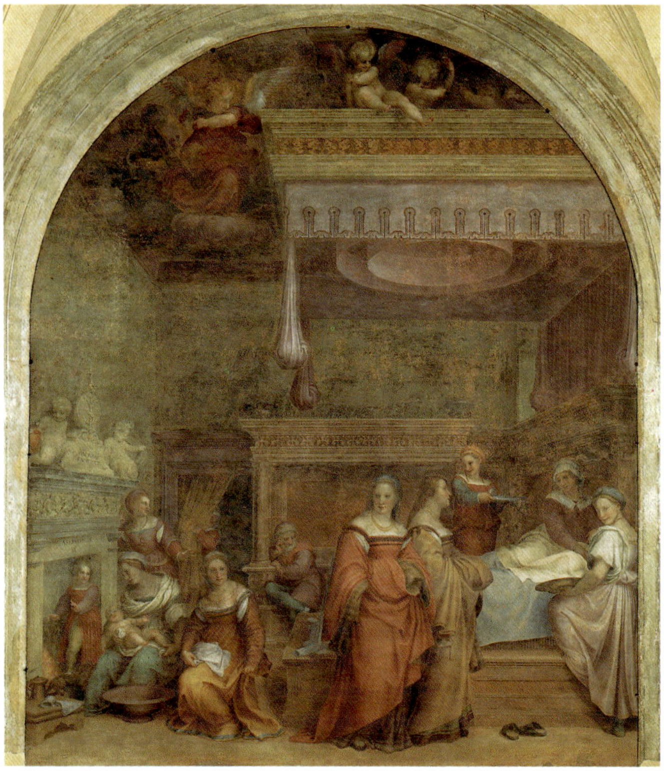

regards its formal arrangement and conception of space. The apostles with their broad, unlined faces, large noses and bizarre expressions, probably correspond to the figures represented in northern engravings, which at the time were widespread. The drapery of their extraordinarily abundant garments invades the space, cancelling the effect of the gradation of planes through the juxtaposition of complementary colours, and even creates an illusionistic annulment of the distance between reality and pictorial representation in the projecting strip around the outside of the painted scene. Another of the painting's peculiarities is the arrangement of the individual figures within this space, at the very limit of measurability: the closed circle formed by the central group from which two almost symmetrical tangential arcs depart. In the upper part of the painting note the refined ambivalence between the prevailing calligraphic effect of the line of the angel ring and the intuitable though undefined spatial reality. Overall, Rosso's fresco departs in no small measure from the harmonious structure of forms and from the gentle tonal gradation of classical painting, communicating instead a diffused sense of irrational excitement.

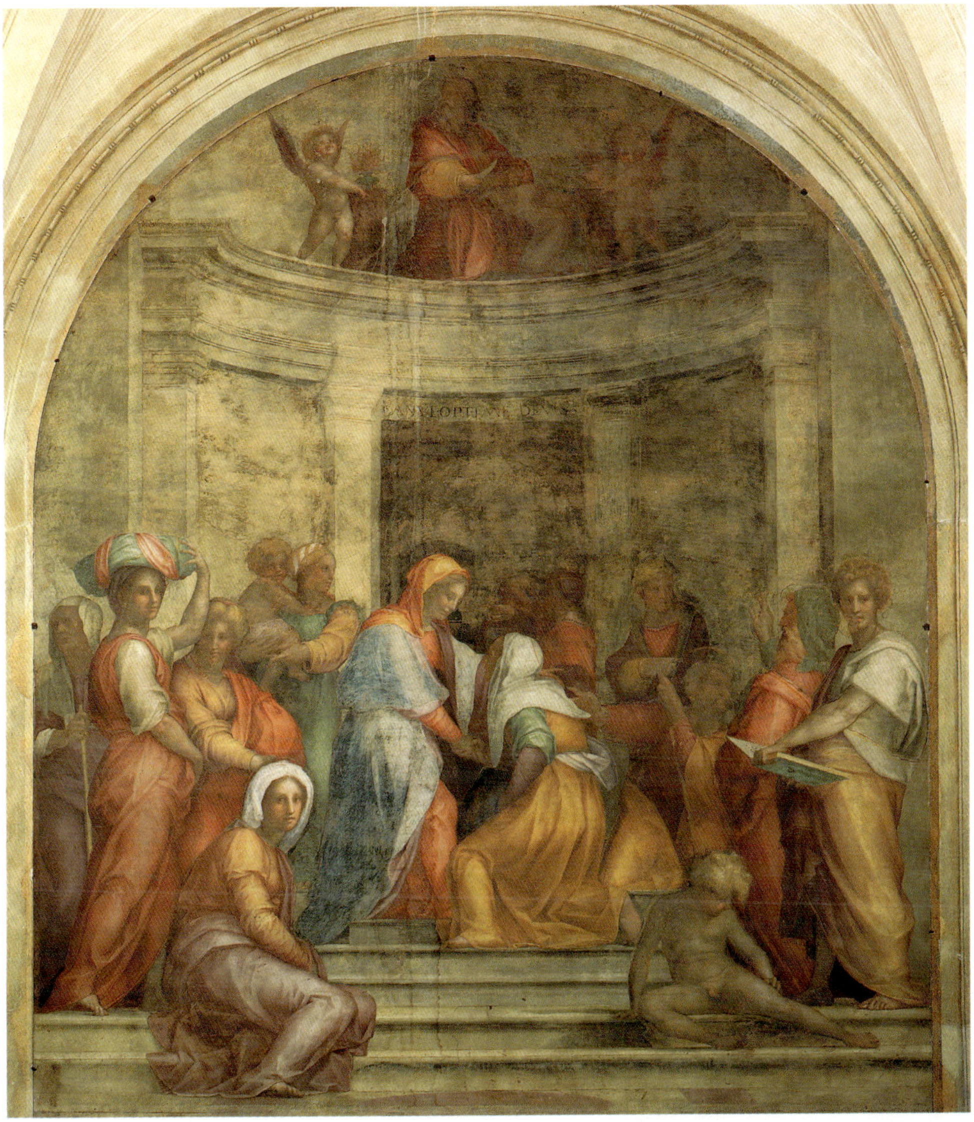

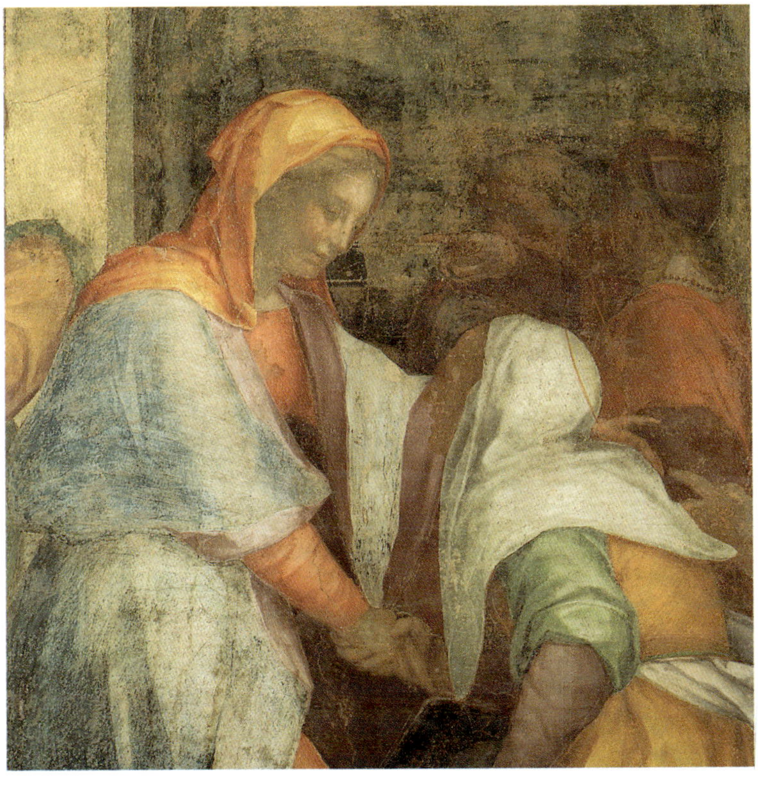

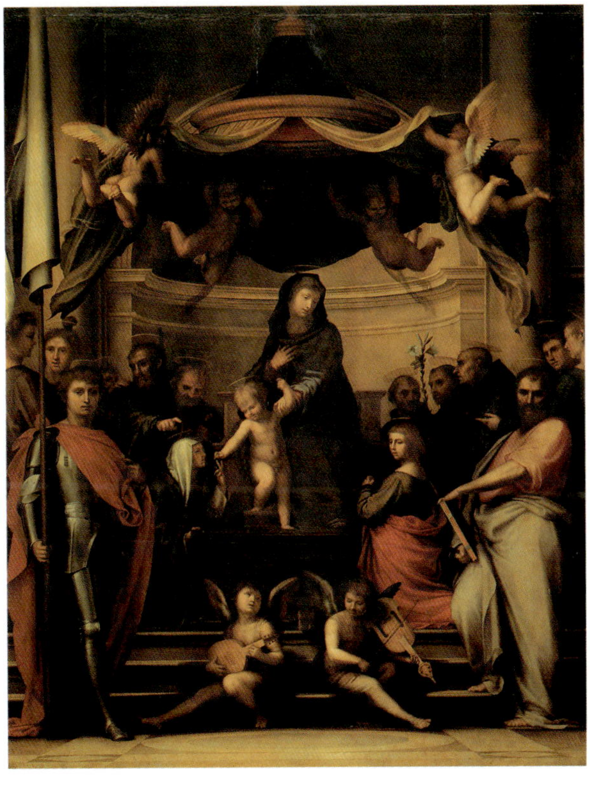

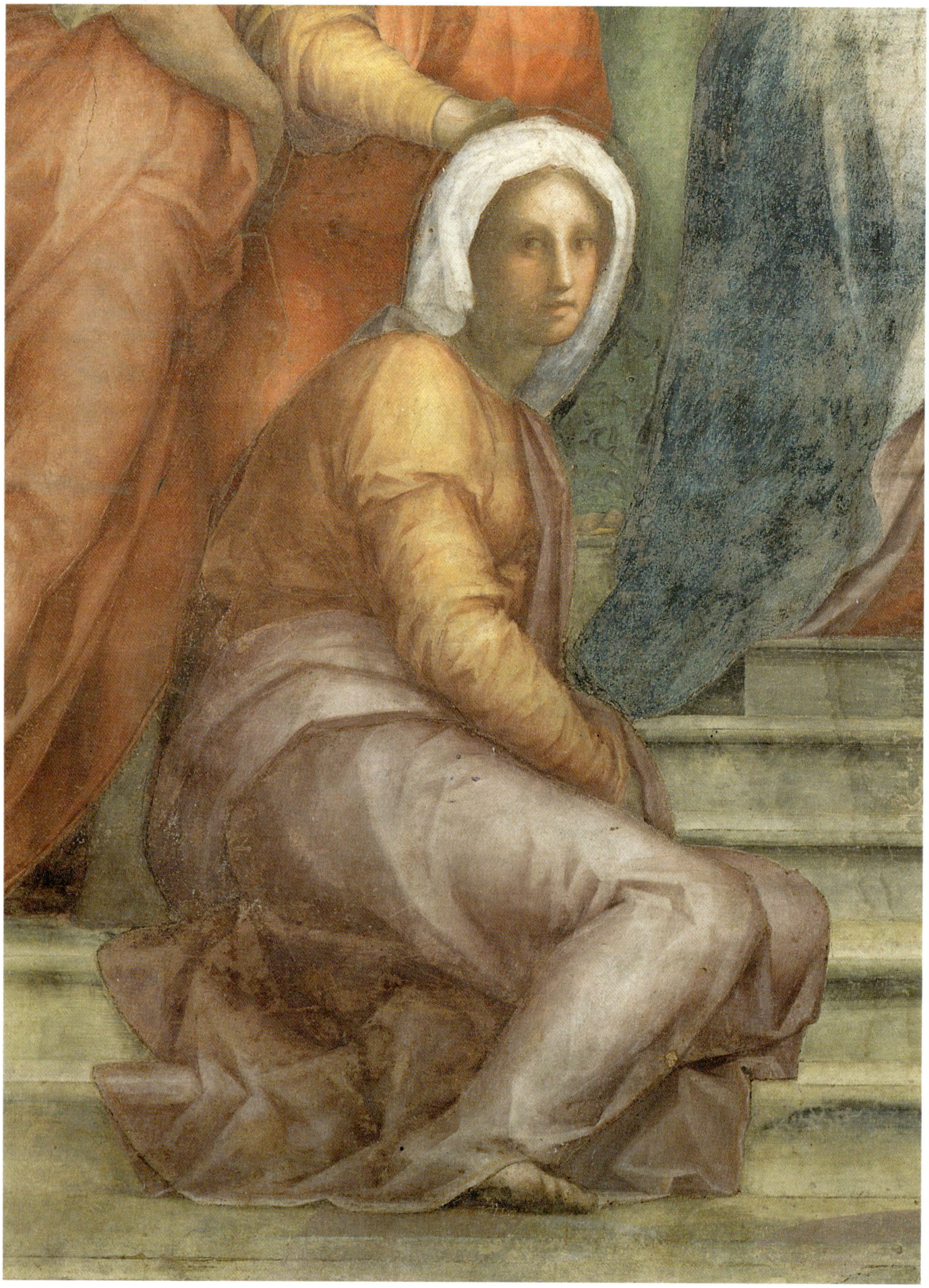

13. Pontormo
Visitation, detail
Florence, Santissima Annunziata

14. Pontormo
Episode from Hospital Life
91x150 cm
Florence, Galleria dell'Accademia

In the *Visitation*, which Pontormo started in 1514 and finished some two years later, the references to the two great Florentine models already evoked by Rosso in his work are even more explicit. The compositional structure is undoubtedly classical in inspiration. The insertion of a pyramid-shaped structure inside a circular space is similar to the one used by Fra Bartolomeo in his *Mystical Marriage of St Catherine* (*Pitti Altarpiece*, 1512). In Pontormo's fresco, however, the central group is surrounded by numerous figures whose varied postures recall the figures painted by Andrea del Sarto nearby, and a certain similarity with the artist's female figures is also found in the faces of the women represented by Pontormo in the right-hand part of the composition. Compared to the frescoes of Andrea del Sarto, in which the scenes are depicted within vast spaces and with narrative emphasis, the event portrayed by Pontormo appears blocked by the stiff, almost statue-like poses of the figures, especially the saint holding a book in the right-hand foreground, the canephore on the left and the woman carrying a child behind the figure of the Virgin. One also has the sensation that the space is not large enough for the crowd that fills it. In their monumentality, the figures again recall the models of Fra Bartolomeo, but diverge from the latter in their slightly charged, restless expressions, like that of the woman sitting in the foreground looking at something outside the scene, or those of the ges-

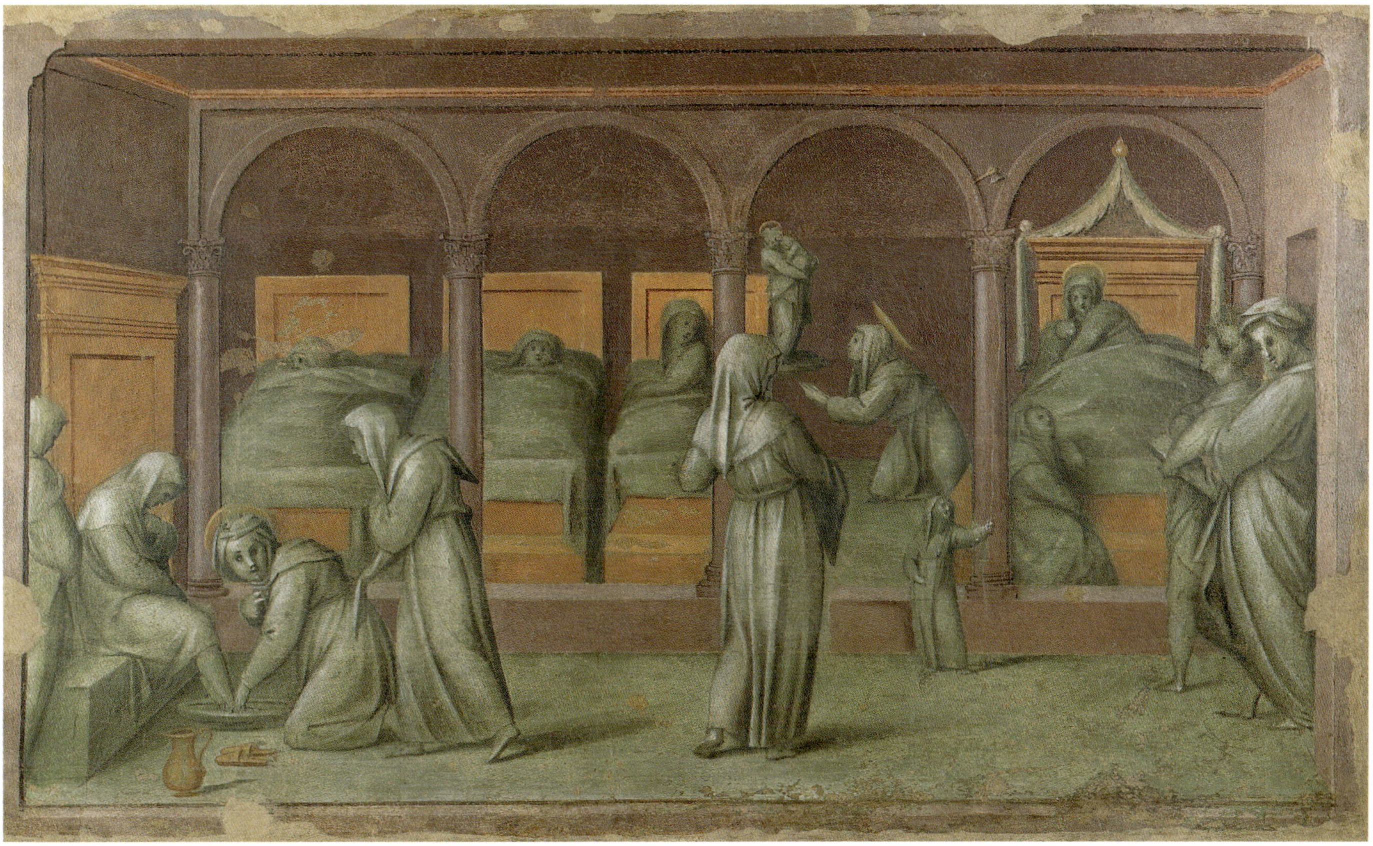

ticulating group in the right-hand background. In addition to the references to Fra Bartolomeo and Andrea del Sarto, there are others to the more or less contemporary works that Raphael was executing in Rome, especially in the first two Vatican Stanze. This would justify the hypothesis of a first journey to Rome probably undertaken by Pontormo, in 1515, a year before the completion of his work. Lastly, we may also identify a reference to the colouristic experimentation of Michelangelo, particularly in the "strident yellow of [St Elisabeth's] garment" (A. Venturi, 1932).

The combined presence of classical references and elements of innovation, aimed at expressing a different direction of figurative research, distinguishes other early works by Pontormo. Originally painted on a wall of the main hall of the Accademia, formerly the women's ward of the old Hospital of San Matteo, the *Episode from Hospital Life* (1514) may be seen as the humble and almost realistic reduction of one of the highest expressions of Andrea del Sarto's classicism, the *Birth of the Virgin* of the Chiostrino dei Voti. The slippers lying on the floor and the basin immediately recall the fresco by Andrea del Sarto, but the drab environment in which the charitable actions of the miraculously healed saint are carried out contrasts sharply with the spacious, elegant room in which Andrea set his scene. The tendency toward an extreme sobriety in Pontormo's fresco is enhanced by the reduction of the range of colours to yellow, pink and green only. If the poses of the figures still feel the decisive influence exerted by classicism, the angularity with which they are delineated, the jerkiness conferred to their movements, and the troubled expressions impressed on faces with pointed chins, round eyes and tiny mouths are quite extraneous to the classical tradition and without figurative precedents.

For the execution of the *Sacra Conversazione* (1514), originally painted on a wall of the church of San Ruffillo and transferred to the chapel of the painters at the Annunziata at the beginning of the 19th century, Pontormo worked on two fundamental models. The compositional structure was that of the Virgin and Child with saints used by the friar (with slight variations as far as the background was concerned) in the *Madonna and six saints* (1509, Florence, San Marco) and in the already mentioned *Pitti Altarpiece*. The *Mystical Marriage of St Catherine*, painted by Andrea del Sarto around 1513 and now in Dresden, was also a probable point of reference for Pontormo's fresco. With this painting, however, Pontormo departed decisively from the two models and presented a personal reworking of the figurative material they contained by dissolving once and for all the harmonious union of forms arranged in a rationally defined and measurable space, a characteristic of the compositions by the two masters. Pontormo reduced the depth and width of the space, producing an effect of compression, the figures being arranged in contrasting poses (standing and kneeling, facing forwards and backwards), and characterized by a marked twisting of the bodies, especially in the Virgin and the Child. The expressions are also anticlassical: the fixed gaze outside the painting of St Lucia, more insistent than the examples of Andrea del Sarto or Fra Bartolomeo, the sigh of ecstasy, almost a grimace, that

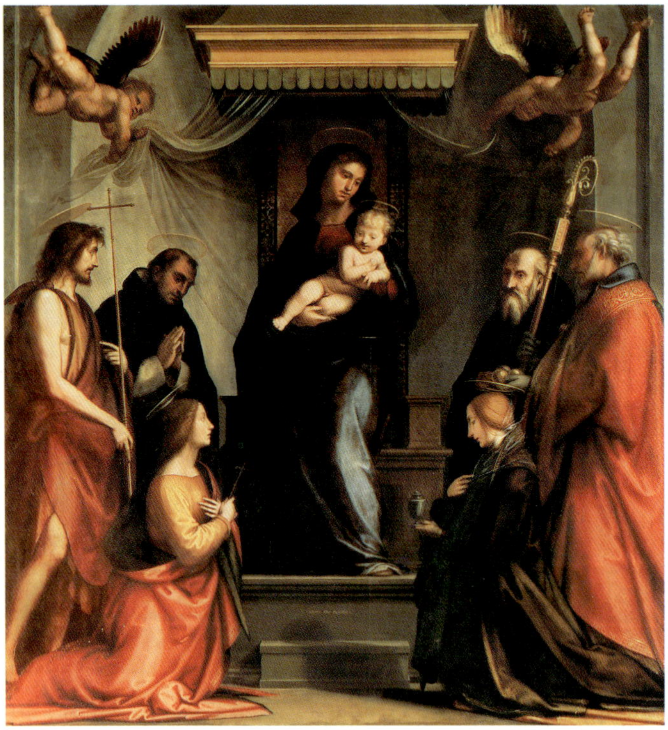

emanates from the presumed figure of St Agnes and expresses all the intensity of an entirely exclusive experience, the petulant and contrary reaction of the Child at the approach of the aged St Zacharias, and lastly the unprecedentedly languid and passionate gaze that the archangel Michael directs toward the Virgin Mary.

The embellishment of the city of Florence on the occasion of the visit of Pope Leo X, an illustrious member of the Medici family, included the decoration of the chapel in the church of Santa Maria Novella, which was used for the pope's daily celebration of Communion. The work was first commissioned to Ridolfo del Ghirlandaio, who executed the *Coronation of the Virgin* on the wall facing the entrance and was finished off by Cosimo Feltrini, who was responsible for the lavish decorative apparatus of the vault that included putti made by Pontormo, the third protagonist of the enterprise. Pontormo also painted the lunette with *Veronica*, which still represented the moment of confrontation with the Florentine pictorial tradition. An illustrious precedent of the scheme of the

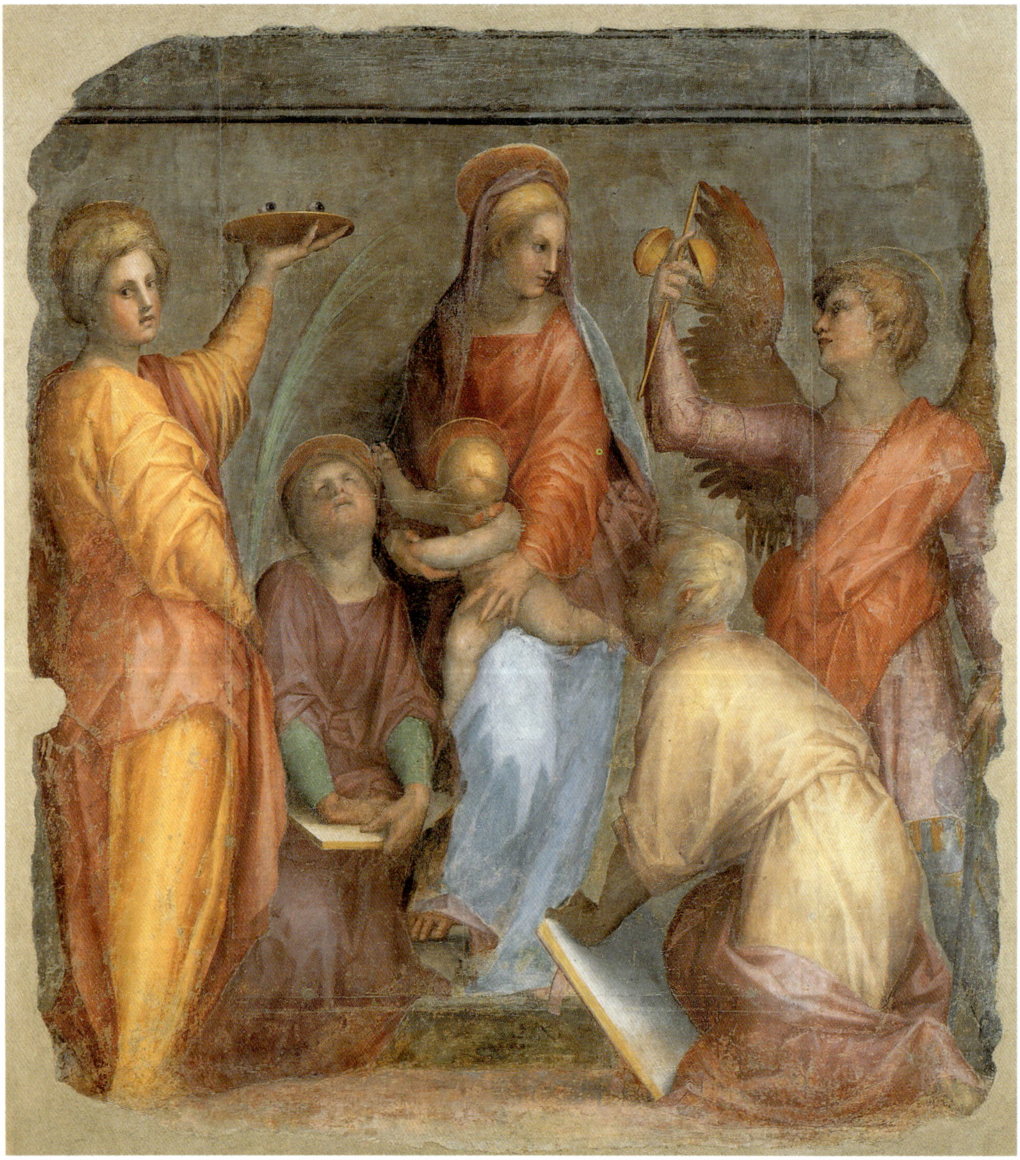

15. Fra Bartolomeo
Madonna and six saints
Florence, San Marco

16. Pontormo
Sacra Conversazione
223x196 cm
Florence, Santissima Annunziata

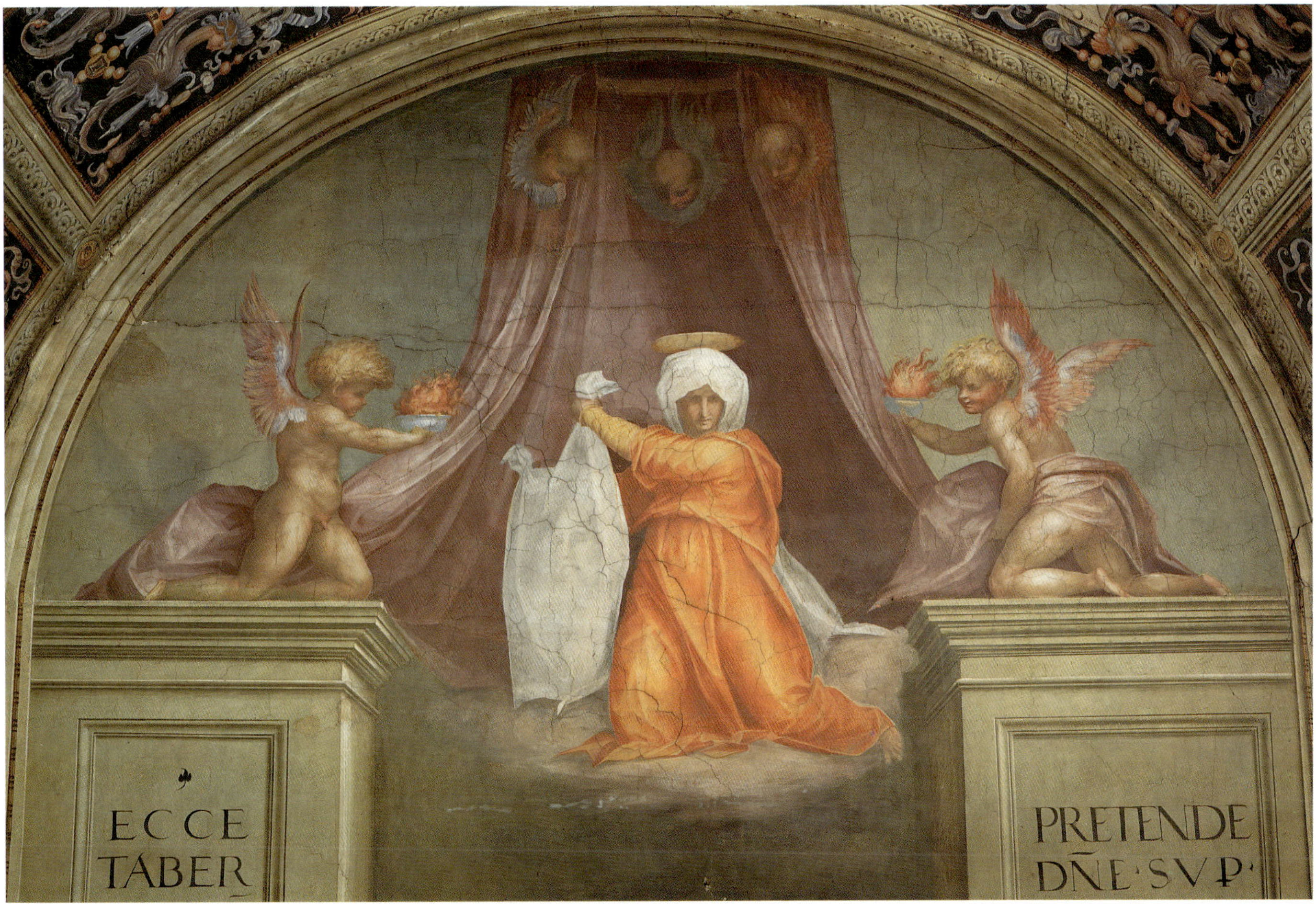

17. Pontormo
Veronica
307x413 cm
Florence, convent of Santa Maria Novella

figure crowned by a pavilion held up by two angels was Raphael's *Madonna del Baldacchino* (1507-8, Florence, Pitti Palace), an idea taken up again a few years later by both Fra Bartolomeo in the *Mystical Marriage of St Catherine* (1511), today at the Louvre, and Andrea del Sarto in the Dresden altarpiece. In the twisting of Veronica's body there is also a classical reference, Michelangelo's *Doni Tondo* (1503-4, Florence, Uffizi), and evident Michelangiolesque inspiration in the bodies of the two naked putti, whose poses reveal here, as in the aforementioned *Sacra Conversazione* in San Ruffillo, the artist's taste for *contrapposto*, for setting different parts of the body on different planes. A display of stylistic finesse is also evident in the striking iridescence of Veronica's robes and in the way that the impression of Christ's face is rendered on the white shroud.

In the first half of the second decade of the century Rosso Fiorentino, like Pontormo, was still busy studying and reworking the figurative styles furnished by classical models. The *Madonna in Glory*, painted by Rosso probably between 1512 and 1513 and today conserved at the Hermitage in St Petersburg, clearly reflects this phase of comparison with the classical figurative tradition. The motif of the Virgin borne up by the group of angels, clearly inspired by Fra Bartolomeo, recalls the fresco of the *Assumption of the Virgin* in Santissima Annunziata (1513-14). The two works also have similar types of angels, with their

18. Raphael
Madonna del Baldacchino, detail
Florence, Galleria Palatina

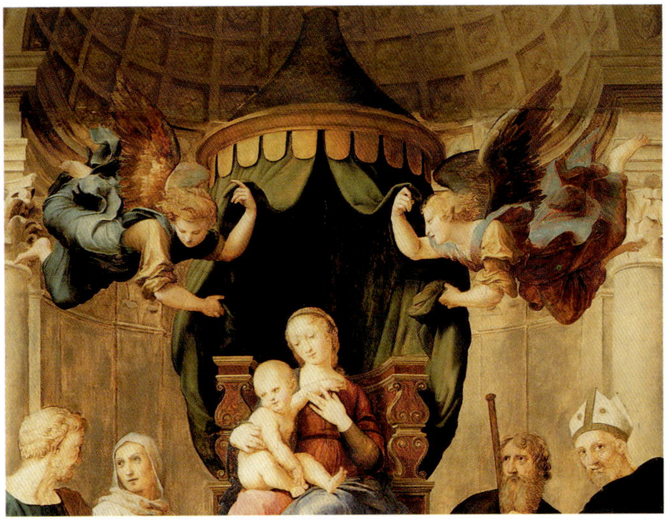

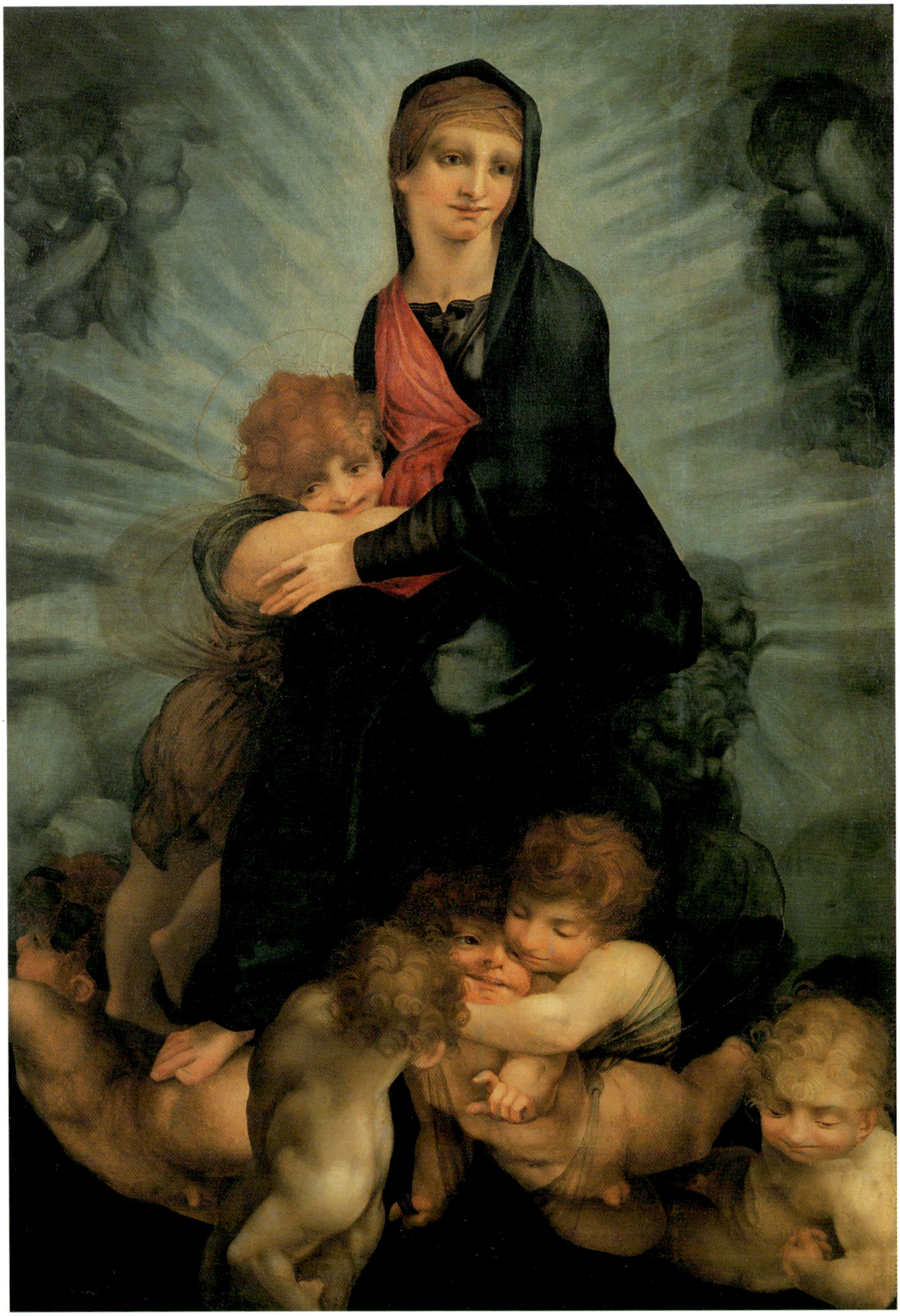

Michelangiolesque bodies and their expressionistically characterized faces, with wide mouths, marked noses and large eyes. The artist also draws on Buonarroti for the basic compositional scheme: a pyramidal structure that tapers towards the top of the painting and is connected to a voluminous base. There are also clear references to some illustrious sculptural works by Michelangelo. The reworking of the compositional idea of the *Bruges Madonna* can be recognized in the tender embrace uniting the Virgin and the Child, who twists his head slightly in clinging to his mother's side. The "unfinished" figures of the small cherubs, enig-

19, 20. Rosso Fiorentino
Madonna in Glory
110x75.5 cm
St Petersburg, Hermitage

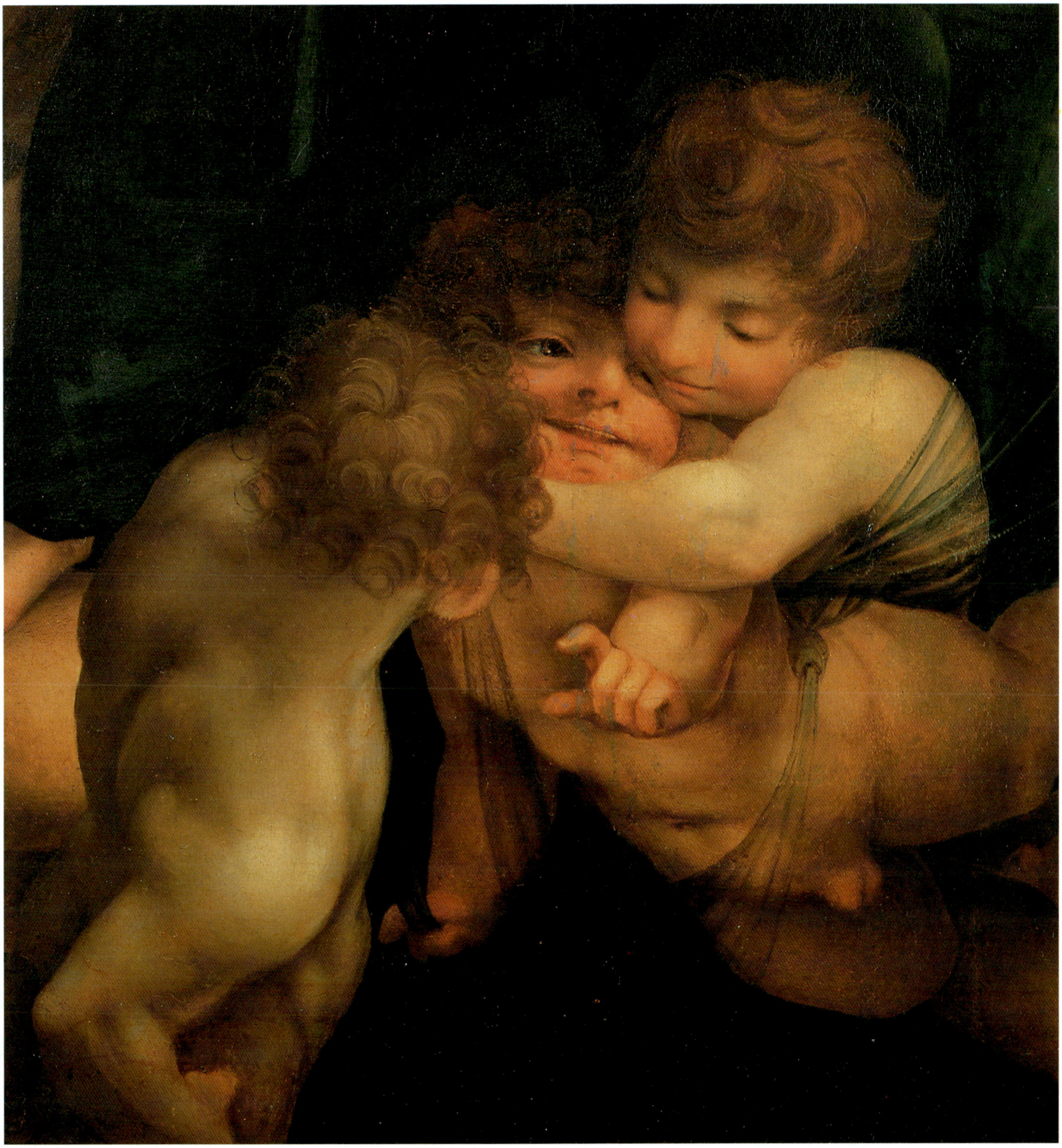

matically emerging from the background, recall those of the *Taddei* (ca. 1502) and *Pitti* (ca. 1503) Tondi. And in the putto depicted in the lower foreground, with its shoulder projected towards the observer, we see the marble *David* of Palazzo Vecchio, seen from above. In the Hermitage *Madonna,* therefore, the links with the classical figurative tradition are still strong. Yet the final solution is highly original, in the foreshortening of the bodies of the angels in the foreground, in the psychological characterization of the faces of the persons portrayed, and particularly in the colour. The explosion of light, which fills the icy blue background, contrasts strongly with the dark blue of the cloak which covers the Virgin's body and which seemingly merges into the dark undefined space in which the angels are flying.

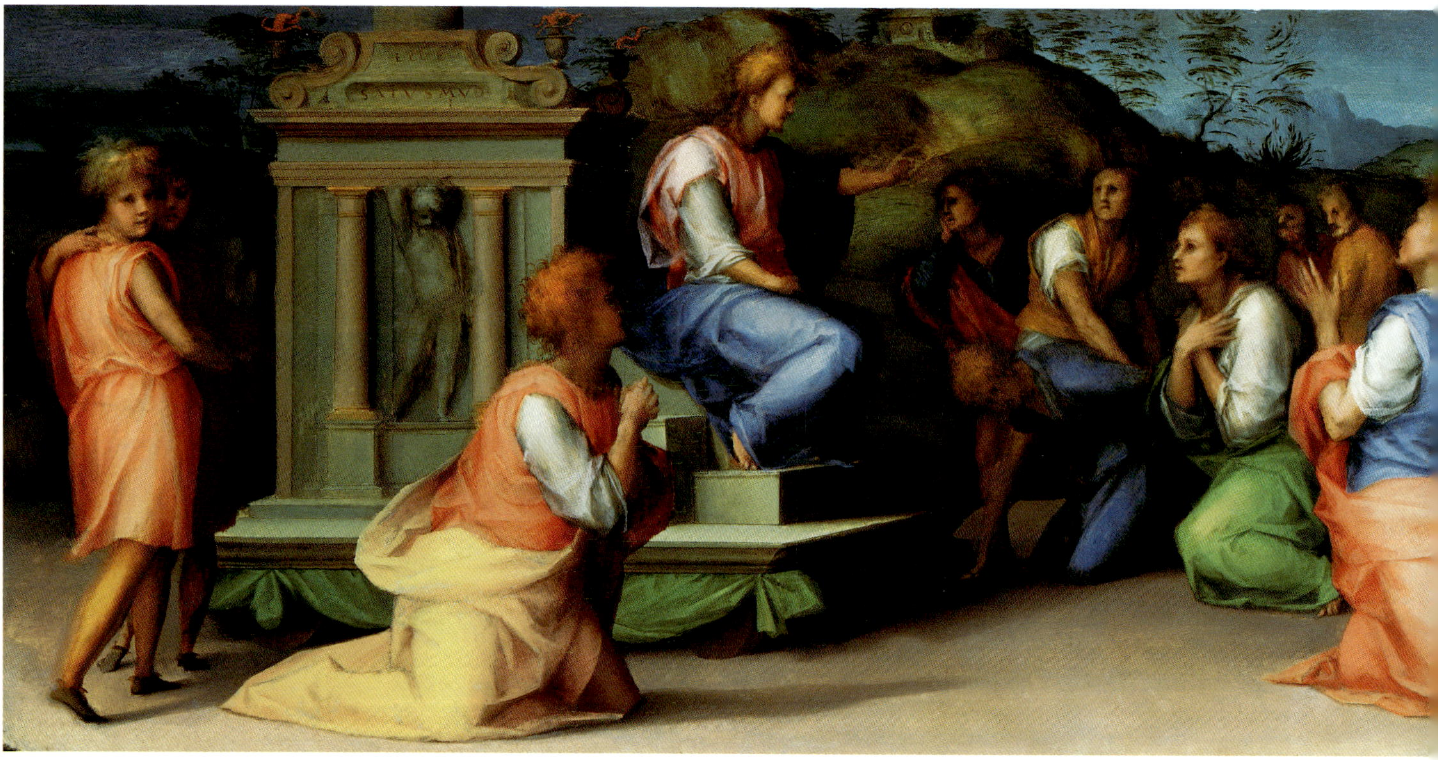

The paths divide: early independent works

From the middle of the second decade of the 16th century the paths of Pontormo and Rosso Fiorentino diverged. Common to both, however, was the creation of an original style that departed from the figurative tradition to which the artists had referred in their early works.

The paintings by Pontormo most representative of this new artistic tendency are the *Scenes from the Life of Joseph the Hebrew* (ca. 1515-18), now in the National Gallery in London. These works, together with others by Andrea del Sarto, Francesco Granacci, Bachiacca and Franciabigio, were intended for the decoration of the nuptial chamber of Francesco Borgherini and Margherita Acciaioli, who were married in 1515. The group of fourteen paintings, broken up at the end of the 16th century, was contained within a wooden decoration made by Baccio d'Agnolo. The chosen theme traditionally comprised the prefiguration of the life of Christ and the exaltation of Divine Providence and Christian virtues.

Compared to the panels executed by the other artists involved in the cycle, the four paintings by Pontormo are distinguished by the originality of the figurative and spatial inventions, the animated action of the figures and the singular use of colours. When describing these fine works, Vasari expressed his sincere approval, admiring particularly the "liveliness of the heads" and the "variety of the expressions" of the small figures, otherwise and more modernly called "macchiette".

The genre of the decoration of panels, predellas and nativity plates, which in past times other eminent artists of the Florentine generation had used to compare themselves, was substantially renewed by Pontormo, with reference to a new figurative model. Indeed, the tense, seething atmosphere immediately noticeable in his *Stories of Joseph*, recalls the crowded scenes portrayed in northern engravings. Around this time the engravings of the Dutch artist Lucas van Leiden and the German Albrecht Dürer were particularly widespread in numerous Italian centres of art. In Florence their works aroused the interest of many artists, including Andrea del Sarto, and the possibility that Pontormo came to know of this new figurative culture through him cannot be excluded.

Of the four works painted by Pontormo, *Joseph revealing himself to his brothers* is probably the first in chronological order. The scene represents the moment when Joseph, now grown up and invested with special authority by the pharaoh, makes himself known to his brothers who have come to Egypt to buy wheat. The land of Canaan, where they live with their father Jacob, is afflicted by a terrible famine. The young men are dumbstruck when they recognize in the pharaoh's generous minister the brother who many years before, out of envy, they had sold to Midianite merchants, and who their father Jacob believed to be dead; they therefore throw themselves at his feet, imploring his forgiveness.

From the point of view of form, the painting still retains some qualities characteristic of the classical figura-

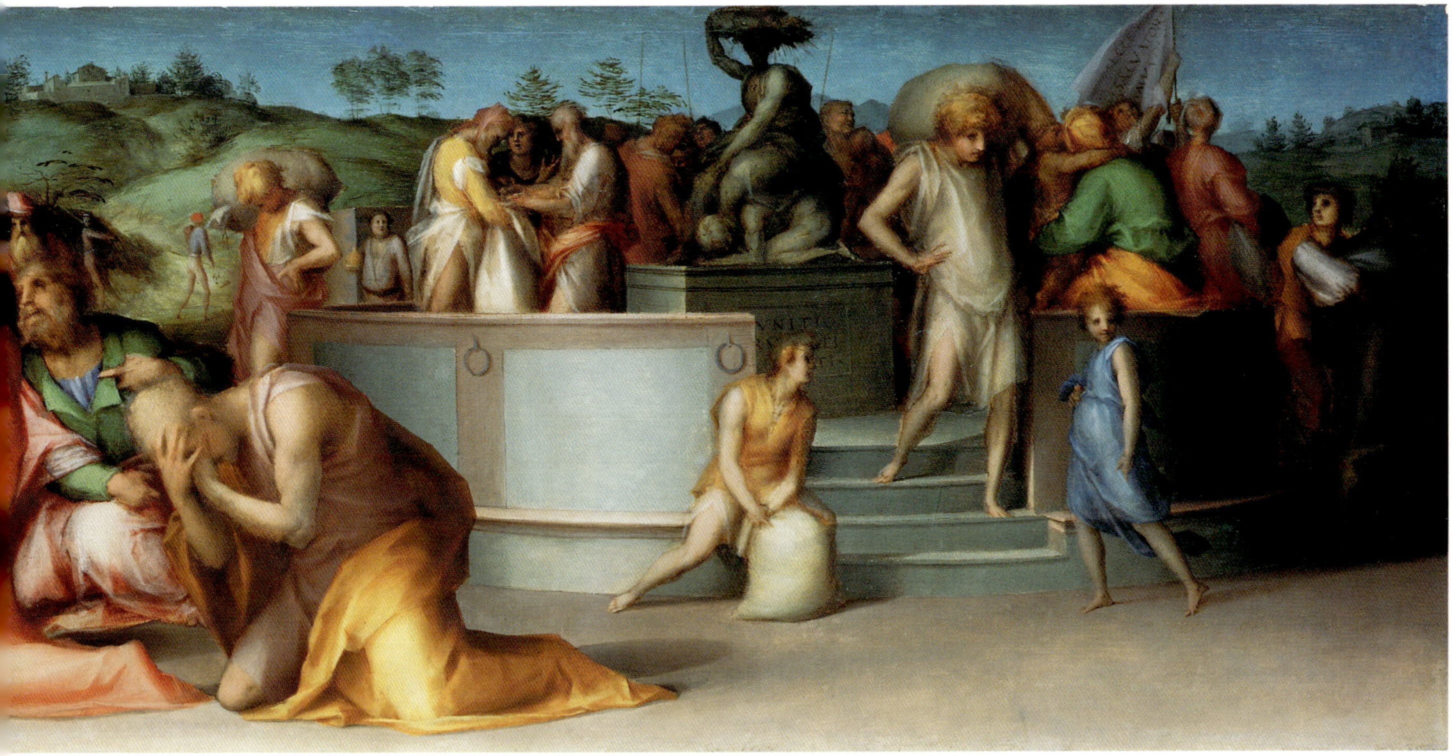

21. Pontormo
Joseph revealing himself to
his brothers
35x142 cm
London, National Gallery

22. Pontormo
Joseph being sold to
Potiphar
58x50 cm
London, National Gallery

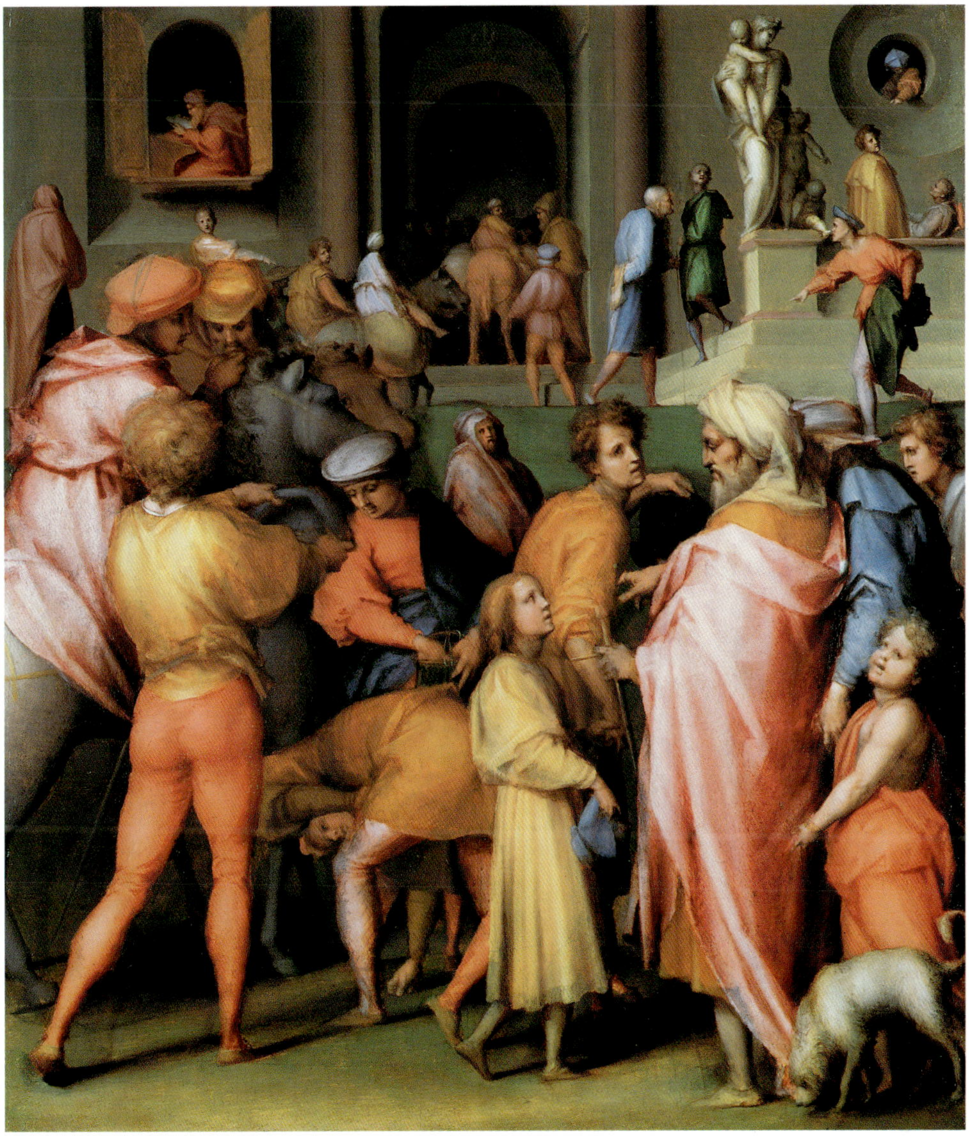

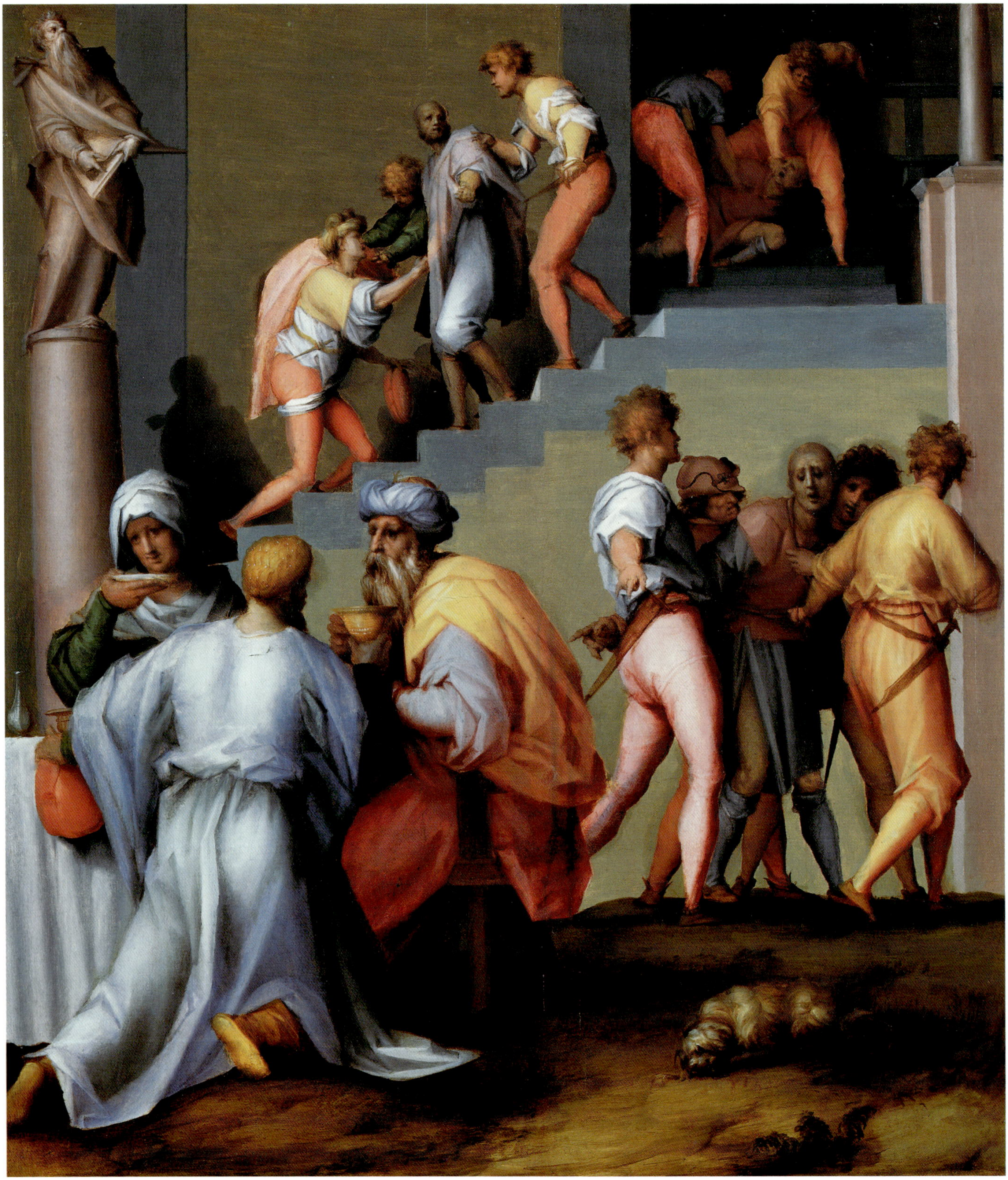

tive culture, for example, the positioning of the bodies of the figures. The composition also has two typical classical schemes, pyramidal and circular, which in a completely original way are not fused into a harmonious structure, but rather split into two parts in which the whole scene can be divided.

Common to the two subsequent paintings is the artist's predilection for a technique that uses the arrangement of figures to guide the onlooker's gaze from the fore-

23. Pontormo
Punishment of the baker
58x50 cm
London, National Gallery

24. Pontormo
Joseph in Egypt
44x49 cm
London, National Gallery

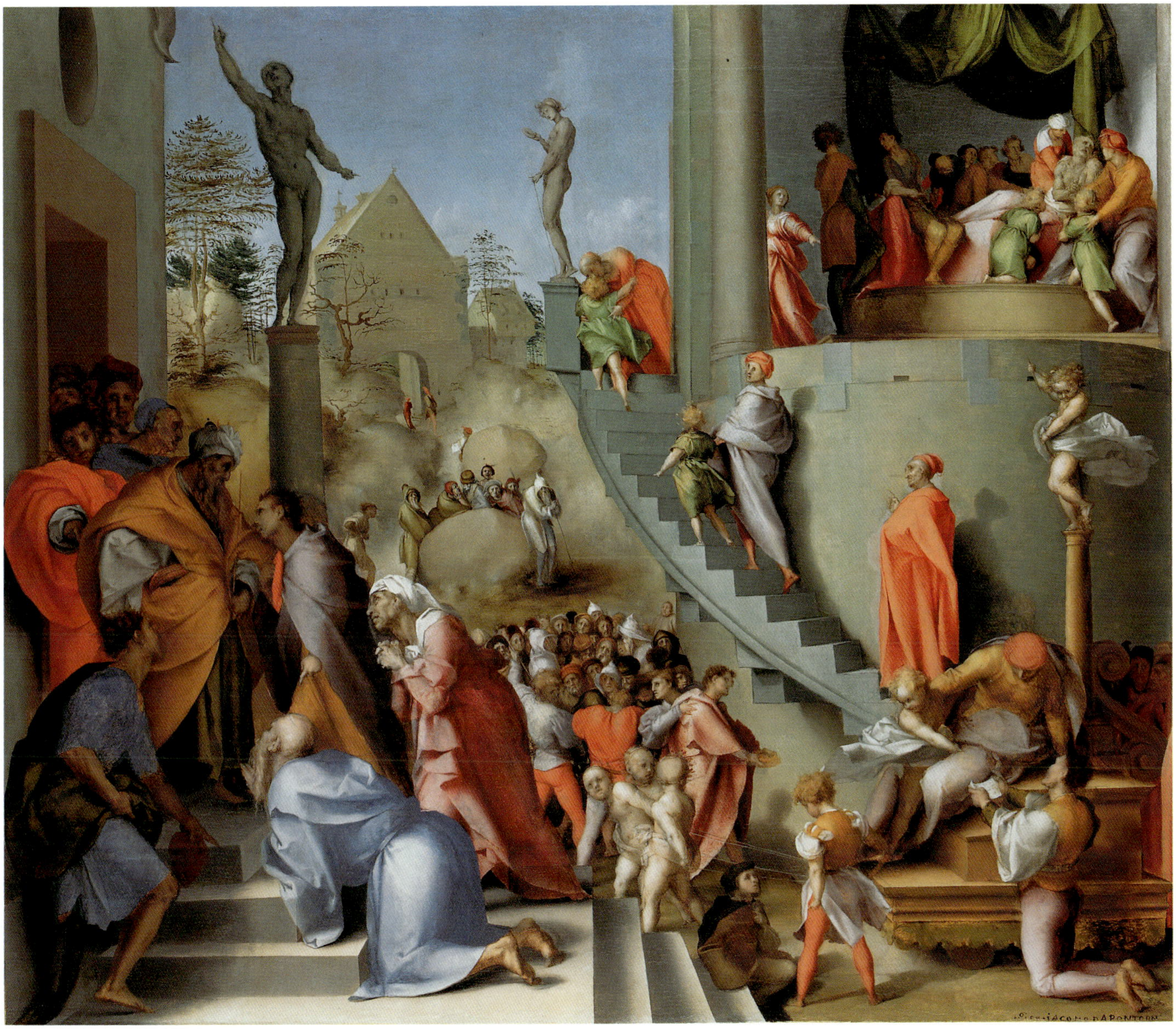

ground towards the background of the painting. In *Joseph being sold to Potiphar*, the action follows a serpentine course, in the scene of the *Punishment of the baker and the forgiveness of the cup-bearer* a zigzagging one. From the pardon of the cup-bearer, newly admitted to serving the pharaoh, the various stages of the baker's punishment are simultaneously represented.

The extreme form of this type of simultaneous representation is only one of the figurative peculiarities characterizing the largest of these remarkable paintings. The work, traditionally entitled *Joseph in Egypt*, depicts the most significant episodes of Joseph reuniting with his family of origin. The painting is divided into four distinct zones. In the left foreground Joseph presents his family, who he invited to move to Egypt, to the pharaoh; according to Vasari, the boy with the dark cloak and brown tunic sitting on the first step of the stairs on which the figures are arranged, is a portrait of the young Bronzino. On the right, Joseph is seen sitting on a triumphal cart pulled by three putti; hoisting himself up with his left arm and clutching firmly onto a putto with the other, he bends toward a kneeling figure who is presenting him a petition or reading him a message; a fifth putto, wrapped in a piece of cloth blown by the wind, dominates the scene from the top of a column, appearing to mime the gesture of one of the two half-living statues represented in the top left and centre of the painting. A restless crowd, curious to see what is going on, throngs the adjacent space between the two buildings in the background. Other mysterious figures, resting against one of the large boulders that dominate the landscape, turn their attention toward the action in the foreground.

The clothes, expressions and features of all these figures are inspired by northern European painting, as is the large castle and surrounding trees depicted in the background. On the unrailed staircase of the imposing cylindrical building to the right, Joseph takes one of his children by the hand; higher up, the other is greeted affectionately by his mother. Lastly, Joseph and his sons, Ephraim and Manasseh, are portrayed inside the room at the top of the building, where Jacob, now old and near to death, imparts his paternal blessing. The curious com-

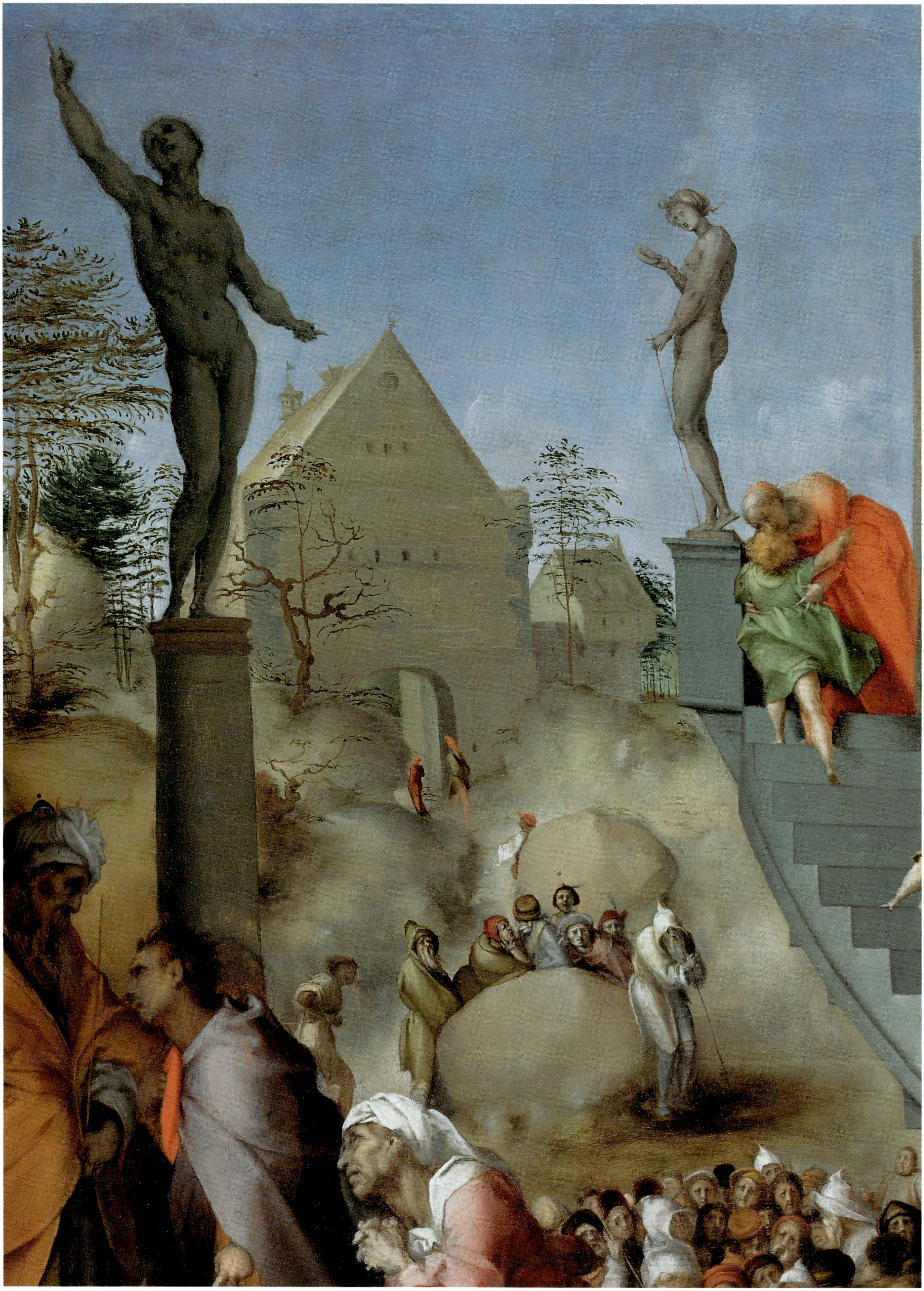

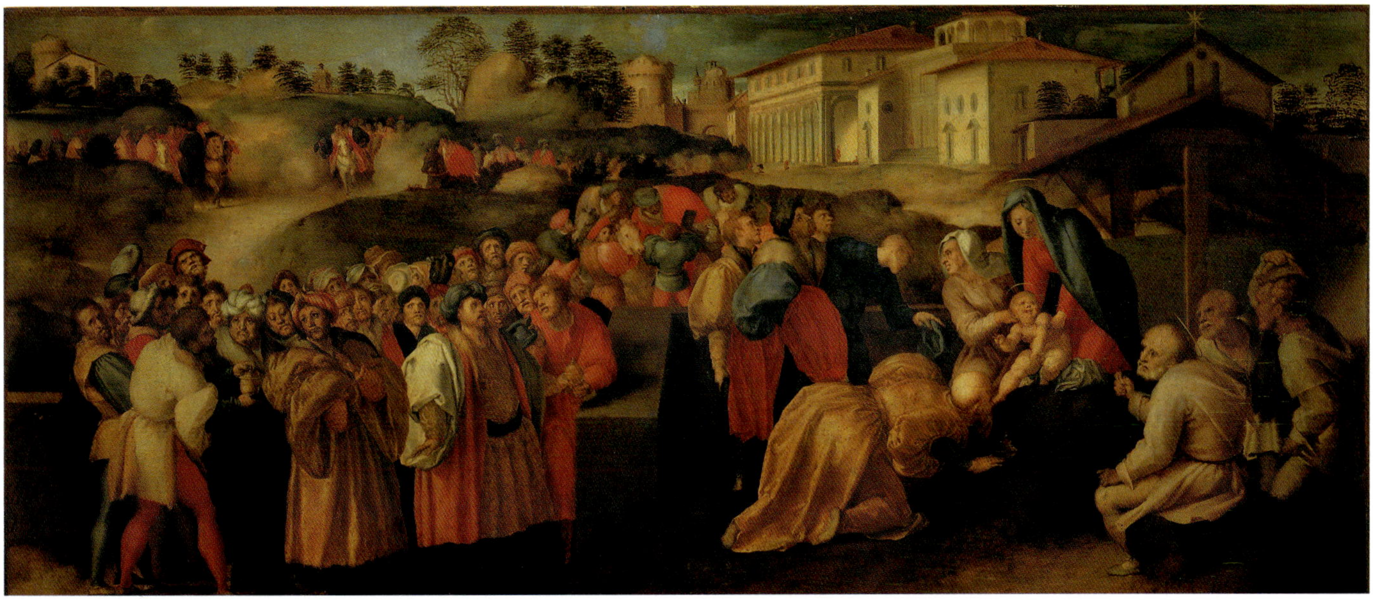

25. Pontormo
Joseph in Egypt, detail
London, National Gallery

26. Pontormo
Adoration of the Magi
85x190 cm
Florence, Galleria Palatina

bination of all these elements confers to the painting an anomalous and intriguing quality.

Two other works by Pontormo can be linked to the stories of the Camera Borgherini. The *Adoration of the Magi* (1522-23), which the artist executed for the chamber of Giovanni Maria Benintendi, has in common with the paintings of the National Gallery the reference to northern figurative culture, which can be perceived in the physiognomical deformation of the characters and in the feverish atmosphere of the whole scene. The background in the painting of *St Quentin* (1517-18), which according to Vasari was executed for the church of San Francesco in Borgo San Sepolcro and is presently conserved in the city's Pinacoteca Comunale, also has certain similarities with the landscape of the *Scenes from the Life of Joseph*. In the old man bent over his walking stick, portrayed in the background to the left of the saint, and in the small figure on the right in the distance pointing nervously at the main event of the painting, the typologies of the two wayfarers meeting in front of the stairway of the scene of *Joseph being sold to Potiphar* are reproposed. Pontormo's predilection for elements of ambiguity and complementarity, already present in his early works, is expressed in the San Sepolcro painting by the contrast between the portrayal of the instruments of torture and the rather languid expression of the saint, who almost seems unaware of the physical pain being inflicted. The painting may also be included among those works by Pontormo in which the references to known sculptural models are more obvious; evident here is the reference to the *Bacchus* of Jacopo Sansovino (1515), now in the Museo Nazionale del Bargello.

In 1518 Pontormo executed the celebrated painting of the *Madonna and Child with saints* for the chapel of Francesco di Giovanni Pucci in San Michele Visdomini in Florence. The painting portrays the Virgin with St John the Evangelist, Joseph, holding the baby Jesus, the young St John, St Francis and St James, the latter being the artist's self-portrait. This work also shows clear references to classical figurative culture, although overall there is a definite break with the effects of harmony and equilibrium. The composition of the figures arranged in two areas, divided by a vertical axis, which forms the height of a triangle, at whose apex is the Virgin's head, recurs in numerous paintings by Fra Bartolomeo. Representative is the so-called *Pitti Altarpiece*, from which the young Pontormo drew inspiration for the *Visitation* of the Annunziata. The painting, which also shows evident references to the psychological characterization and *sfumato* of Leonardesque works, nonetheless represents a moment of exasperation and overall saturation of classical motifs. In the composition both the right part and the left part, although symmetrical and populated by an identical number of figures, are organized very differently. The complex twisting of the bodies and the many different directions of the gestures suggest the use of a grid of extremely complicated and dynamic geometrical schemes. The lines of vision go in all possible directions; in no instance do they cross or match, this emphasizing the psychological isolation of the figures. The facial features and expressions of the older Joseph and St John the Evangelist, as well as the laughing putti, are exaggeratedly pronounced. In short, everything combines to create an atmosphere of restless instability. The effect of suffocating compression produced by the reduction of spatial depth, and by the dense chiaroscuro that attenuates the colours, is counterbalanced by a centrifugal

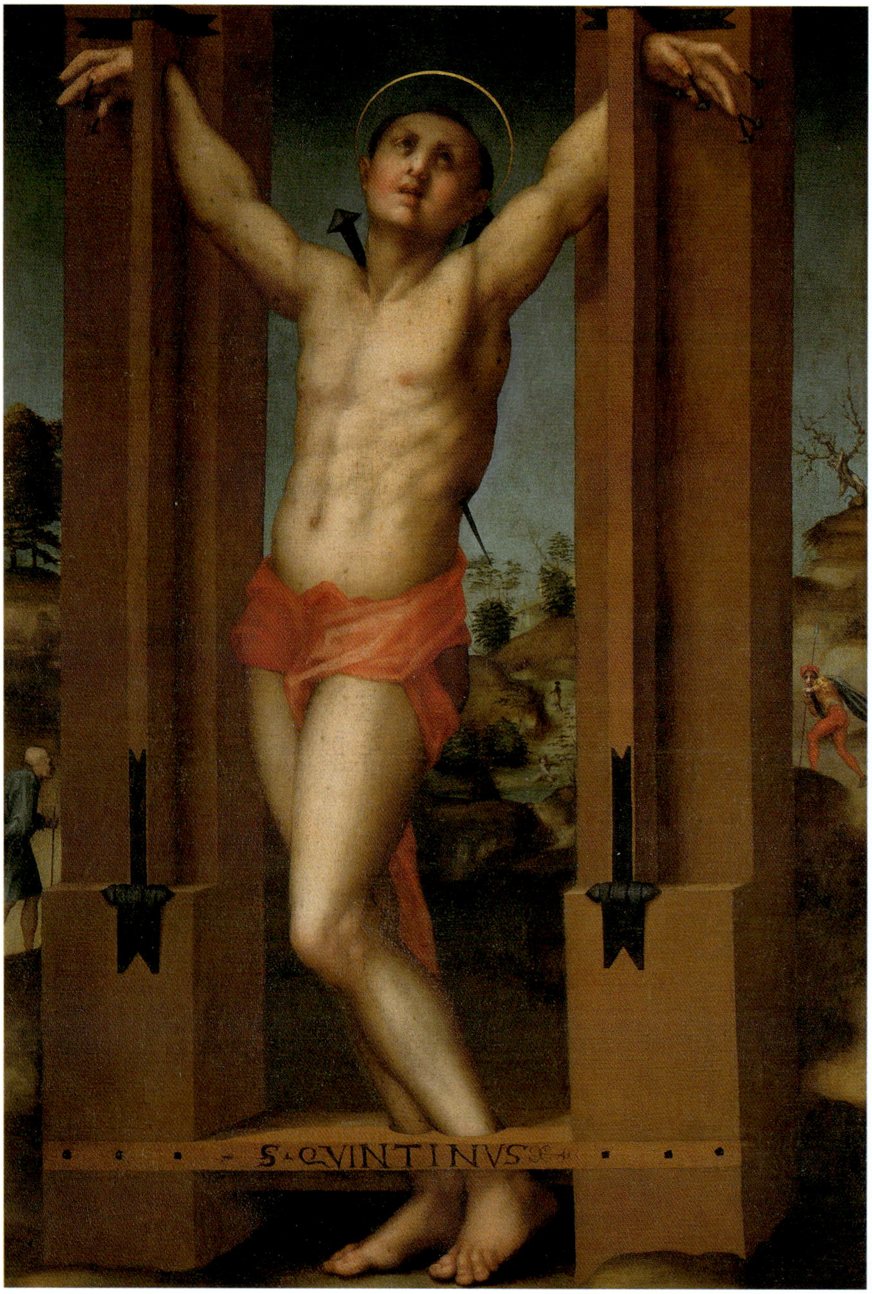

energy generated by the agitation of the figures. This definitively breaks the harmonious unity of the classical compositional structure.

Pontormo's detachment from the contemporary pictorial tradition was decisively affirmed in the *St John the Evangelist* and the *St Michael Archangel*, painted probably in 1519 for the Cappella del Santissimo Crocifisso in the church of San Michele Arcangelo at Pontorme, where they now are. In the case of the two saints of Pontorme, as in the already mentioned *St Quentin*, the model for the construction and positioning of the figures is undeniably sculptural. In the *St John the Evangelist*, for example, the left leg crossing over the right, with the foot resting on its toes, recalls that of the *Levite* (1506-11), sculpted by Giovanni Francesco Rustici and placed to the right of the figure of the Baptist above the north door of the Baptistery in Florence. But perhaps more than because of the evident similarities with sculpture, the paint-

27. Pontormo
St Quentin
163x103 cm
Sansepolcro, Pinacoteca Comunale

28. Pontormo
Madonna and Child with saints (Pucci Altarpiece)
214x185 cm
Florence, San Michele Visdomini

29-30. Pontormo
St John the Evangelist and St Michael Archangel
173x59 cm each
Pontorme (Empoli), San Michele

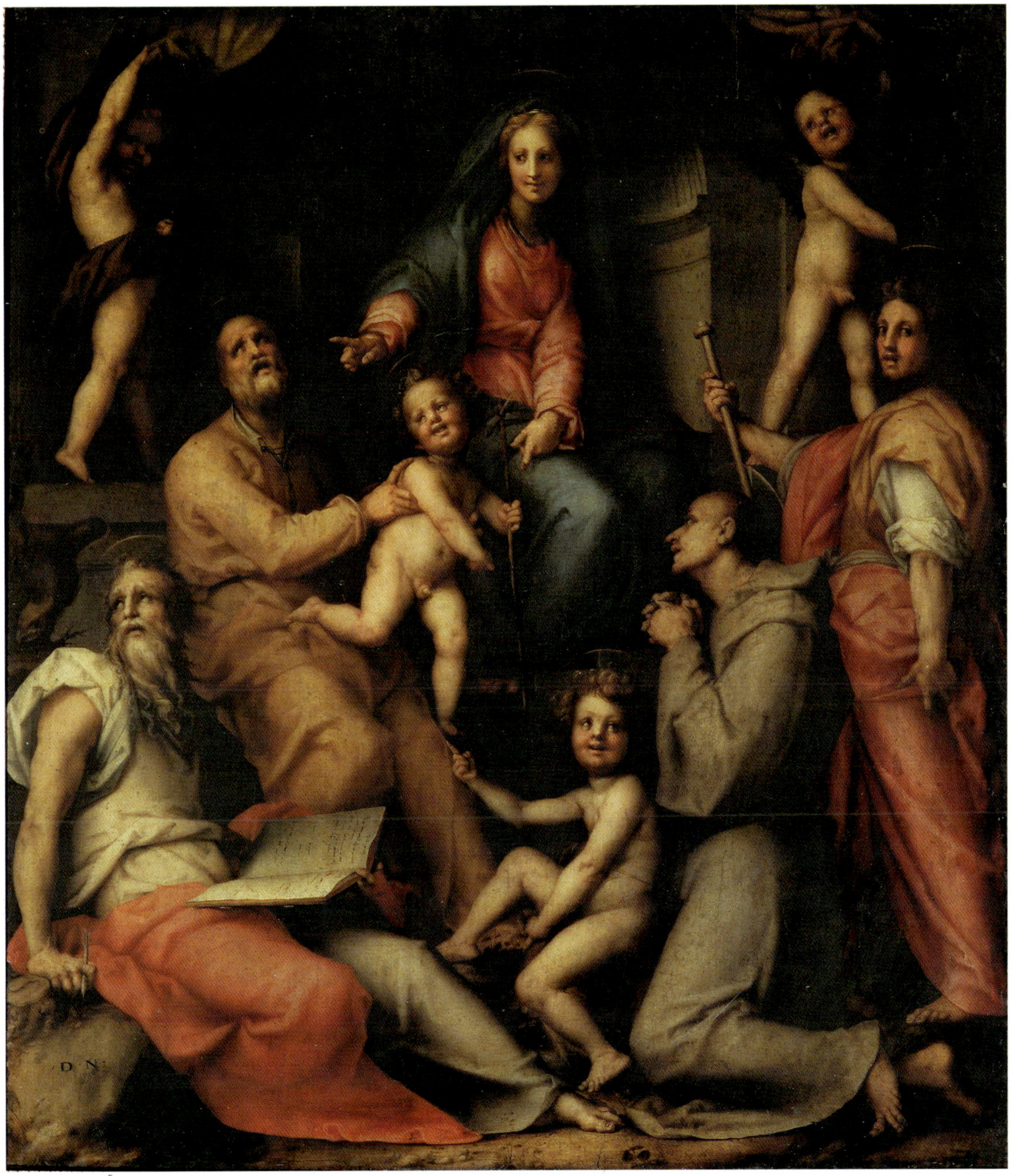

ings in question play a role of particular importance within Pontormo's pictorial production because they usher in a phase of refined formal research.

First of all, there is a deliberately clear-cut demarcation of the edges of the surfaces of the bodies, drapery and other details, which bestows particular emphasis on the paintings' complex linear articulation. In addition to the calligraphic elegance, the play of colours also reinforces the formal refinement of the paintings. In both cases the red of the drapery that surrounds the figures, although having a noticeably different tonality, lighter in the case of *St John the Evangelist*, brighter and stronger in that of *St Michael*, invades the painted surface and contrasts sharply with the darkness of the background and the blue-grey tints of the clothes. This dominant colour contrast forms a kind of formal connection between the two paintings. A bizarre element is added to the portrayal of *St Michael* in the presence of the putto with its hooked wings and ass's ears, representing the demon. With a stunned expression, the putto clutches a cup of the scales held by archangel Michael and, turning it over, shows its underside; still fresh is the wound that the saint has inflicted on its back.

The *St Antony Abbot* of the Uffizi (ca. 1519) reminds us of the figure of *St John the Evangelist* of Pontorme by virtue of the obvious facial similarities. This bald and long-bearded old man, holding a scroll in his right hand and clutching a gnarled staff with his left, is also reminiscent of Michelangelo's celebrated figures of prophets in the Sistine Chapel, while his furrowed brow and visionary expression also recall some typologies of figures portrayed in the engravings of Dürer. Compared to the variegated tints and colour shades of the saints of Pontorme, the severe, sober use of colour in this painting, being essentially limited to shades of black and brown, almost tending to monochrome, represents a

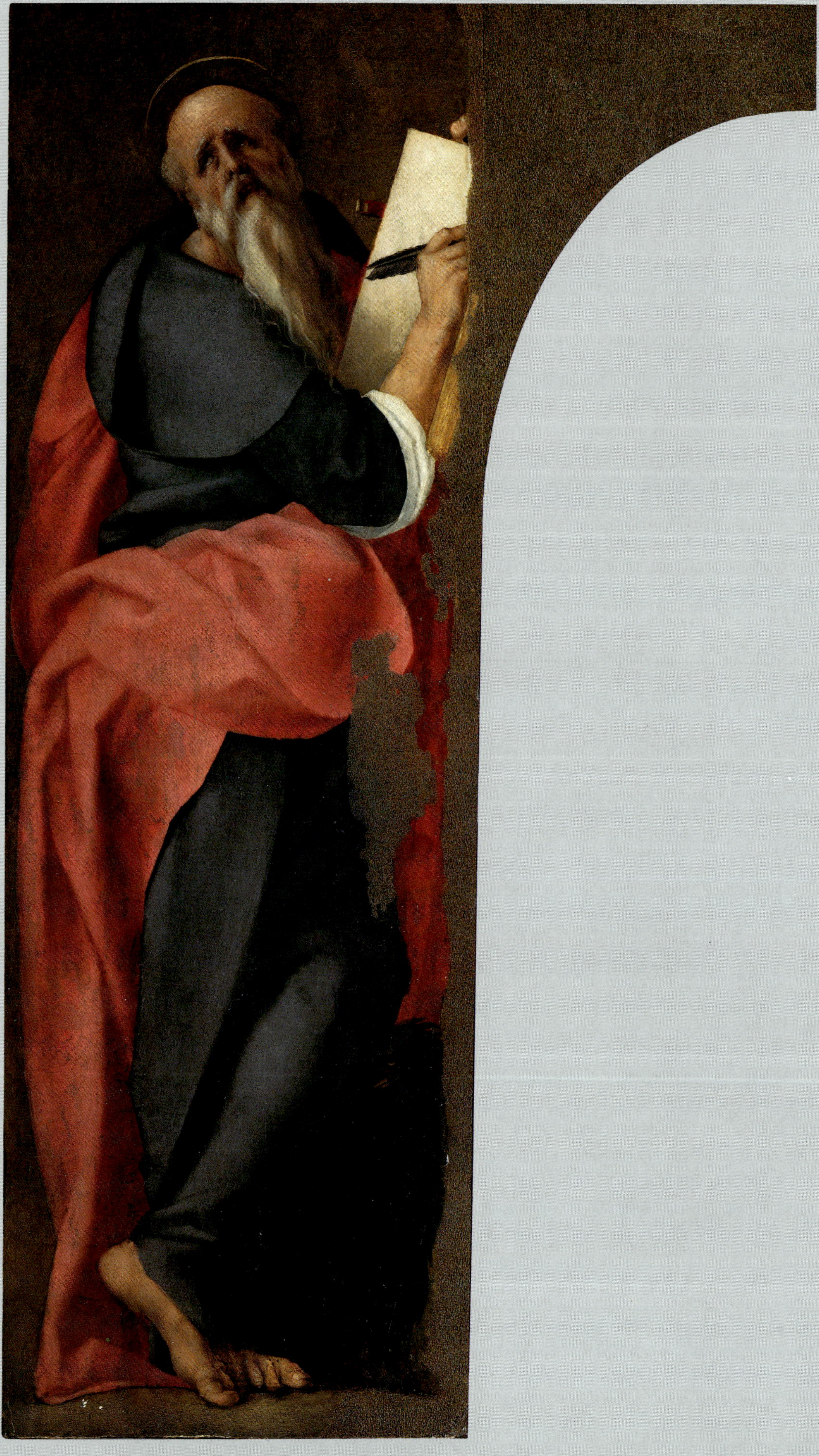

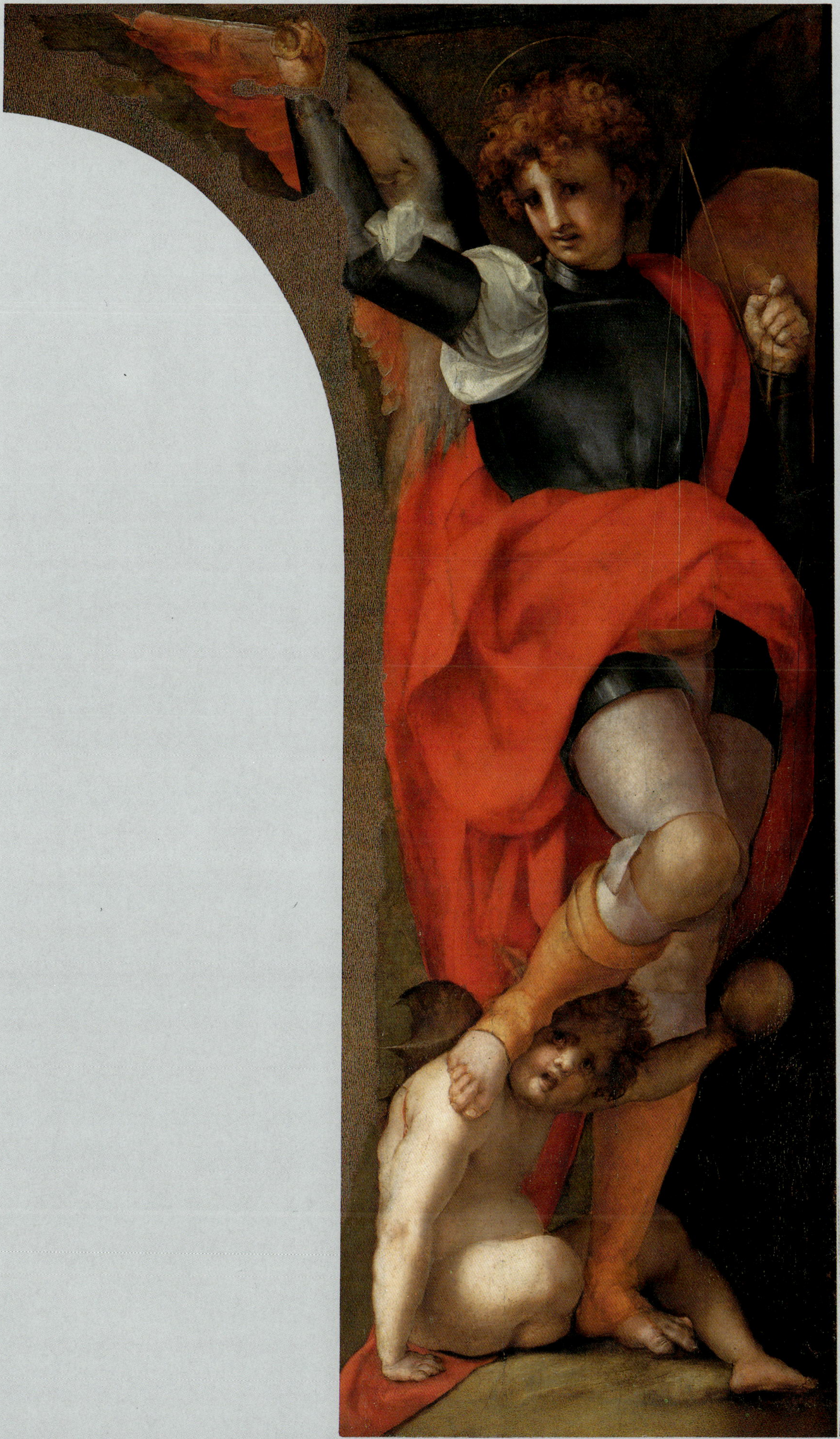

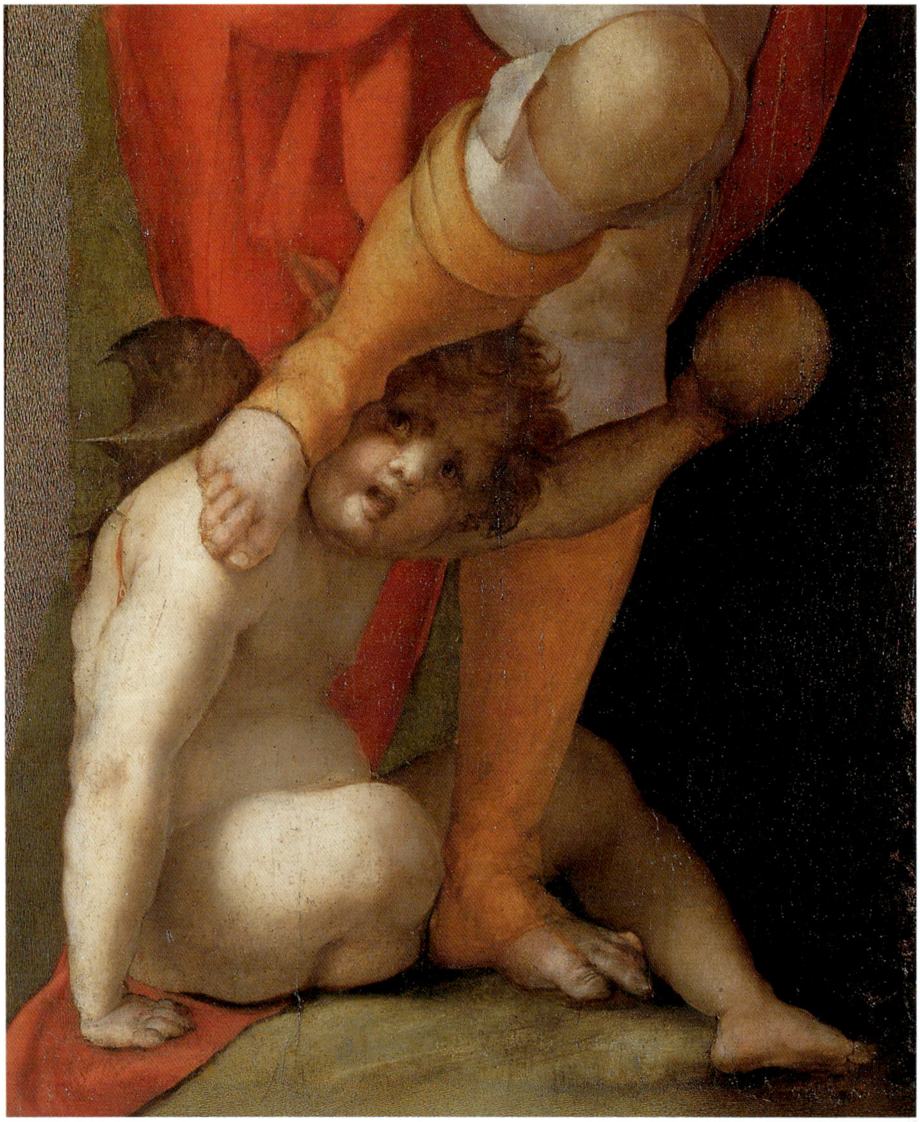

31. Pontormo
St Michael Archangel, detail
Pontorme (Empoli), San Michele

32. Pontormo
St Antony Abbot
78x66 cm
Florence, Uffizi

33. Rosso Fiorentino
Macabre Allegory
Florence, Prints and Drawings
Collection of the Uffizi, no.
6499 F

different, though no less refined, formal direction.

Strong colour contrasts and calligraphic effects reappear in the *Madonna and Child with two saints* (ca. 1522) of the Uffizi, a work whose attribution to Pontormo is the object of some debate. In this painting the spatial depth, already considerably reduced by the closing of the background by means of a wall with a parapet, is completely annulled by the juxtaposition of the various colours which, it as has been noted, creates an effect of "polychrome intarsia" (A. Venturi, 1932). Here, as in the *Pucci Altarpiece*, the harmony of the classical compositional structure is disrupted by the varied, diverging directions of the postures, expressions and gestures of the figures, most noticeably the nervously outstretched hand of St Francis. The prevailing movement, however, produced by the forked opening of the bodies of the two angels sitting in front of the Virgin, is away from the centre of the composition.

Rosso responded to the opening of the classical scheme, a result which Pontormo achieved in the examples described, with a tendency to close the composition towards the centre. This is clearly revealed by comparing the above-mentioned pair of angels painted by Pon-

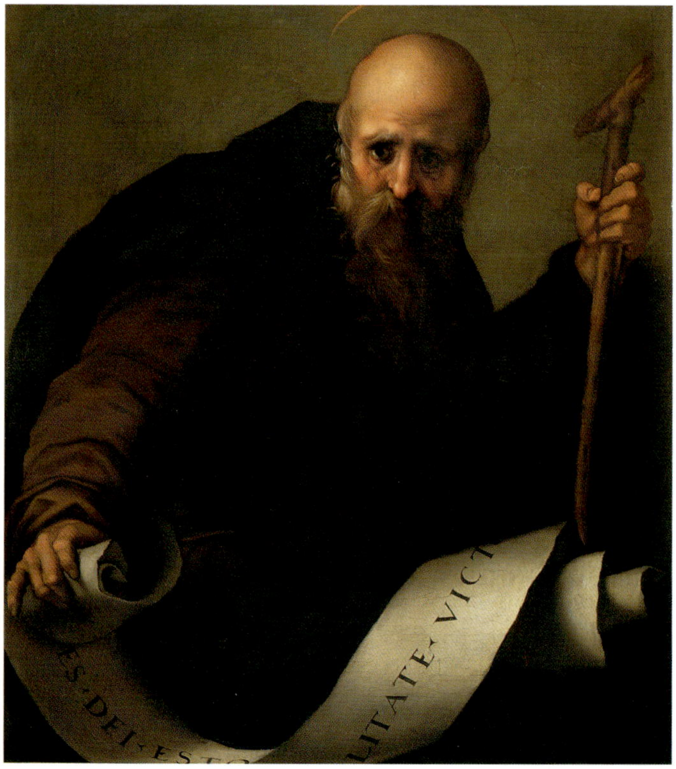

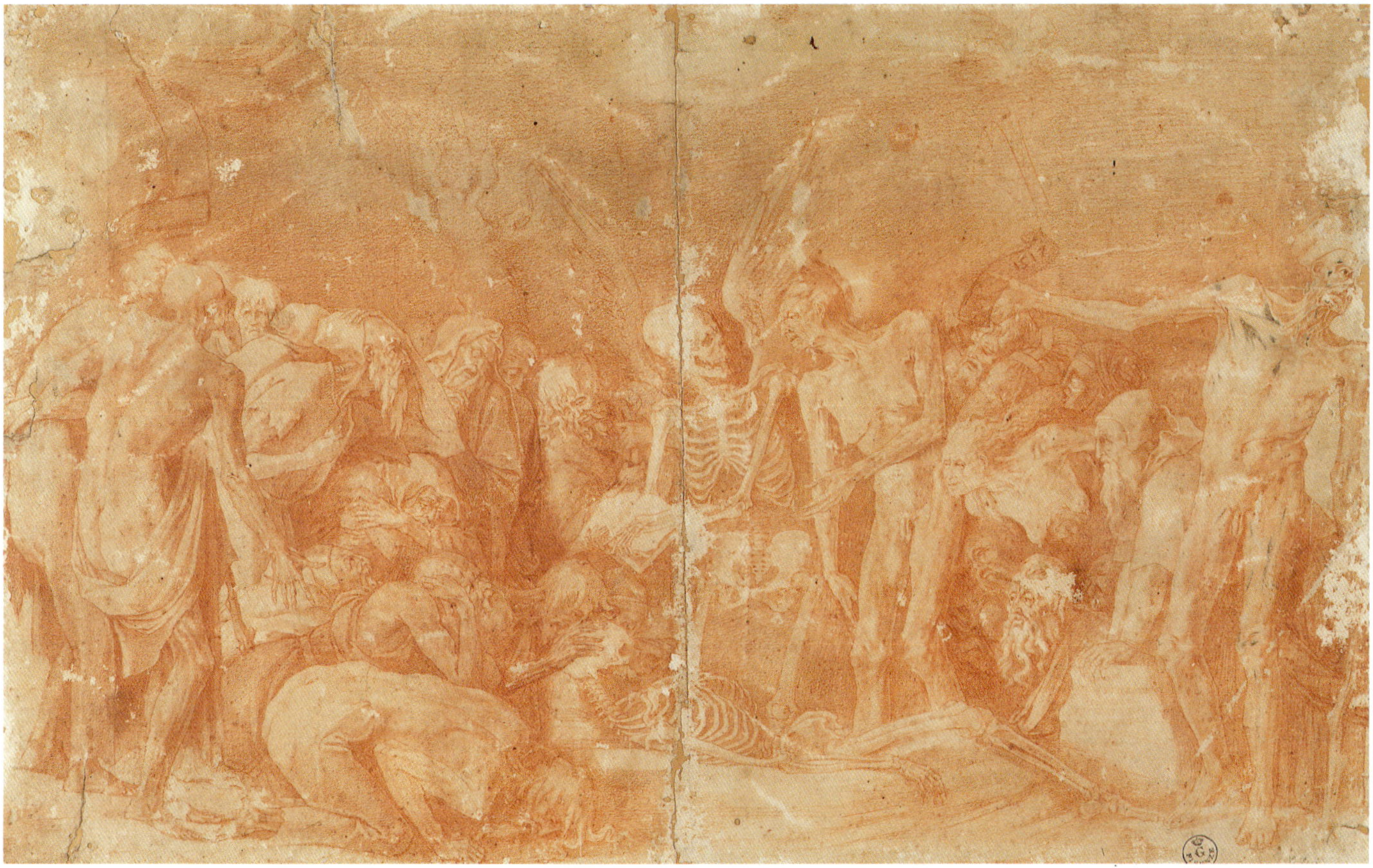

tormo with the two angels crouching in the foreground of the celebrated *Ognissanti Altarpiece*, which Rosso Fiorentino executed in 1518. This painting, now in the Uffizi and also known by the title *Madonna enthroned with four saints*, portrays the Virgin and Child between St John the Baptist, St Antony Abbot, St Stephen and St Jerome. The work was commissioned by Leonardo Buonafede, the "spedalingo" of Santa Maria Nuova, for a chapel in the church of Ognissanti, in accordance with the testamentary will of Francesca de Ripoi, a Catalan widow who had lived in Florence. The painting never in fact occupied the place it had been intended for, very probably due to the dissatisfaction of the person who commissioned it, who, according to Vasari, saw it while it was being prepared and was decidedly unimpressed. The presence of the saints, with their rather diabolical features and their "cruel and desperate expressions", which provoked the reaction of Buonafede, is undoubtedly one of the most innovative characteristics of this painting. The faces of the saints, darkened by heavy shading, are utterly devoid of that serenity which characterizes the figures in traditional altarpieces, absorbed in meditation or rapt in mystical ecstasy. Their expressions are not harmonized into a gentle collective interaction, but instead are questioning and visibly astonished, conveying a sense of overall tension that is enhanced by the nervous gestures of St Jerome, the Child and St John the Baptist. The general unease of the upper group seems to have no effect on the two angels sitting at the Virgin's feet, who are totally absorbed in their reading. This same quality of relaxed and total absorption in a particular activity is also

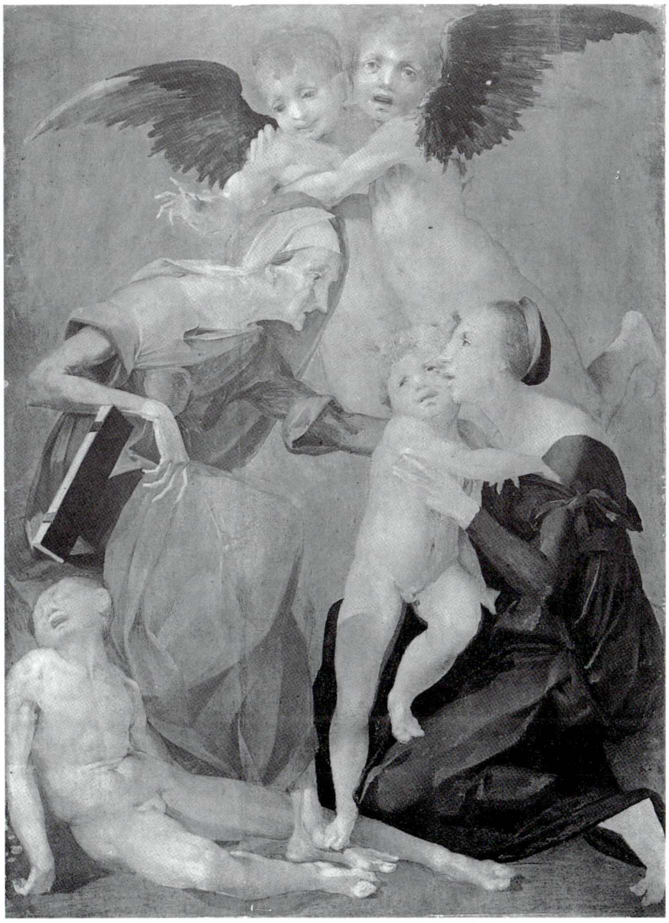

34. Rosso Fiorentino: Holy Family, 161x117 cm Los Angeles, County Museum

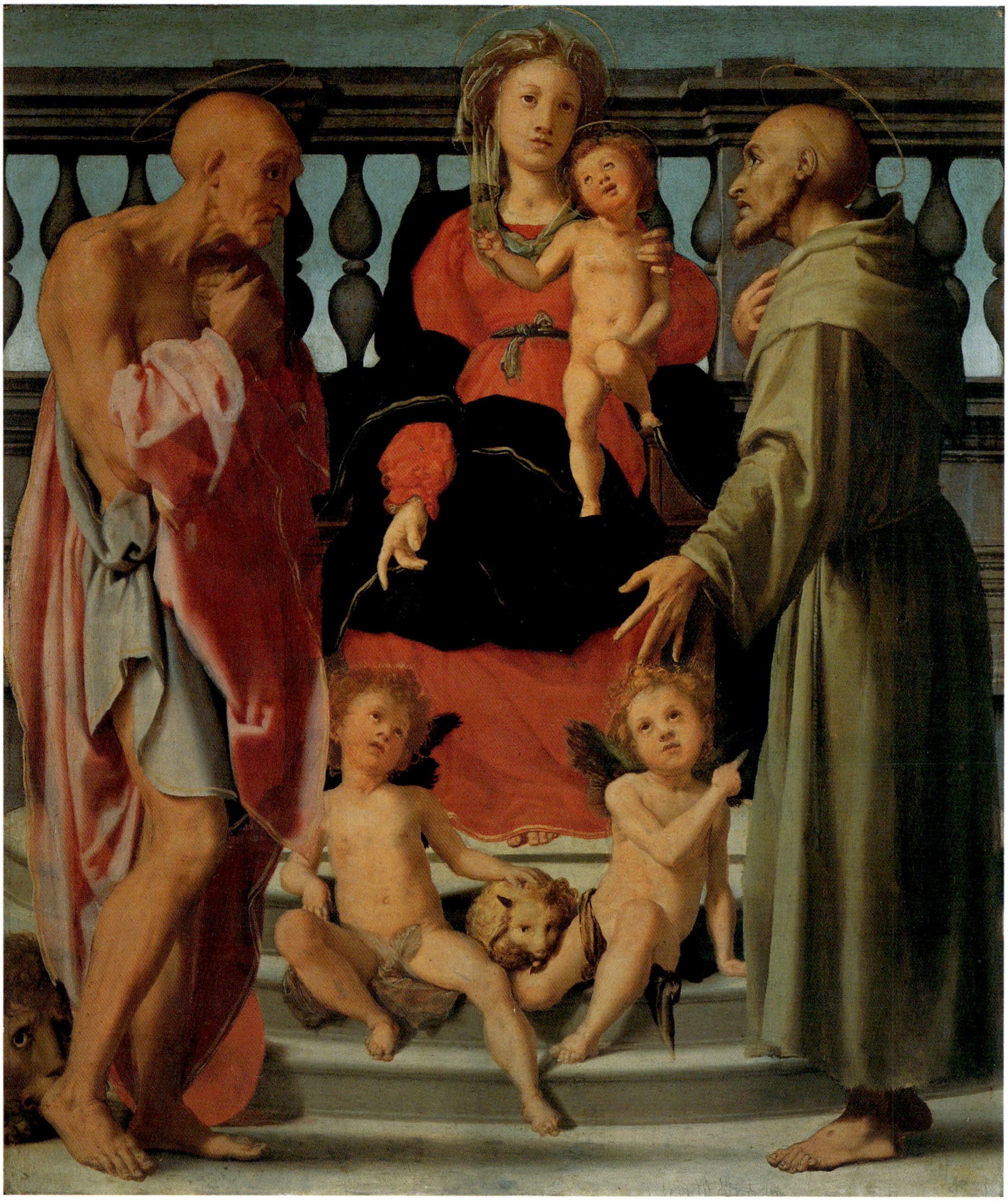

present in the extraordinary *Musician Angel* of the Uffizi, the angel's curly-haired head resting delicately on the lute on which it is playing some chords. According to the most recent critics the small painting probably has a chronological placing during Rosso's second Florentine period (ca. 1522) and is probably the fragment of a larger work.

In the *Ognissanti Altarpiece* the disruptive figurative innovations are accompanied by references to the tradition, in Bartolomeesque and even High Renaissance models, of the niche-like arrangement of the group of saints and the postures of the individual figures. As with Pontormo's more or less contemporary examples, these are visibly compressed by the marked reduction of spatial depth. Although the folds of the clothing and drapery are stiff and angular, they are distinguished by a complex range of colours and delicate *cangiante* effects. The typology of St Jerome, with the "cruel" and at the same time "desperate" expression referred to by Vasari, is new. In this figure, the sunken abdomen, the prominent sternum, ribs and collar-bone of the chest area, and the skeletal thinness of the neck, arms and fingers, reveal unquestionable links with the studies of decomposing or flayed bodies that began to interest a great number of Tuscan artists from the 15th century; among them we may therefore also include Rosso. The two flayed figures portrayed at the extreme sides of the composition in the enigmatic *Macabre Allegory* of the Uffizi (1517) may be associated with similar experiences. And in this context we might also include the figures of the emaciated St Anne and the young St John of the *Holy Family* of Los Angeles, pervaded by a funereal and anguished atmosphere. Here Rosso affirms his clear detachment from the traditional portrayals of one of the most commonly painted iconographical themes of the early years of the 16th cen-

35. Pontormo
Madonna and Child with two saints
72x60 cm
Florence, Uffizi

36. Rosso Fiorentino
Madonna enthroned with four saints (Ognissanti Altarpiece)
172x141 cm
Florence, Uffizi

37. Rosso Fiorentino
Musician Angel
47x39 cm
Florence, Uffizi

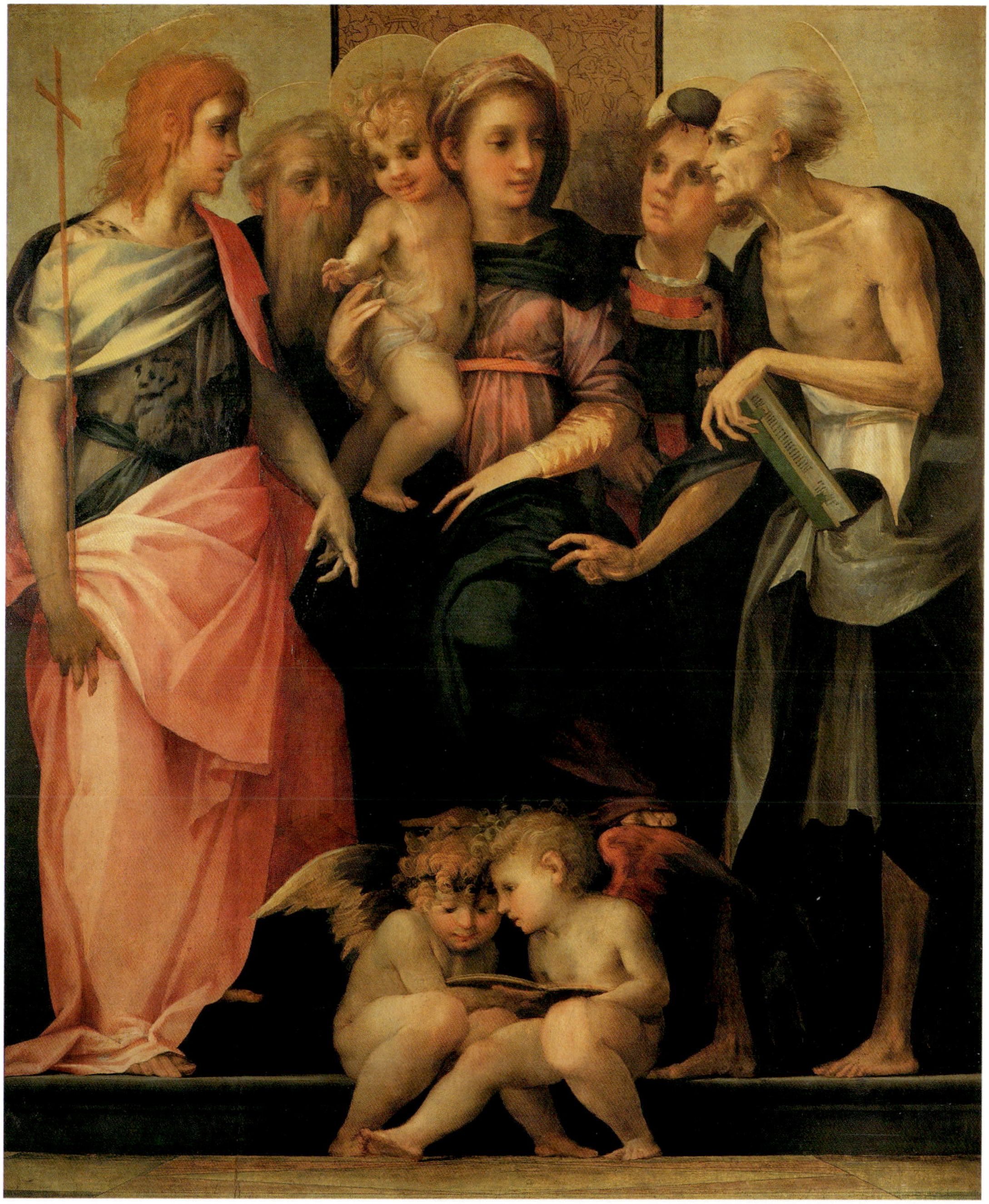

tury, the Madonna and Child with the young St John, to which is sometimes added the figure of St Anne. Every trace of the grace and softness in the expressions and postures of the figures, depicted in numerous proto-16th-century examples, has been lost. The serene, luxuriant natural environment that customarily surrounds the holy group has been replaced by an indefinite space from which two disturbing figures of demon-angels with dark, menacing wings emerge. In addition to the innovative figurative inventions, the painting is shot through with a haunted atmosphere produced by eccentric changing colour effects, unfinished parts and the substantial dissolution of the plastic form, especially apparent in the lower part of the work. The painting thus heralds that period of audacious formal and expressive experimentalism that would reach its height in the works of the Volterran period.

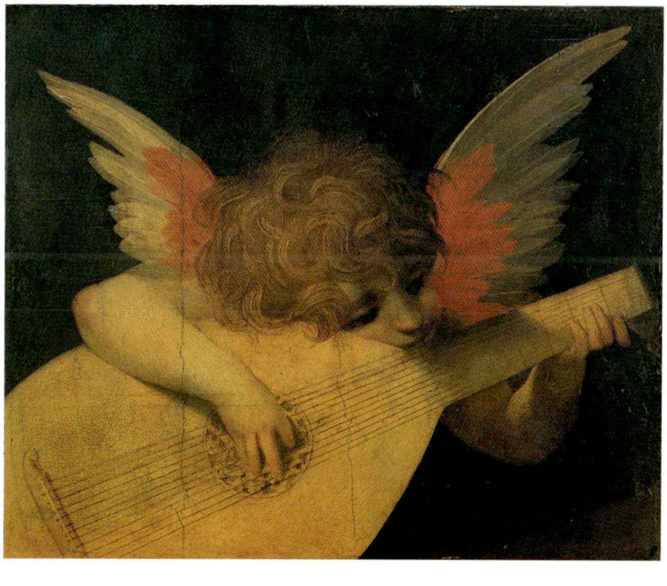

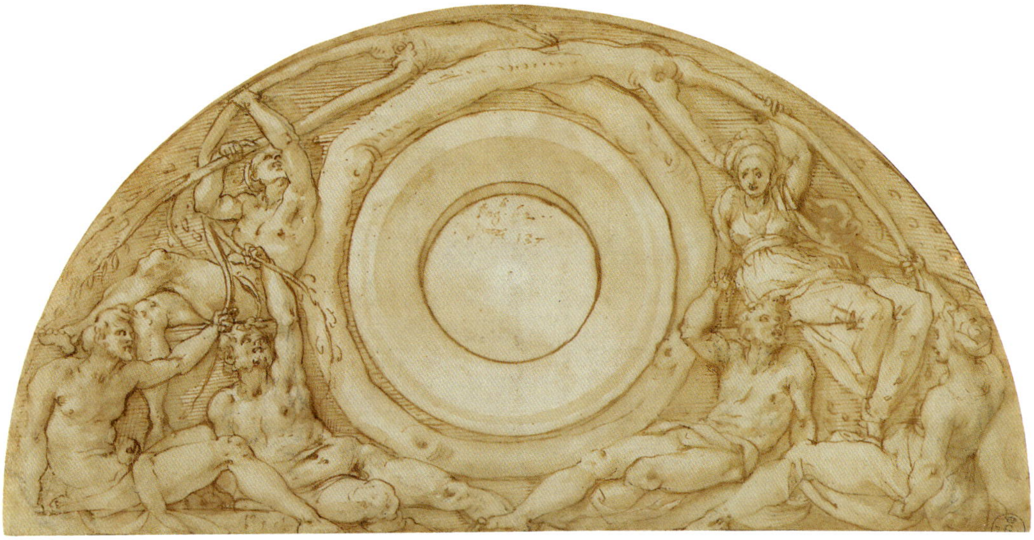

Pontormo at Poggio a Caiano

In 1519 Pontormo took part in the decoration of the salone of the Medicean villa of Poggio a Caiano. He received the commission from Ottaviano de' Medici, who presided over the works on behalf of pope Leo X, formerly Cardinal Giovanni de' Medici, and Cardinal Giulio, his cousin, the future Clement VII. The iconographical programme, designed by the historian Paolo Giovio, aimed to evoke the celebrations of the Medici house through a series of episodes drawn from Roman history. Following the specifications laid down by Giovio, the other artists involved in the decorative cycle, Andrea del Sarto and Franciabigio, painted two walls of the great hall. In 1521, due to the death of Leo X, the works were suspended for over a decade. In 1532 the new pope Clement VII again summoned Pontormo to complete the cycle of frescoes. For this second commission, which the artist never executed, there survive some extraordinary preparatory cartoons, which we shall consider further on. As regards the programme of Paolo Giovio, the theme chosen by the painter is undoubtedly an isolated episode. This was, according to Vasari, the pictorial representation of the classical myth of Vertumnus and Pomona taken from a story in Ovid's *Metamorphosis*.

In Pontormo's fresco the two deities are represented at the two ends of the lower area of the lunette with the same attributes that distinguish them in Ovid's story, the sickle of Pomona and the basket of Vertumnus. They are both wearing peasants' clothes, like the other adult figures in the group. Around the oculus of the window are four naked putti: the two lower ones are holding the two ends of a festoon of leaves and fruits, while the two above are sitting on large trunks, from which slender laurel branches grow outwards, holding two standards aloft. A fifth ignudo, a boy, is sitting on the low wall behind the old peasant representing Vertumnus and the young companion sitting beside him. Dangling his legs, he rests his right forearm on the wall and extends his left upwards, raising a pale mauve-coloured cloth to touch a bayleaf. The airy atmosphere and the relaxed attitudes of the figures are those of a peasants' moment of leisure on a hot day of rest. The classical myth is therefore reworked here in a rustic-

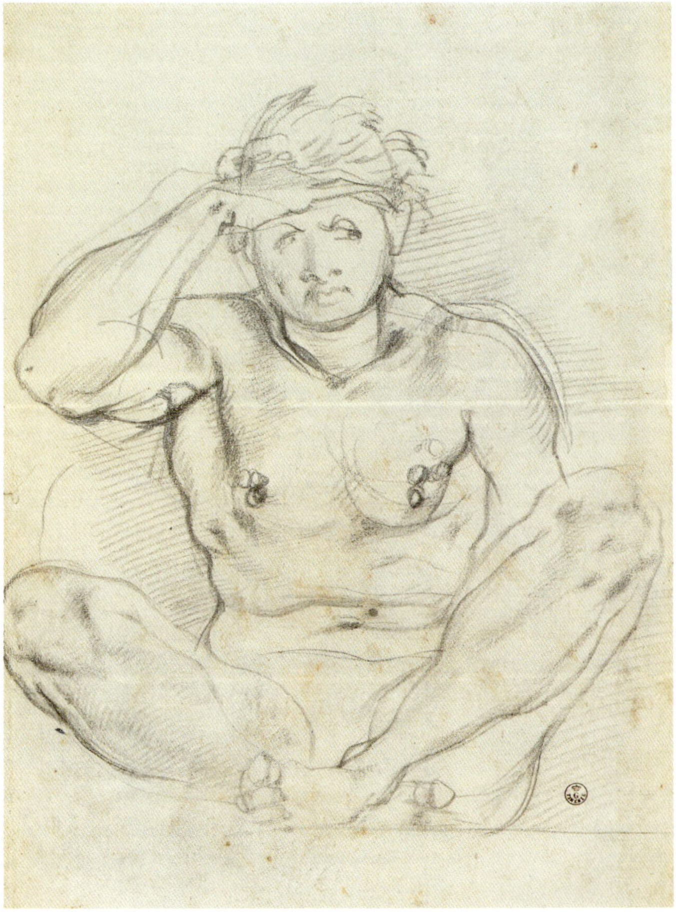

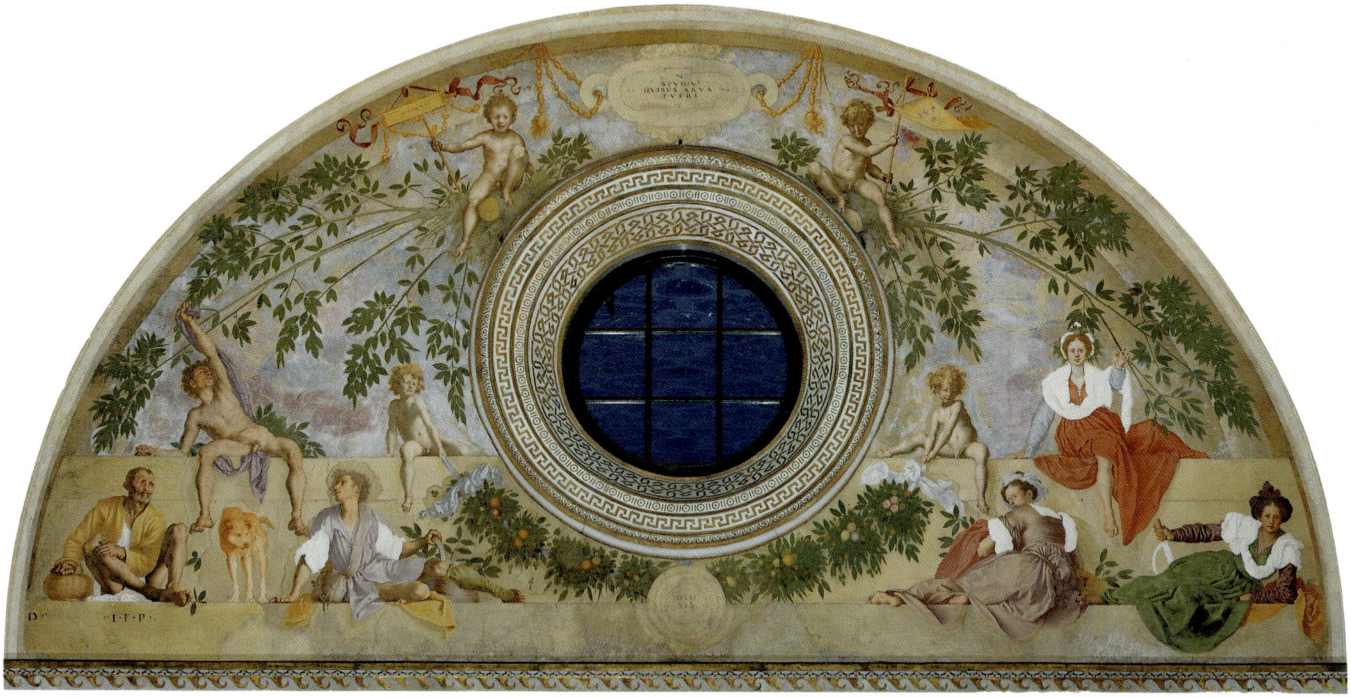

38. Pontormo
Study for the lunette with Vertumnus and Pomona
Florence, Prints and Drawings Collection of the Uffizi, no. 454 F

39. Pontormo
Figure study for Vertumnus and Pomona
Florence, Prints and Drawings Collection of the Uffizi, no. 6685 F r

40. Pontormo
Vertumnus and Pomona
461x990 cm
Poggio a Caiano (Florence), Medici villa

popularesque way. The general naturalistic character reaches the height of realism in the portrayal of the peasant Vertumnus, his face furrowed by the ravages of time and his gnarled hands deformed by the hardships of work in the fields. To his right is a skinny dog with a grumpy expression, almost ready to bark, undoubtedly one of the most unusual and bizarre details of the fresco. It was probably the example of northern engravings that inspired Pontormo to develop this particular interest for the representation of the natural world, in which animals and plants have a dignity equal to that of human beings.

The inscription on the plaque, which crowns the oculus, refers to the rustic theme. It is in fact a quotation from the first book of Virgil's *Georgics*, in which the author invokes the gods and goddesses whose task is to protect the fields: Diique deaeque quibus arva tueri (*Georgics* 1, 21). The exaltation of country life was a perfectly appropriate theme for the decoration of a Medicean "villa". Indeed, Lorenzo il Magnifico, in various passages of his celebrated literary works, had already extolled the beneficial effects of country life as opposed to the tensions of political and social commitments in the city.

According to one critical interpretation, the fresco's appearance as an innocent rural fable may conceal a more complex allegorical significance, linking the theme chosen by Pontormo to the other scenes depicted in the salone. Together with these, the representation of the classical myth of Vertumnus and Pomona would form a single complex political metaphor designed to exalt the destiny and immortality of the Medicean dynasty. The various branches of the powerful Florentine family would be represented by the trunk of laurel situated in the upper part of the lunette. The renewal of the dynasty in the course of the years and the consequent immortality of Medicean power would be evoked by the idea of the regeneration of nature with the passing of time, in the passing of the days and the seasons. In this context, the companions of Vertumnus and Pomona would also be seen as divine figures: thus, the young ignudo sitting on the low wall and the peasant woman corresponding to him on the other side, would be respectively Bacchus, the god of wine, and Ceres, the goddess of agriculture, both linked to the theme of the renewal of the natural world and mentioned by Virgil in the passage of the *Georgics*. Beside Vertumnus, traditionally associated with winter, would be represented Apollo, the sun; on the other side Diana, the moon, the only other deity cited by Vasari, and Pomona, or spring. The series of figures arranged in the foreground in the lower area of the fresco would therefore allude to the passing of the days and months.

Observing the fresco with particular attention we also notice that the scene has no descriptive or narrative

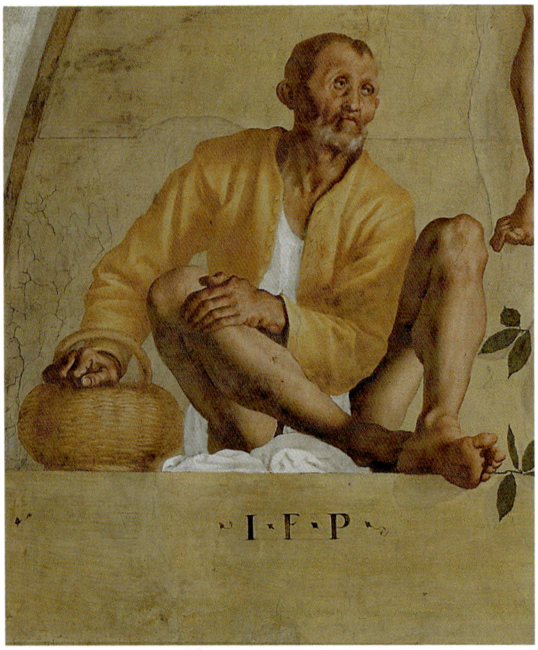

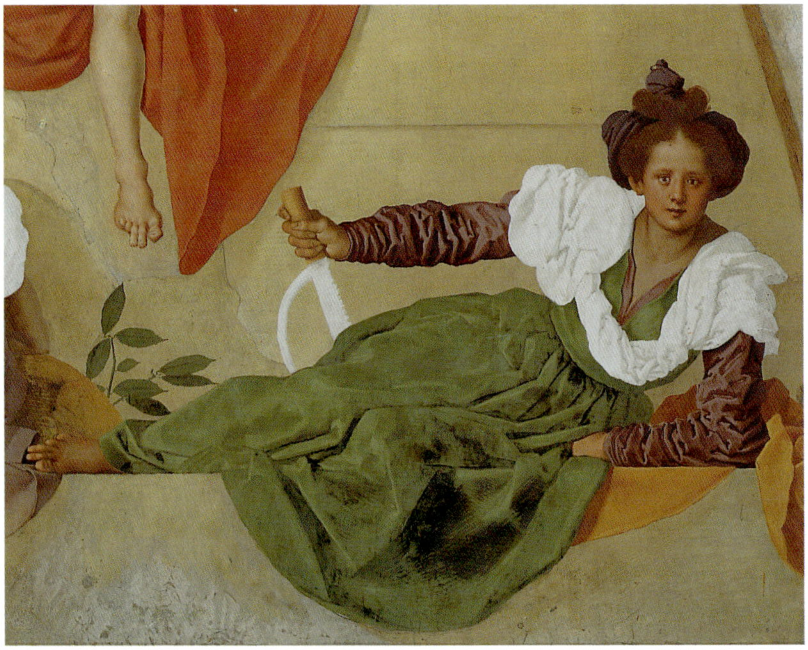

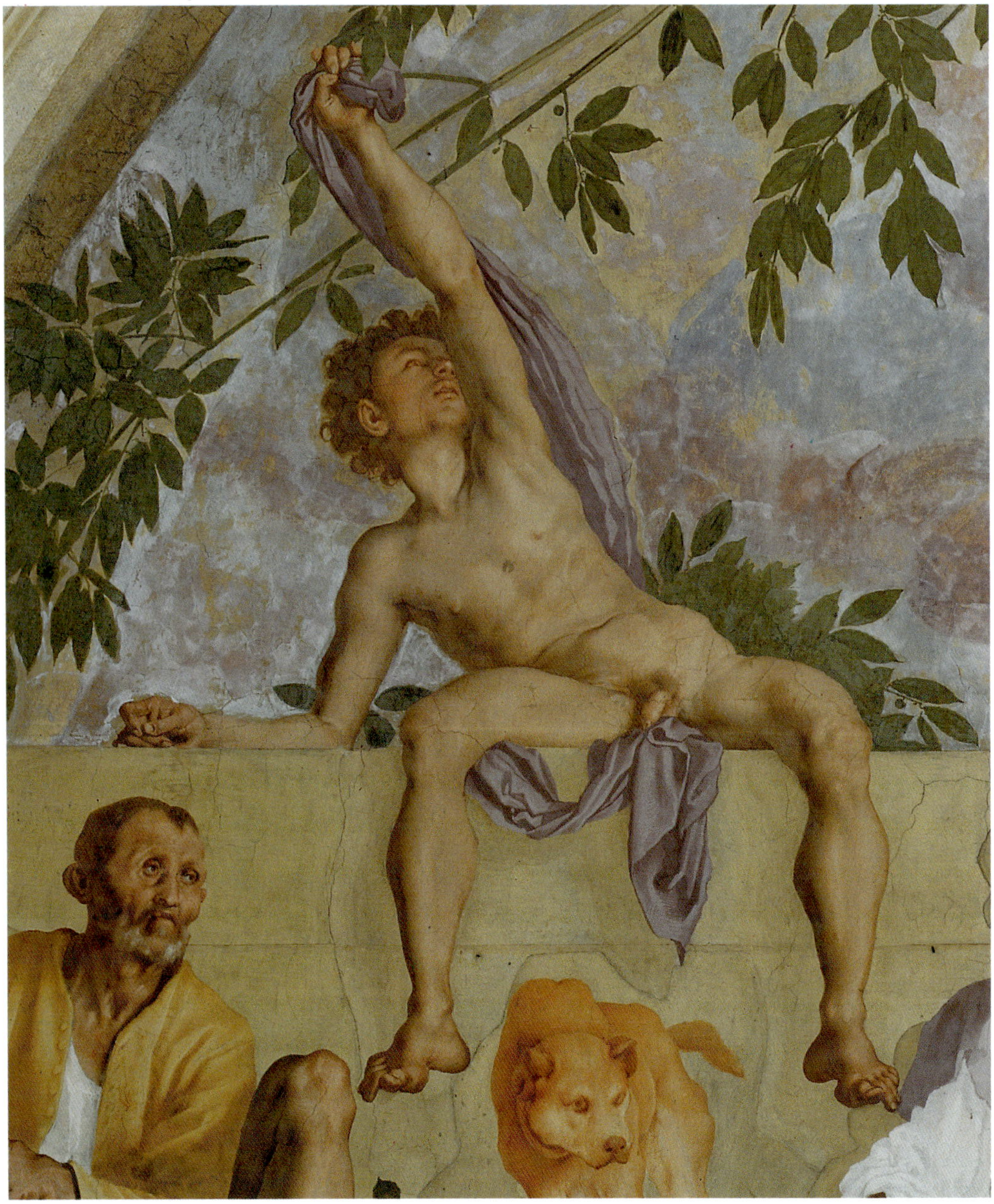

41-43. Pontormo
Vertumnus and Pomona, details
Poggio a Caiano (Florence), Medici villa

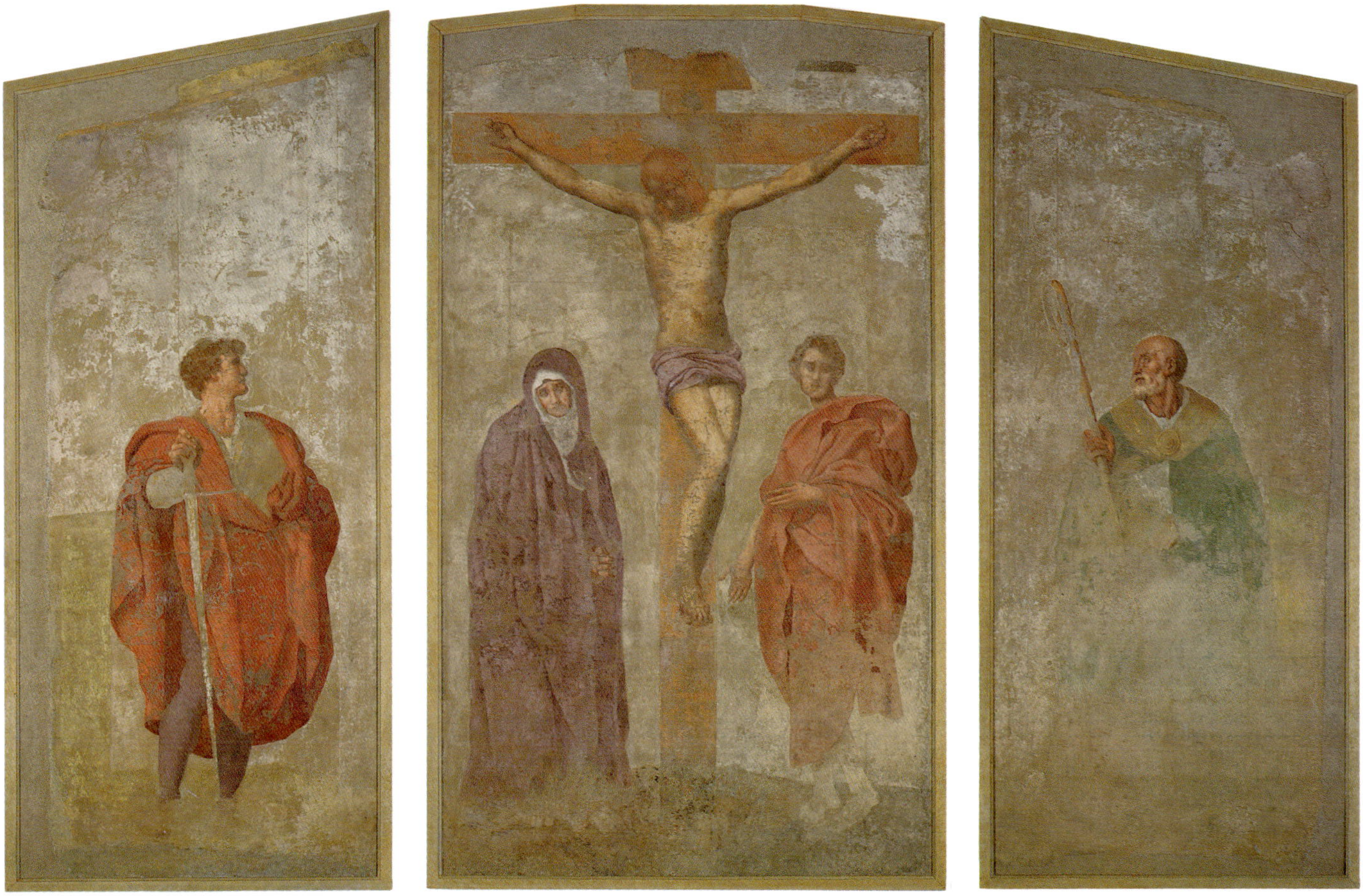

44. Pontormo
Tabernacle of Boldrone
Crucifixion with the Virgin and St John, 307x175 cm; St Julian and St Augustine, 307x127 cm each
Florence, Accademia delle Arti del Disegno (deposito)

content, it tells us no story, and the natural environment is evoked only by the presence of the laurel fronds and the clothing of the figures. The apparent naturalness of the whole scene coexists with, or rather, is dominated by a refined formal research which, as in the other works by Pontormo so far analyzed, very probably represented the artist's main interest.

This aspect is testified primarily by the long and complex process of graphic preparation that preceded the final execution of the fresco. Of this period of elaboration there remain today three designs relative to the decoration of the whole surface of the lunette and some preparatory drawings for the individual figures. Some of these drawings remained at the level of ideas, among them the unforgettable drawing of a young ignudo sitting cross-legged and shielding his eyes from the sun.

Proceeding to a brief examination of the formal aspects of the fresco of the large lunette, we notice at once a clear reduction of the spatial depth. The sensation of an open environment is, in fact, only apparent. The hazy sky of the background and the low wall close the space, reducing to the minimum its capacity to accommodate figures. The arrangement of the figures is regulated by a relatively simple schema, characterized by a thoroughly studied symmetrical equilibrium: two figures in the foreground on the right and two on the left on the first ledge of the wall, two on each side on the second level and another two in the upper area of the oculus. Inside this basic structure, however, the harmony of the whole scene is compromised by the plurality of the directions suggested by the extremely articulated postures of the figures: seated, reclining, viewed frontally and from behind.

The facial features of the old peasant Vertumnus recalls those of St Augustine depicted on the left of the crucified Christ in the fresco executed by Pontormo for a tabernacle at Quarto, near the Benedictine monastery of Boldrone. Also traceable to the decoration of the lunette of Poggio a Caiano is the chromatic delicacy of this work, a work, on the other hand, which by virtue of the unmistakably northern characteristics of the Madonna and St John the Baptist is also linked to the cycle of frescoes for the Carthusian monastery of Galluzzo. The fresco must have been completed, therefore, in an intermediate period between the two works mentioned, that is, between 1521 and 1522.

The works for the Carthusian monastery of Galluzzo

In 1523, writes Vasari, "there being some mild outbreaks of plague in Florence [...] Jacopo had the opportunity of going some distance away and leaving the city". In the company of Bronzino, Pontormo took refuge in the Carthusian monastery of Galluzzo, where he worked until 1527. The isolated environment, far from the tensions of city life, was particularly suited to the meditative and solitary nature of Pontormo, who in this phase of his artistic activity was observing with particular attention a new figurative model, the northern one, from which he had already drawn much inspiration in the panels of the Camera Borgherini. The cycle of frescoes with *Scenes of the Passion*, which he executed in the monastery cloister, marked a stage of authentic exploration into that variegated and complex figurative universe. Although attempts were made in the past to identify the influence of Dürer in each of the scenes, today it would seem more accurate to ascribe a generally northern taste to the entire decoration. We see it, unquestionably, in the elongated profiles and clothing of the figures, and above all in the psychological penetration perceptible in the dramatic spirituality of their expressions. Sharply drawing attention to this evident characteristic, Vasari reproached Pontormo in the frescoes for the monastery for having abandoned "his early style, which was given to him by Nature, full of delicacy and grace", and for having assimilated "the unadorned German style in everything - in the garments, in the expression on the faces and in the poses". It is thanks to this intense period of study of the northern figurative culture, however, that Pontormo broke all ties with the Florentine tradition and gave vent to a highly personal formal research.

Although the frescoes are in a very poor condition it

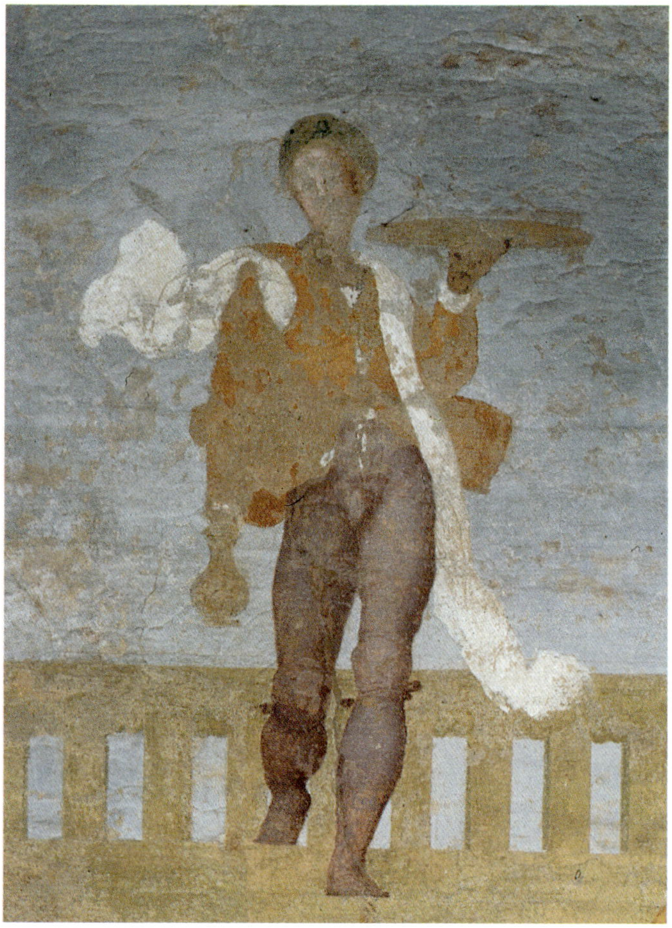

45-50. Pontormo
Cycle with Scenes of the Passion
Certosa del Galluzzo (Florence)

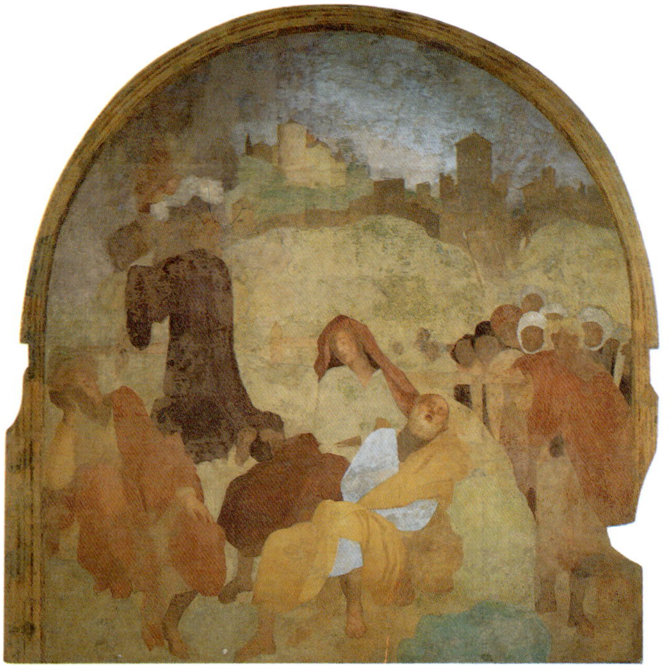

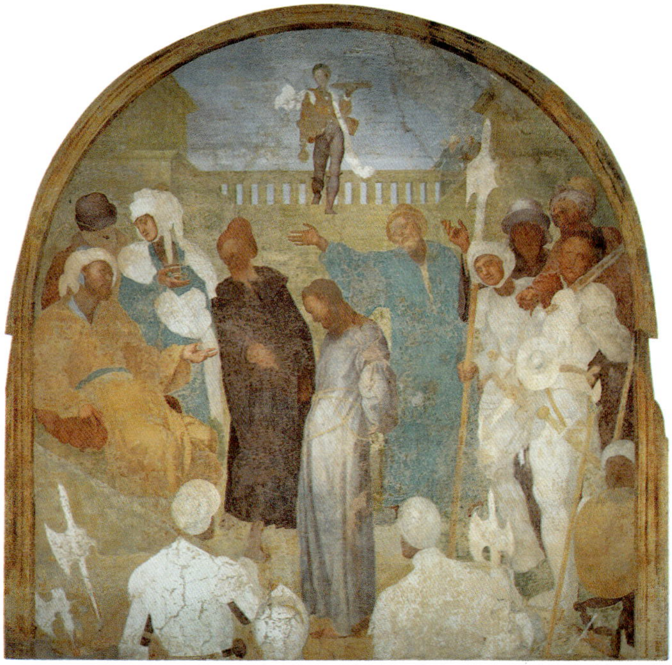

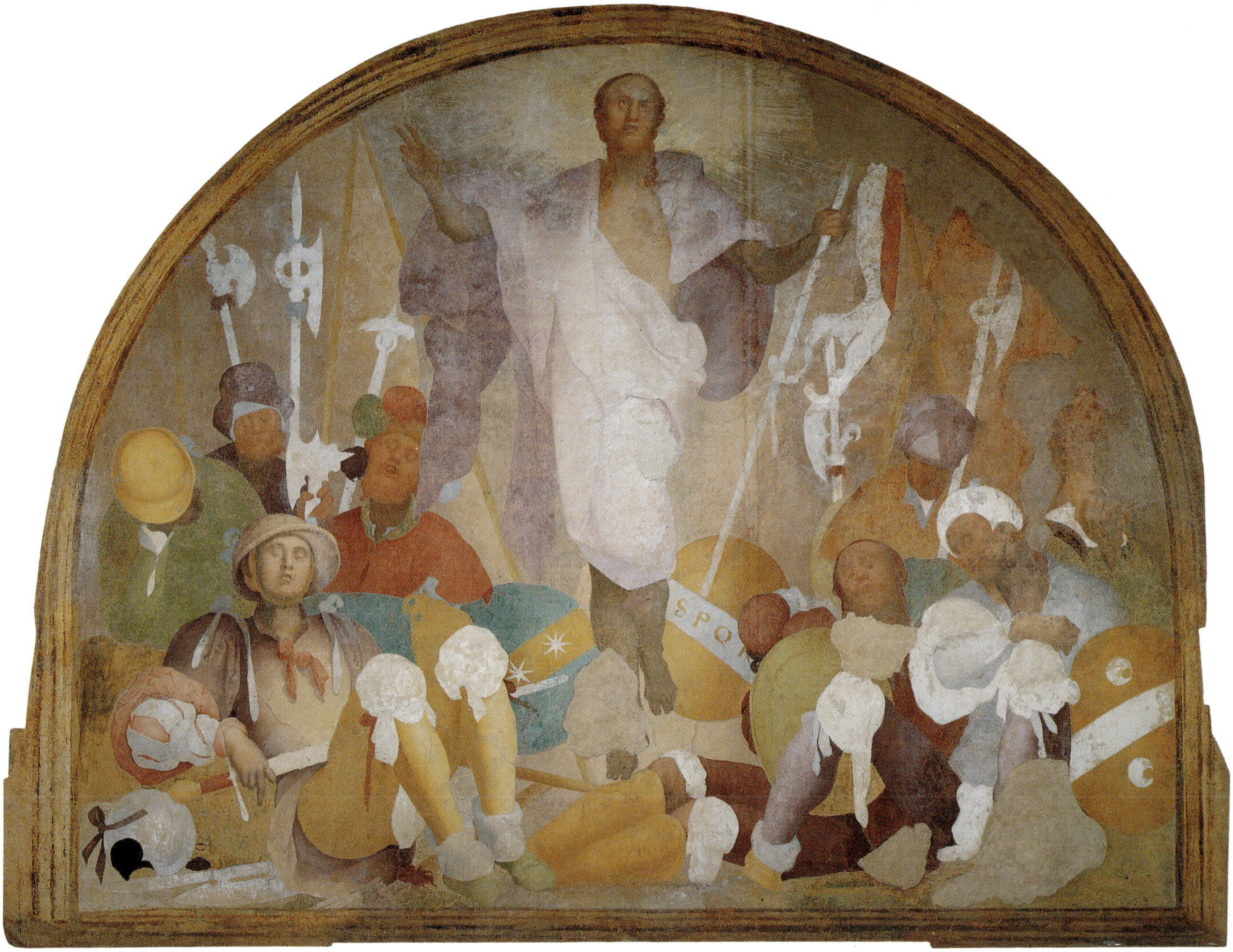

45. *Agony in the Garden*

46, 47. *Christ standing before Pilate*

48. *Resurrection of Christ*

49. *Ascent to Calvary*

50. *Deposition*

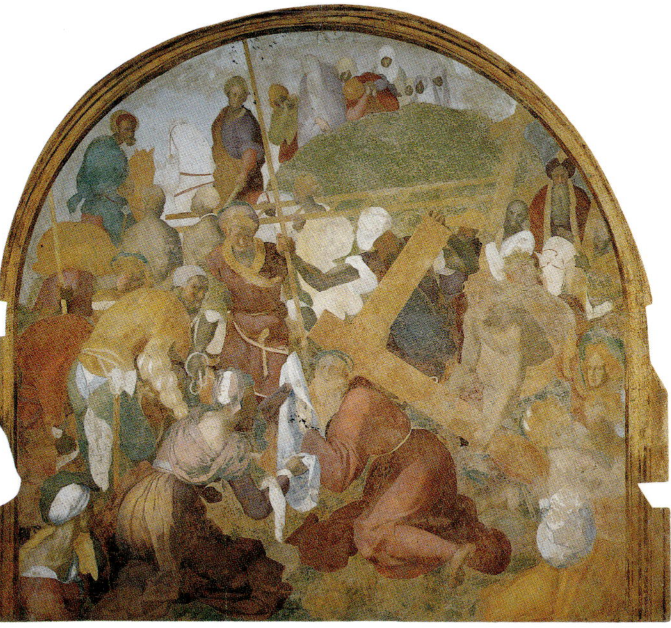

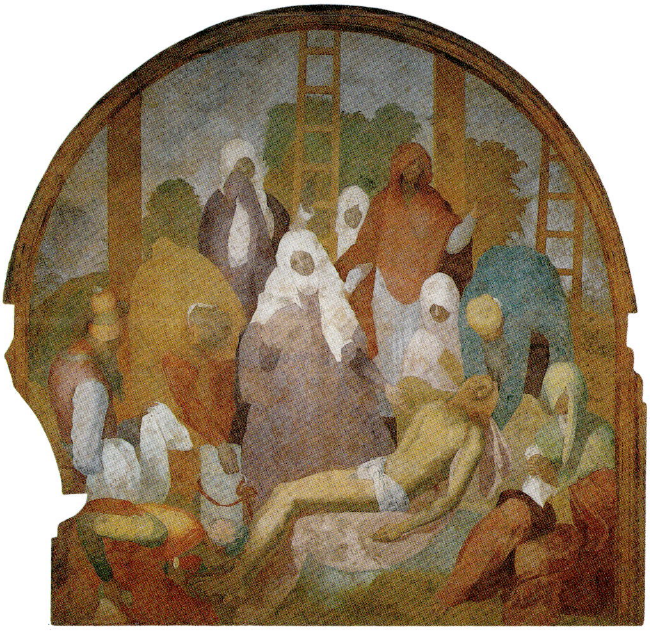

is still possible to appreciate some of the principal formal characteristics. From what Vasari says, the effect of moonlight in the *Agony in the Garden*, traces of which can be discerned in the background of the scene, where the outline of a town is, must have been striking. Silence seems to pervade the left part of the fresco, where in the foreground Peter, James and John are immersed in a deep sleep. A little higher up is the kneeling Christ, turned away from us, presenting his Father with a last human appeal: "[...] if thou be willing, remove this cup from me". The impassioned group of soldiers on the right side of the painting is led by Judas, who has tied to the belt of his tunic the bag of money received in return for his betrayal.

In *Christ standing before Pilate*, a crowded circle of figures surrounds the body of Christ, who holds his head slightly bowed in a gesture of profound humility and resignation towards the accusations directed at him by the city elders and high priests. The composition is divided into two parts by an undulating central axis formed by the profiles of the figures of Christ and the cup-bearer, who, nimbly descending the steep flight of stairs in the background, is bringing Pilate the jug and basin with which to wash his hands. The decorative taste for a highly elaborate linear articulation, by now a hallmark of Pontormo's style, is revealed here too, as it was in the fresco of Poggio a Caiano, by the cancelling of perspective through an emphatic reduction of spatial depth, which tends to push every element of the composition towards the foreground, and by the juxtaposition of pure colours with their soft shades, the dazzling white being particularly striking. In the *Ascent to Calvary* the scene revolves around the episode of Christ's meeting with Veronica, who offers him the headcloth. An essentially dynamic element is bestowed upon the composition by the animated variety of postures of the figures and by the different directions suggested by the tangle of cross, sticks and ladders that cut through the procession of the condemned, ministers of justice, accusers and curious onlookers. Intensely northern in inspiration is the group of mourners placed behind the hill in the background, a touch of intense dramatic force being produced by the deep anguish of the Virgin and John, the favourite apostle.

In the *Deposition*, the animated state bestowed on the composition by the alternation of bent and erect figures animates in a highly bizarre way the pyramidal structure traditionally used for this kind of representation. In keeping with northern figurative culture are the clothes of the figures and some particular facial characteristics, which Vasari previously referred to, greatly admiring the figures of "two old men done to represent Joseph of Arimathaea and Nicodemus, who, though done in the German style, have the most beautiful faces and expres-

51, 52. Pontormo
Supper at Emmaus
230x173 cm
Florence, Uffizi

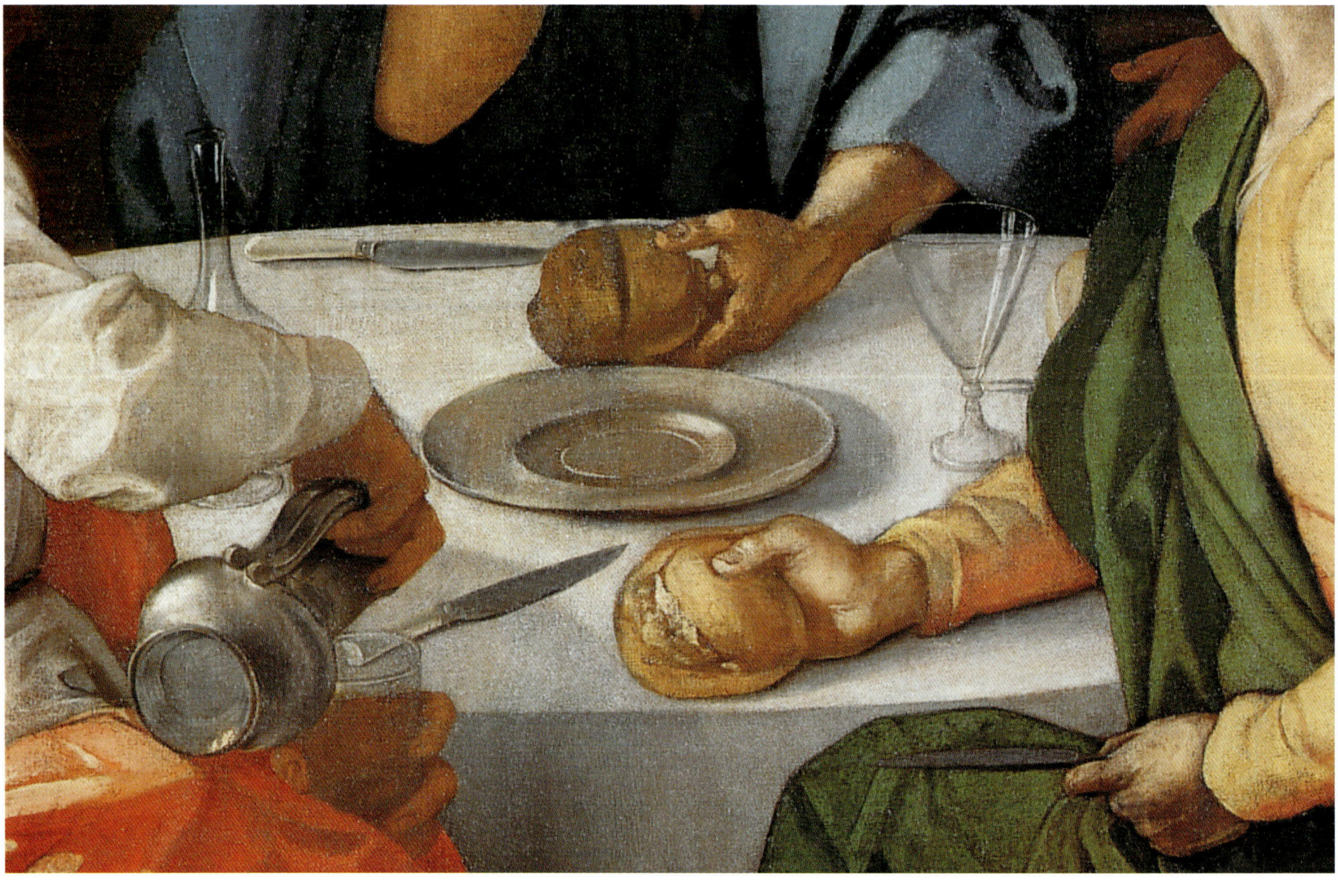

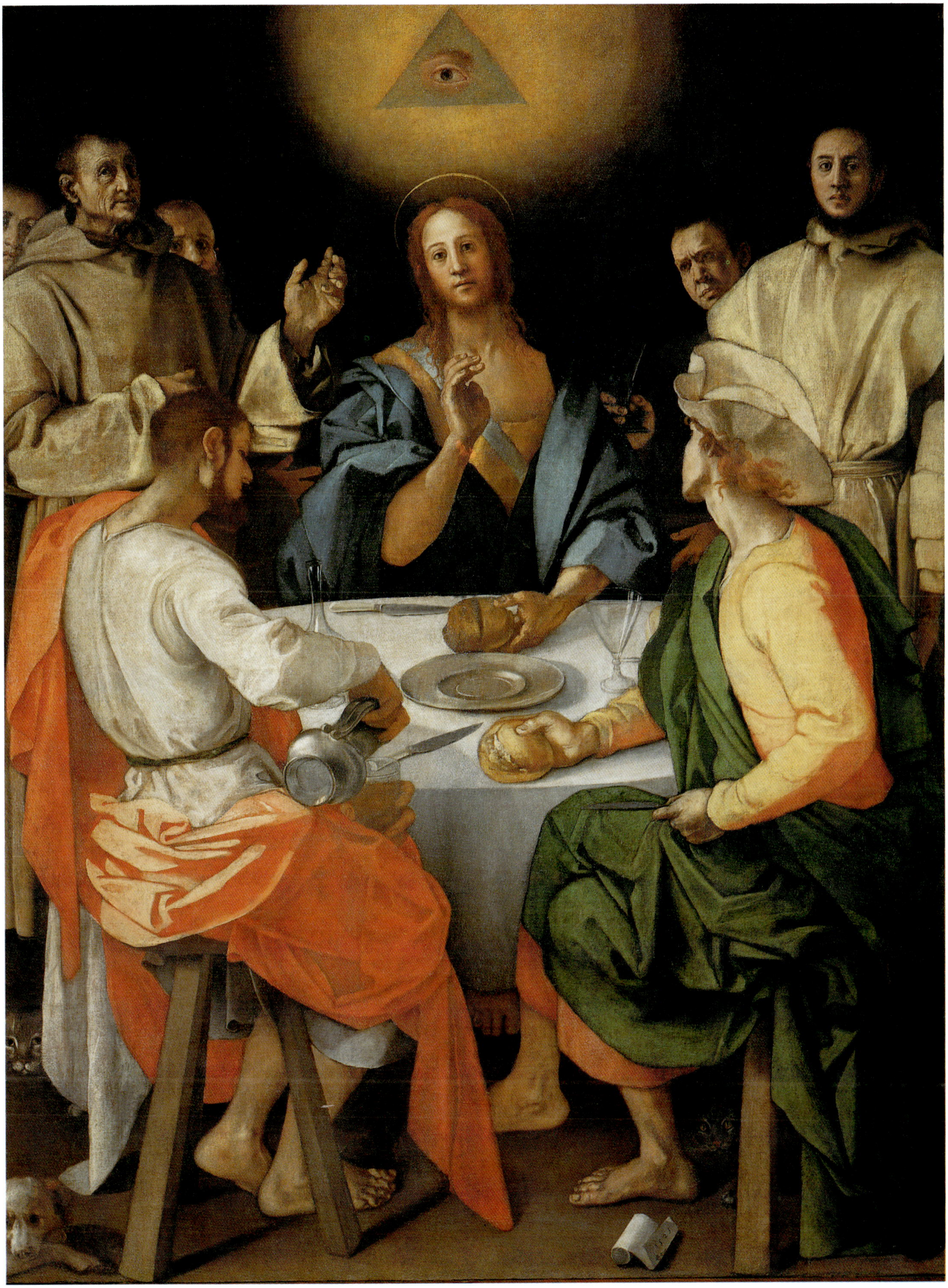

53. *Pontormo*
Birth of the Baptist
54 cm diam.
Florence, Uffizi

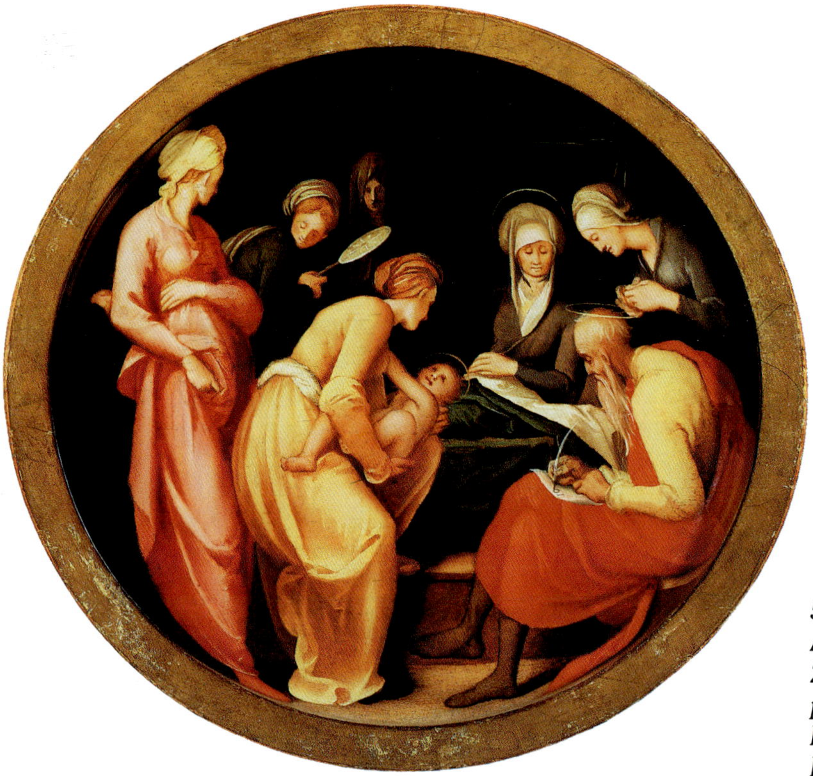

54. *Pontormo*
Annunciation
250x110 cm each part
Florence, Santa Felicita

sions that could be seen in old men, with soft beards coloured with marvellous delicacy". The play of colour contrasts, with the use of intense tones reaches a high degree of formal refinement in the attempted *cangiante* effect on the robes of Mary Magdalene.

The formal refinement reaches a peak in the last scene of the cycle, the *Resurrection of Christ*, where the roundness of the faces of the sleeping soldiers and the single parts of their bodies, the helmets and the shields form a "series of polychrome discs" (A. Venturi, 1932) with a kaleidoscopic variety of yellows, whites, greens, greys and purple.

At the end of the fresco decoration of the cloister, for the monastery guest-quarters or store-rooms, Pontormo executed a canvas portraying the episode in which the now risen Christ, repeating the same act of breaking the bread that he had made during the Last Supper, is about to be recognized by two of his disciples. The canvas, now in the Uffizi, is dated 1525. It seems that the eye of God, painted above Christ's head, was added later by Empoli, who executed a copy of the precious painting.

In the *Supper at Emmaus*, as in the frescoes of the cloister, the inspiration behind the figurative concept is certainly Dürer. With some variations, the general idea of the painting derives, in fact, from an engraving belonging to the series of the *Little Passion* published by the German artist in 1511. Dürer and northern figurative culture in general were also the inspiration behind one of the most striking characteristics of the canvas, the close adherence to an everyday reality that has frequently induced authoritative scholars of Pontormo to interpret this extraordinary work as heralding the realistic research of Caravaggio, Velázquez and Francisco Zurbarán. The elimination of the distance between painted event and spectator and the foreshortened contact with reality are effects created by the inclusion of portraits of people living at the time and participating in the event, and the large naked feet of the disciples in the lower part of the painting, where the heads of cats can be seen, their inquisitive gazes directed towards the onlooker. A crouching puppy can just be seen in the lower left corner of the painting. The same attention to realism is also evident in the careful representation of the group of objects forming a still life on the table, subtly rendered even down to the definition of the materials: the linen of the tablecloth, the transparent glass of the chalices and the shiny metal of the jug, knives and plate. In accordance with Pontormo's predilection for combining extremely diversified characteristics in the same painting, this aspect of sincere adherence to reality coexists with an intensely mystical atmosphere centred on Christ's gesture of blessing, which is repeated in the gesture of the Carthusian monk portrayed to his right. The expression of profound spiritual intensity of this figure, the same that characterizes the figure on Christ's left, is countered by the doubting, apprehensive expressions of the monks that appear in the background. In this lofty example of Pontormo's art there are also refined colour effects.

In the wooden *tondo* with the *Birth of the Baptist* (ca. 1526) of the Uffizi, as in the frescoes of the cloister in the monastery of Galluzzo, the elongated typologies of the figures and their facial characteristics betray clear links with northern figurative culture.

The formal research intensifies

At the end of the third decade of the 16th century Pontormo intensified his formal research. This phase of the painter's artistic career is marked by the decoration of the Cappella Capponi in the church of Santa Felicita in Florence. The chapel, designed by Brunelleschi, and formerly patronized by the Barbadori family, was bought by Ludovico Capponi in 1525, the year in which Pontormo started to work there with the assistance of Bronzino. According to Vasari, God the Father and Four Patriarchs, now lost, once decorated the hemispherical cupola, which was apparently replaced by a vault in the 18th century.

Four tondos with the *Evangelists* still adorn the pendentives that once supported the old cupola. Except for the painting of St John, the precise authorship of the other three portraits has posed considerable problems for scholars, who are unable to agree on the extent to which Bronzino contributed in the execution of the paint-

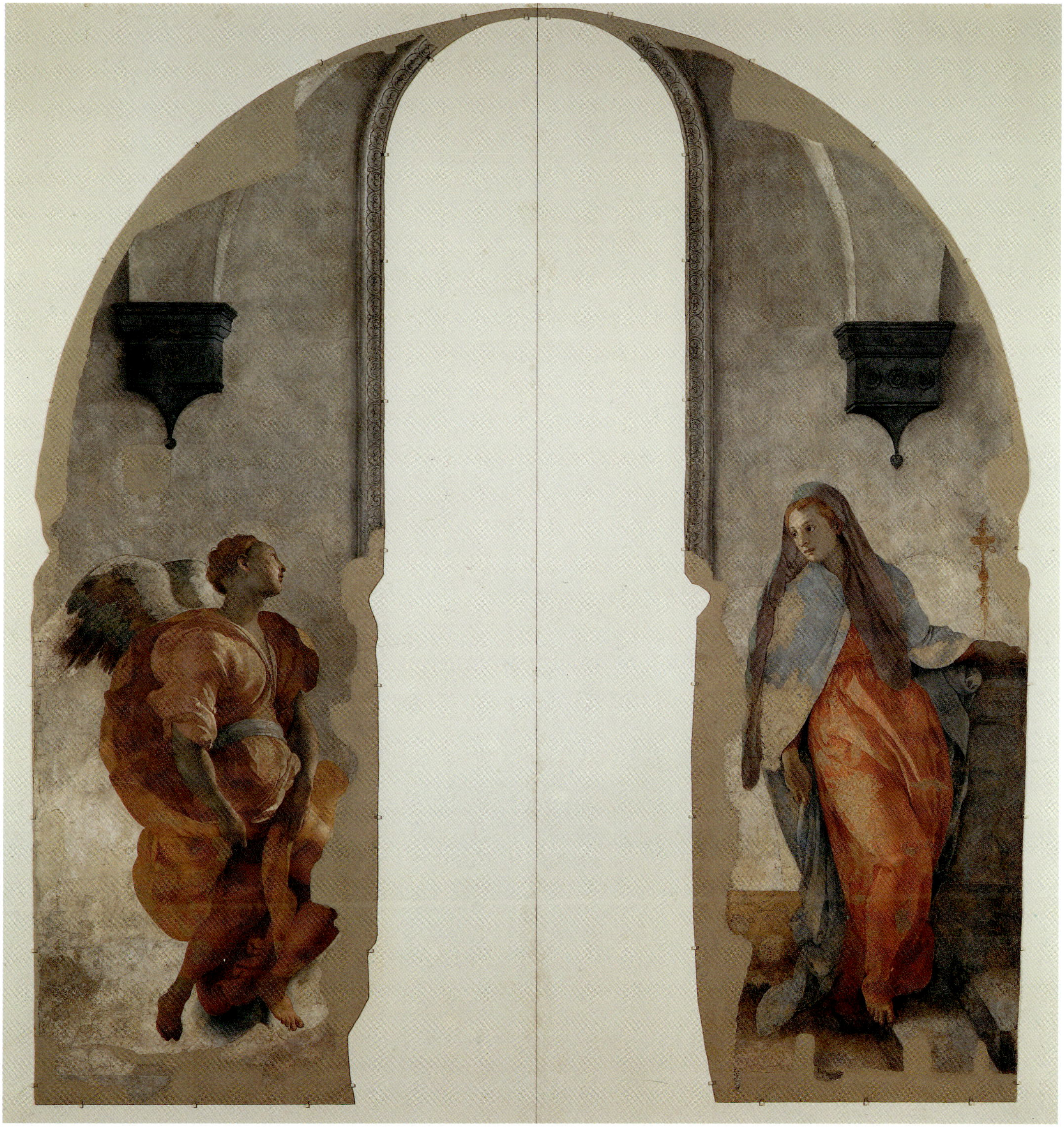

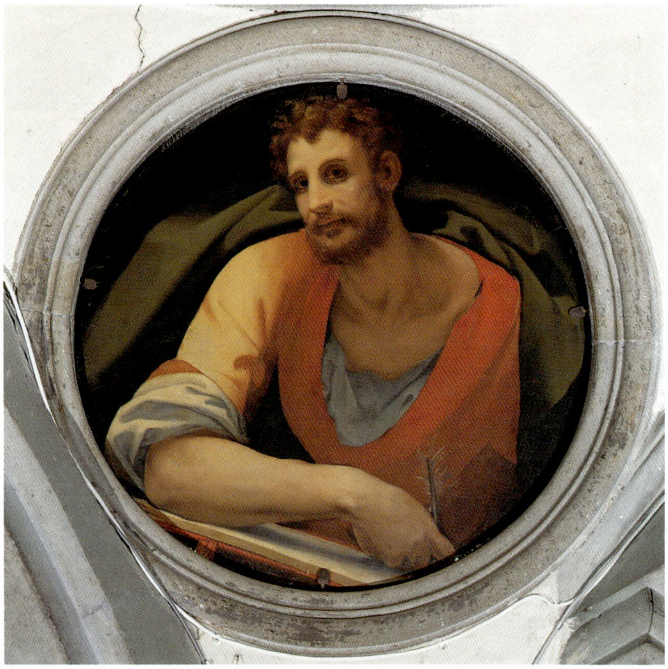

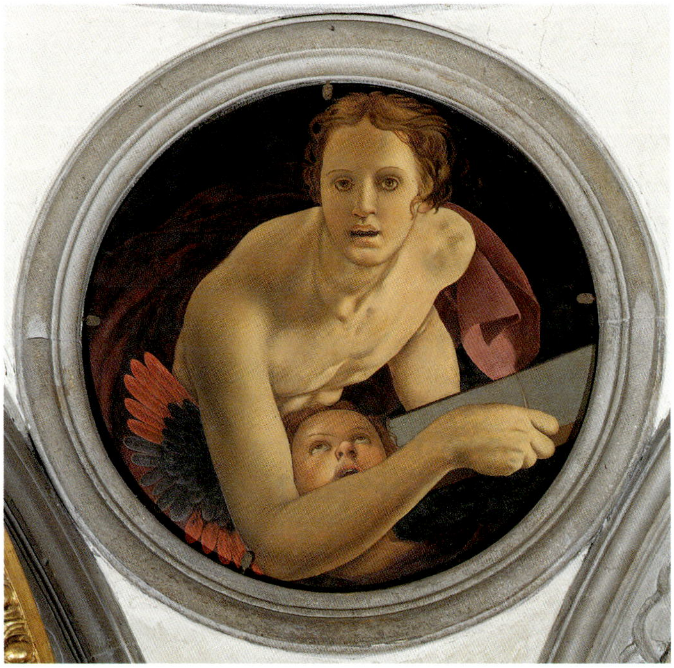

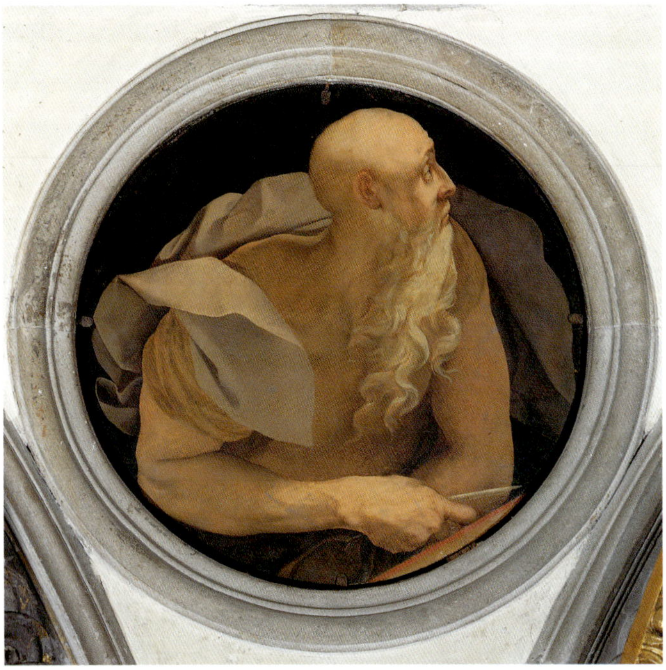

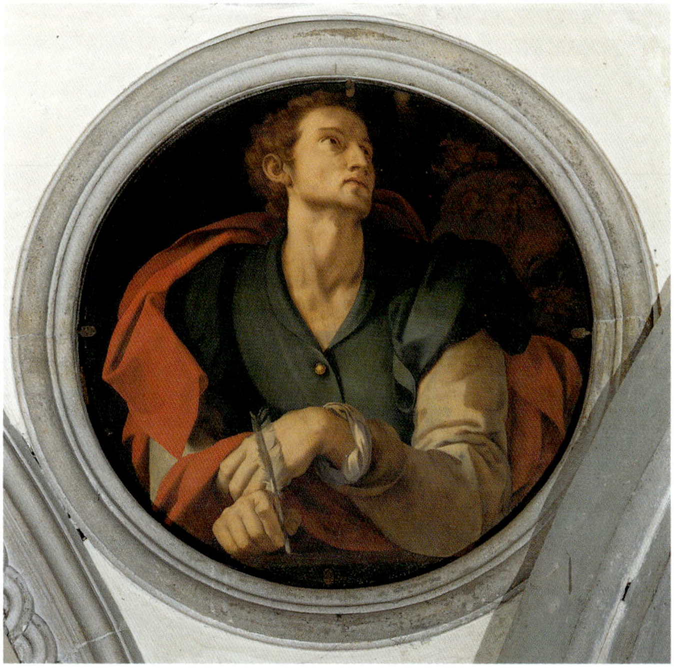

ings. The figures of the Evangelists, with their distinctly Michelangiolesque flavour, have a vigour deriving from the way their heads are twisted and pushed forward. They are wrapped in ample robes, whose bold colours stand out against the dark backgrounds. This play of strong contrasts, which exalts the delicate outlines of the coloured surfaces, is in keeping with the refined style of the entire decoration. Yet the most significant expression of Pontormo's new artistic tendency is undoubtedly the chapel's altarpiece, the painting of the famous *Deposition* (1525-28), which can perhaps justly be described as the artist's masterpiece. It was presumably the highly singular artistic innovation of this painting that prompted Pontormo, as Vasari points out, to build a "turata", a kind of screen, which for three years prevented anyone from entering the chapel. The compositional idea

55-58. Pontormo and Bronzino
The Evangelists Mark, Matthew, John and Luke
70 cm diam. each
Florence, Santa Felicita

59-61. Pontormo
Deposition and details
313x192 cm
Florence, Santa Felicita

is, indeed, extravagant and totally unprecedented: an "inextricable knot of figures" (A. Venturi, 1932) and drapes that pivots around the bewildered youth in the foreground and culminates above in the two lightly hovering figures emerging from a vague background. This com-

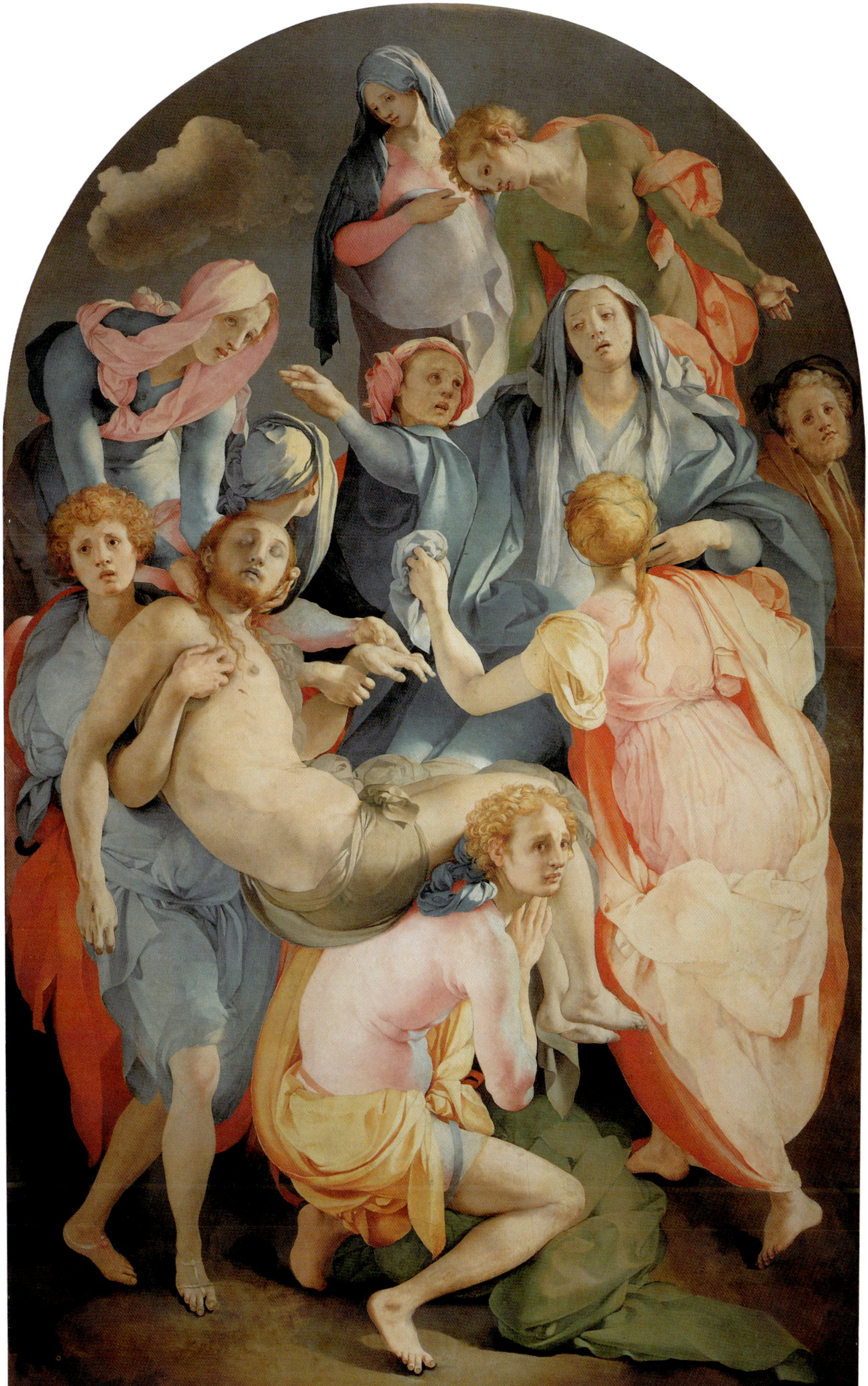

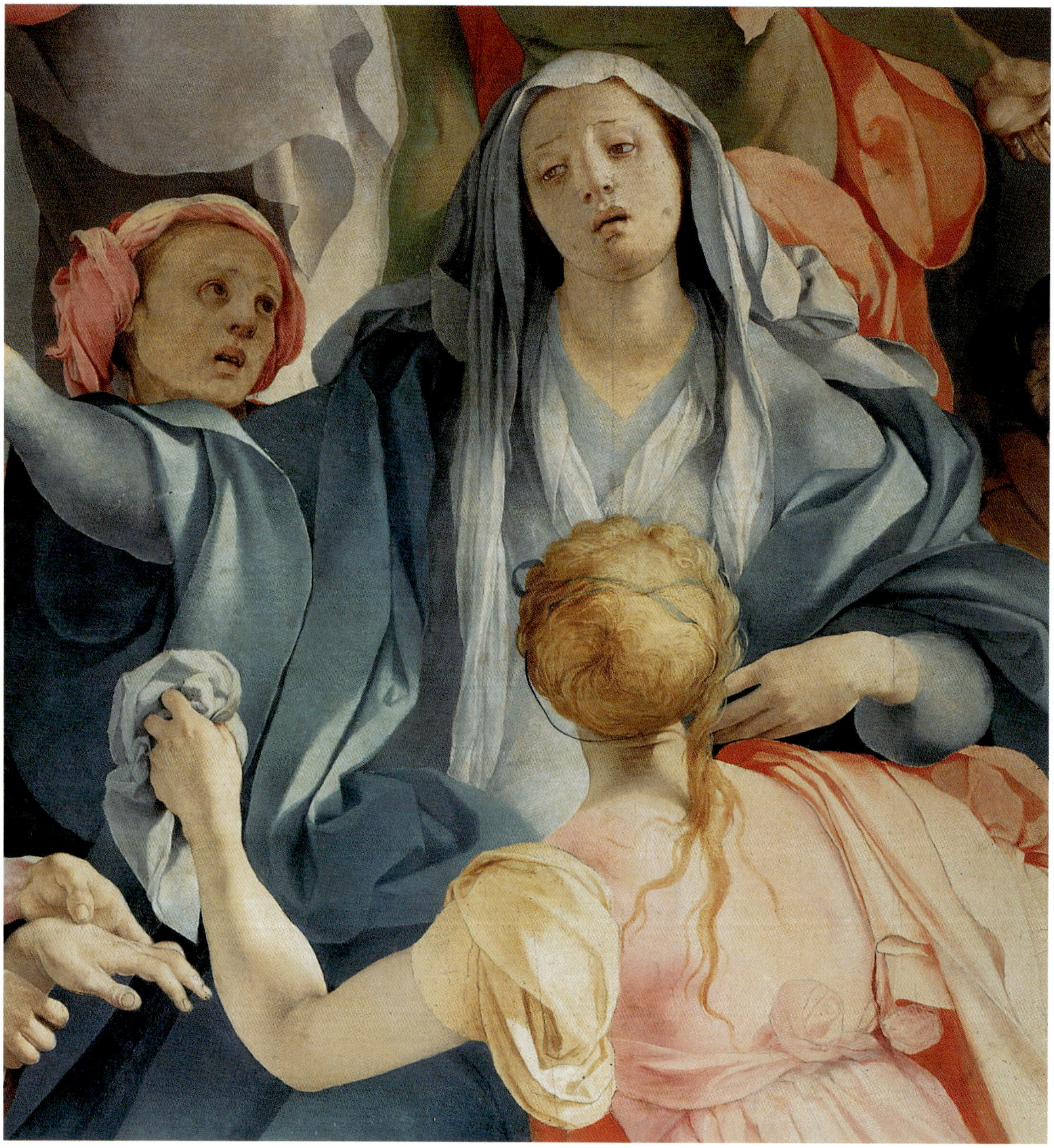

plicated "bunch" (L. Becherucci, 1944) of forms arranged in the shape of an upturned pyramid defies any attempt at a rational exploration or identification of planes. The compositional complexity is accompanied by a significant and probably deliberate ambiguity in the representation of the subject, which may be interpreted as halfway between the theme of the Deposition and that of the Pietà or Lamentation over the Dead Christ. The painting appears to represent the moment in which the body of Christ, having been taken down from the cross, has just been removed from the mother's lap. The Virgin, visibly distraught, and perhaps on the point of fainting, still gazes longingly towards her Son, and gestures with her right arm in the same direction. In the centre of the painting, the moment of the separation is underlined by the subtle contact of Mary's legs with those of Christ, now freed from his Mother's last pathetic embrace. The twisted body of Christ, with its right arm firmly held up, is reminiscent of Michelangelo's Vatican *Pietà* (1498). An intense spiritual participation in the grief of the event profoundly affects the expressions and attitudes of all the figures present, even that of the woman turned away from the onlooker, probably Mary Magdalene, who communicates her anguished psychological condition by reaching out sympathetically towards the swooning body of the Virgin. Some scholars have interpreted the two young figures holding up the deceased's body as angels in the act of drawing Christ away from the main group and leading him finally into the arms of his Father, once represented in the cupola of the chapel. The general direction of the movement is, in fact, a rising one, and is created by the ethereal quality of the weightless figures, and their slow, almost dance-like rhythm. The two presumed angelic presences, moreover, seem to be unaffected by the weight of the lifeless body, and the figure in the foreground appears to be in the act of raising himself up by lightly pressing down on the front part of his foot.

The intricately connected group of figures, involved

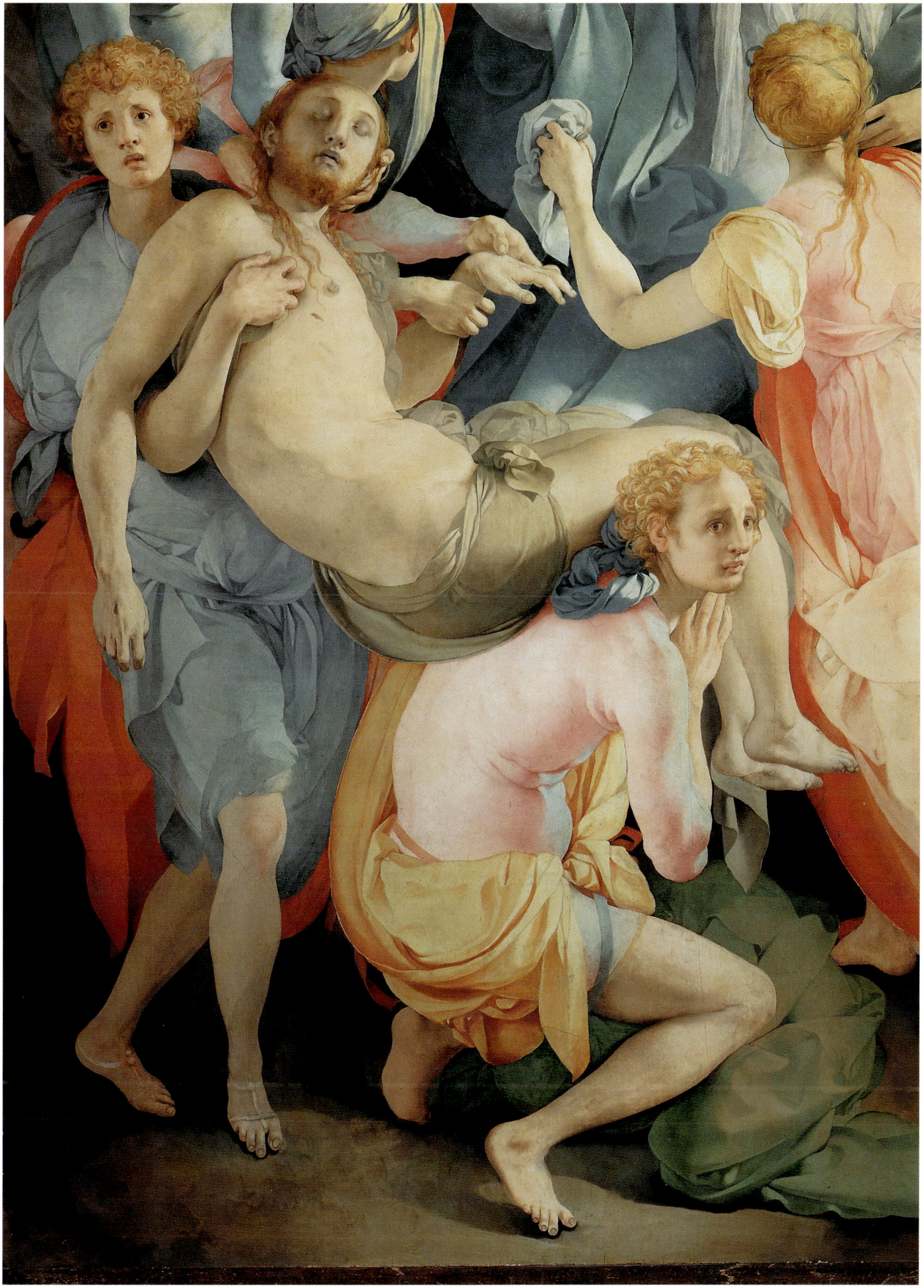

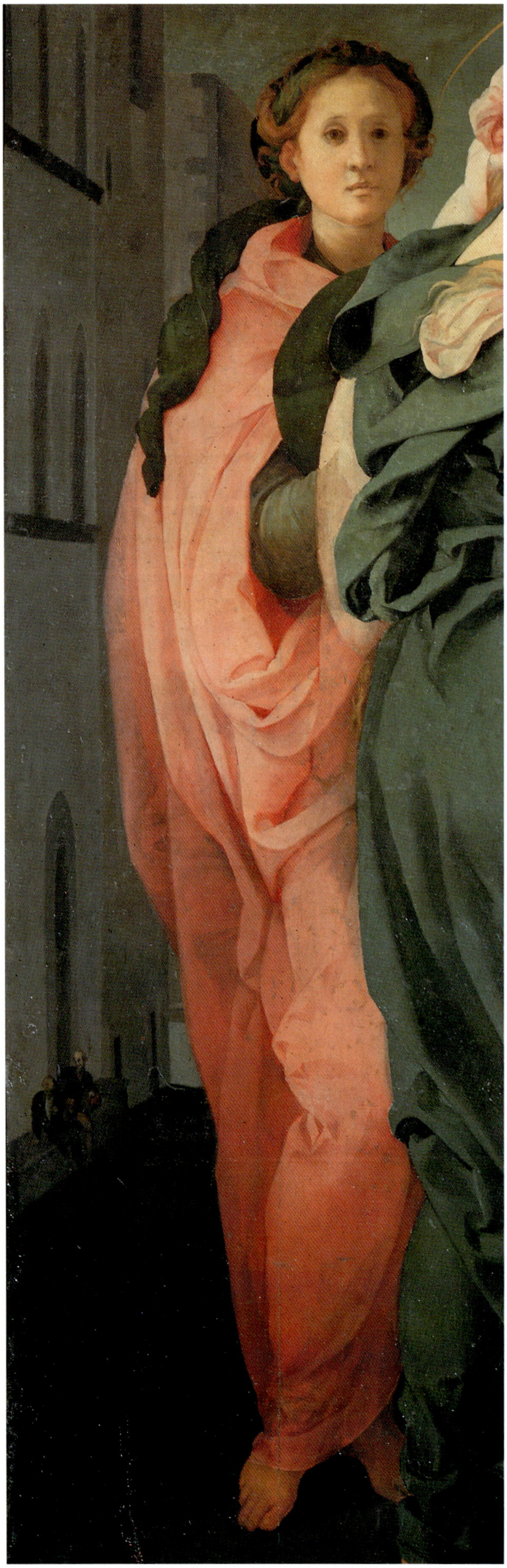

in a highly dramatic atmosphere, takes on the appearance of a rich frieze in the harmony of highly refined colour tones of pinks, blues and greens. The glaring light creates splendid *cangiante* effects: yellows with reddish tints, and reds highlighted with yellow. The transparent shadows do not annul the colours, but actually become them, in the flesh tones invested with subtle shades of pink and green. The cloaked man wearing a strange hat, almost imperceptible against the background of the painting behind the arm of the Virgin, may possibly be the artist himself. Staring at something beyond the confines of the painting, and looking as though he were about to leave the pictorial space, he presents us with this complex and refined decoration of colours, forms and lines which for him have a value beyond any noble content.

The decoration of the Cappella Capponi in Santa Felicita is completed by the figure of the *Heralding Angel* and the *Annunziata*, frescoed on the wall of the window (ca. 1527-28), two paintings representing an expression of sublime artistic refinement.

The "extravagant and new" manner that Vasari refers to when describing the highly personal figurative inventions of the Santa Felicita altarpiece is also evident in another painting by Pontormo, the celebrated *Visitation* of the parish church of San Michele at Carmignano, a work inexplicably ignored by the Aretine biographer. The painting, dating to the years 1528-30, is still conserved inside the church today, above the second altar on the right for those entering the nave, where it is framed by 17th-century decoration. The lozenge-shaped arrange-

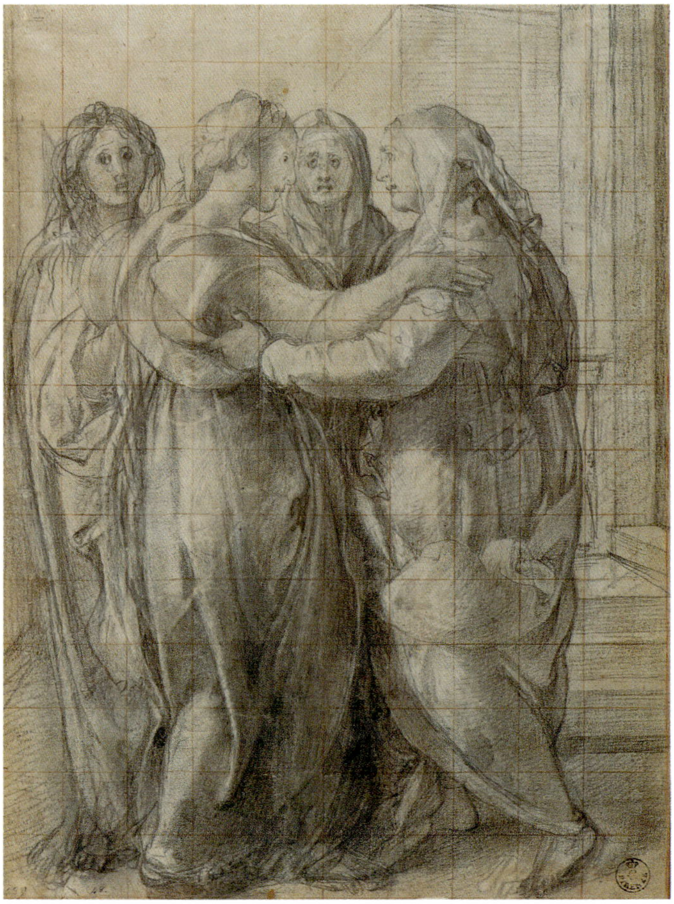

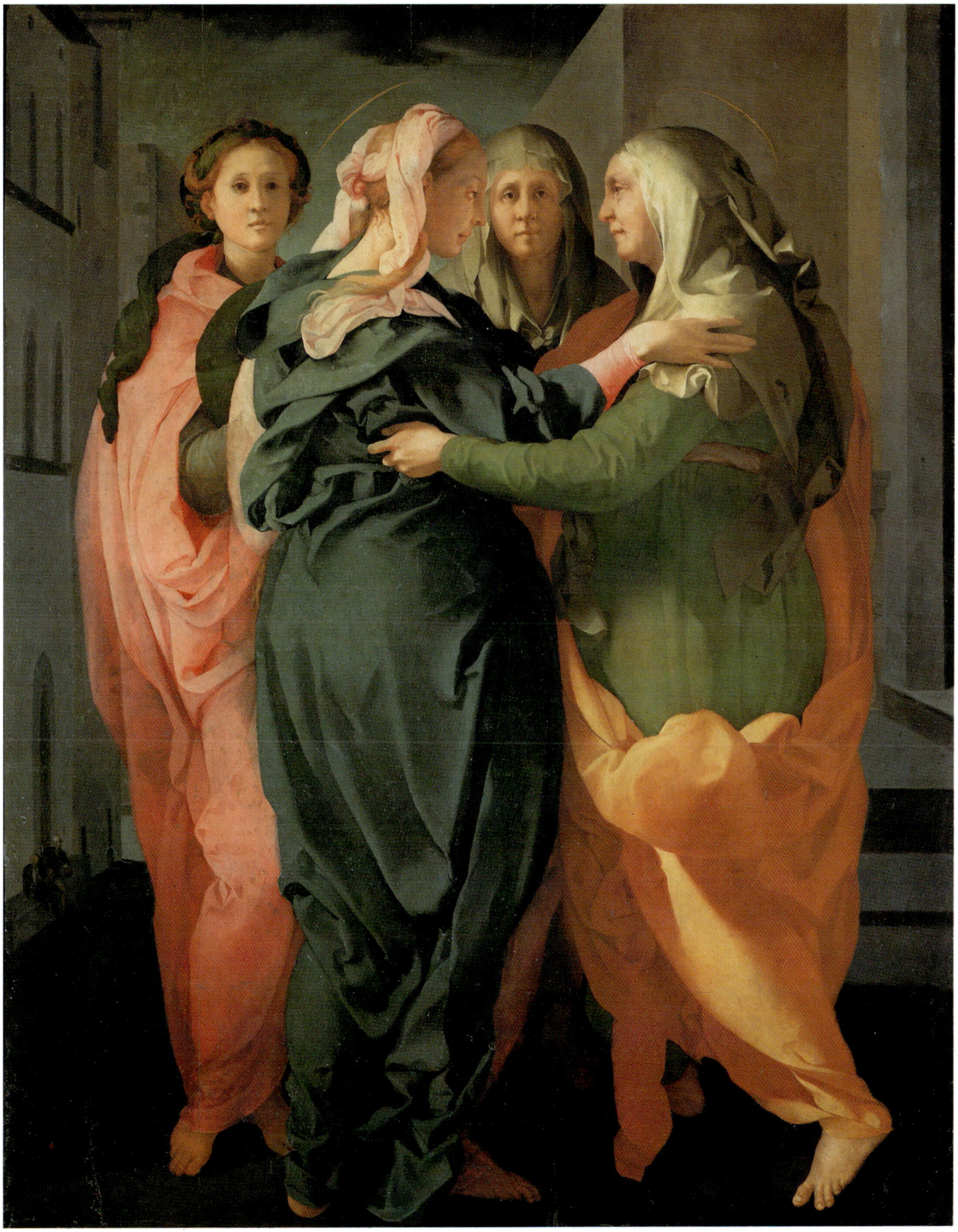

62, 64. Pontormo
Visitation
202x156 cm
Carmignano (Florence), parish church

63. Study for the Visitation
Florence, Prints and Drawings Collection of the Uffizi, no. 461 F

ment of the four figures represented in the foreground of the painting was probably suggested to Pontormo by Dürer's engraving portraying the *Four Witches* (1497). Entirely original, on the other hand, are the intertwining "arcs of arms and fabric" (A. Venturi, 1932) that firmly unites the two protagonists whose distinctly enlarged bodies dominate the painted surface.

An initial idea for the scene of the *Visitation* of Carmignano can be seen in a drawing in the Uffizi, which reveals some significant differences compared to the painted version. The preparatory design shows the two women in a frontal pose, and more to the left compared

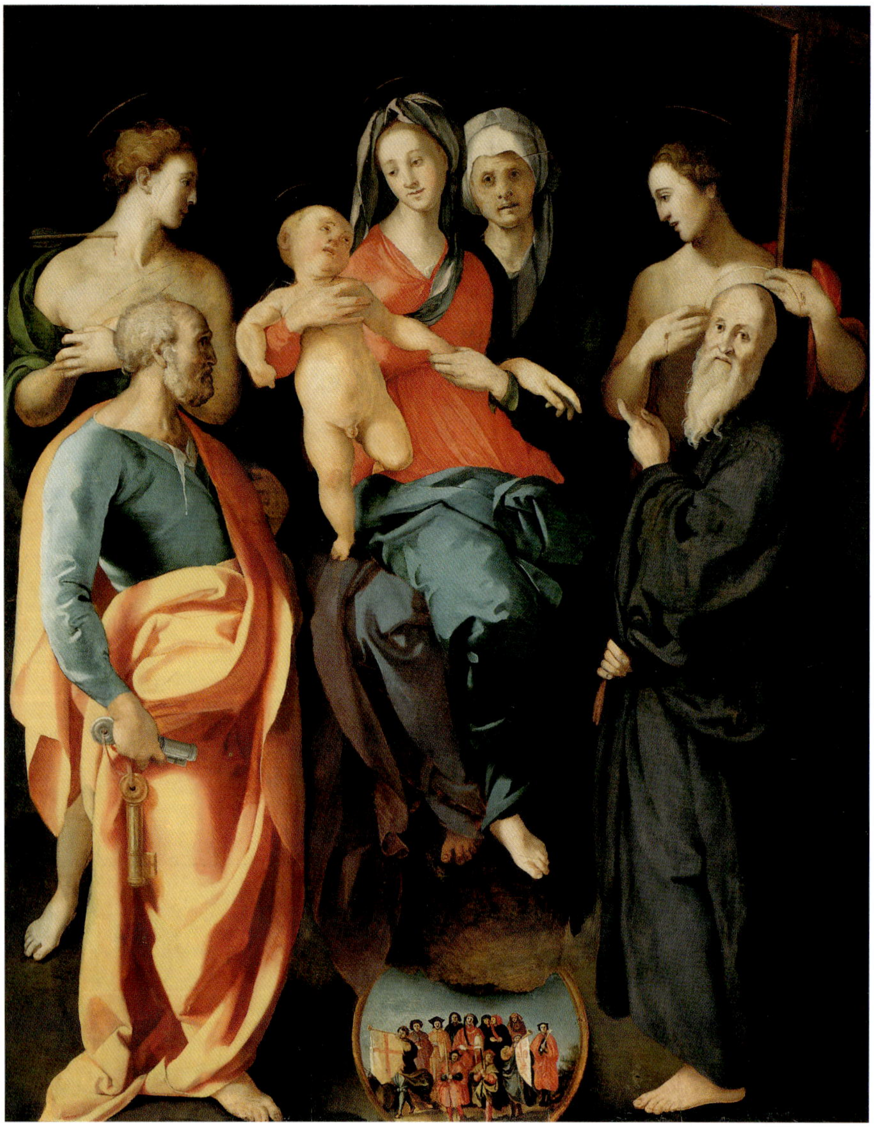

65. Pontormo
Madonna and Child with St Anne and four saints
228x176 cm
Paris, Louvre

to their position in the painting. In the preparatory drawing the drapery around the four figures is less ample and thus diminishes the group's compactness, while the brisk pencil strokes delineating the faces of the companions or maidservants of the protagonists express in them a certain psychological agitation, which in the painting is totally absent. In keeping with Pontormo's taste, the painting possesses an extremely studied compositional typology, full of strange combinations of counterbalanced elements. The profile portrayal of the two main figures embracing each other with extreme delicacy and exchanging looks of intense mutual affection is set against the rigidly frontal position of the two bystanders in the background. Immobile, almost petrified, the latter keep their eyes fixed on something outside the scene, revealing their total lack of emotional participation in the event. The age difference between these two women and their facial resemblance with the protagonists invite an interpretation of the two maidservants as the doubles of Mary and Elisabeth. Their expressions convey a rather melancholy tone to the scene's general atmosphere of high spirituality. In the painting of the *Visitation*, the compositional inventions are accompanied by an elegant play of colour contrasts and harmonies with refined *cangiante* effects.

The juxtaposition of the glorious yellow of St Elisabeth's cloak and the dark green tones of Mary's robes reappears in the drapery enfolding the frowning St Peter and the Virgin in the *Madonna and Child with St Anne and four saints* of the Louvre. This work has recently been dated to the years 1524-26, although on the basis of Vasari's indications it is traditionally dated 1528-29. The painting was executed for the convent of Sant'Anna in Verzaia, just outside Porta San Frediano. From 1370 to 1529, when the building was destroyed during the siege of Florence, every year on 26 July, the saint's feast day, the painting marked the destination of a procession dedicated to the celebration of Florentine liberty. On this day the people remembered the revolution of 26 July 1343, which resulted in the overthrow and exile from Florence of the tyrant Walter de Brienne, Duke of Athens. It seems the painting was commissioned by the captain of the infantry and by other servants of the Signoria of Florence who are represented in the tondo beneath the group of the Holy Family, together with the "trumpeters, pipers, mace-bearers, commanders and pages".

The reflection on Michelangelo

From the end of the second decade of the 16th century up until his last artistic ordeal, the decoration of the great chapel in the basilica of San Lorenzo in Florence (1546-56), Pontormo devoted himself to an attentive reflection on various works of Michelangelo, his aim being to compare himself openly with Buonarroti and demonstrate how his art was capable of re-elaborating in an original way the references to the great master's illustrious figurative inventions.

A clear reference to Michelangelo's nudes for the *Battle of Cascina* (1505-6) is discernible in the painting which the artist executed between 1529 and 1530 for the nuns of the Spedale degli Innocenti. This work, now conserved at Palazzo Pitti in Florence, portrays the martyrdom of eleven thousand Christian soldiers of the Theban legion who, together with their commander Maurice, refused to participate in pagan rites and were barbarously slaughtered on the orders of Emperor Maximianus (end of 3rd century AD). The titles which commonly distinguish the painting are the *Martyrdom of the Theban Legion* or *The Eleven Thousand Martyrs*. The painting shows the moment of the emperor's sentence and that of the subsequent martyrdom, for whose representation the artist used a preparatory drawing, presently conserved in Hamburg, which he executed some time beforehand in the fresco decoration of a lunette of the Compagnia dei Martiri of Camaldoli. This work, for which Perin del Vaga designed the scene of the death sentence, was never finished by Pontormo, who used the same preparatory design for a second pictorial version, representing only the martyrdom, which he intended for Carlo Neroni and which is traditionally identified with the painting today housed in the Uffizi, where a large number of art scolars have recognized the intervention of Bronzino. In the painting of Palazzo Pitti, a further explicit reference to the art of Michelangelo is represented by the figure of the emperor, who in the right foreground imparts his order to an executioner. The latter, whose back is turned away from the observer, is strikingly distinguished by a profusion of robes of varying colours, including a dazzling yellow. The posture of the body of Maximianus recalls the statues of the Medici dukes placed above the celebrated tombs of the New Sacristy in San Lorenzo (ca. 1520-1534). The painting of the *Madonna and Child with the Young St John* of the Uffizi, recently dated 1534-36, interesting for the twisted body of the Virgin that brings her face into contact with the pathetic figure of the young St John and for the projection of the Child's leg, also refers to the sculptures of San Lorenzo and in particular the *Madonna and Child* of the Medici Chapels.

66. Pontormo
The Eleven Thousand Martyrs
65x73 cm
Florence, Galleria Palatina

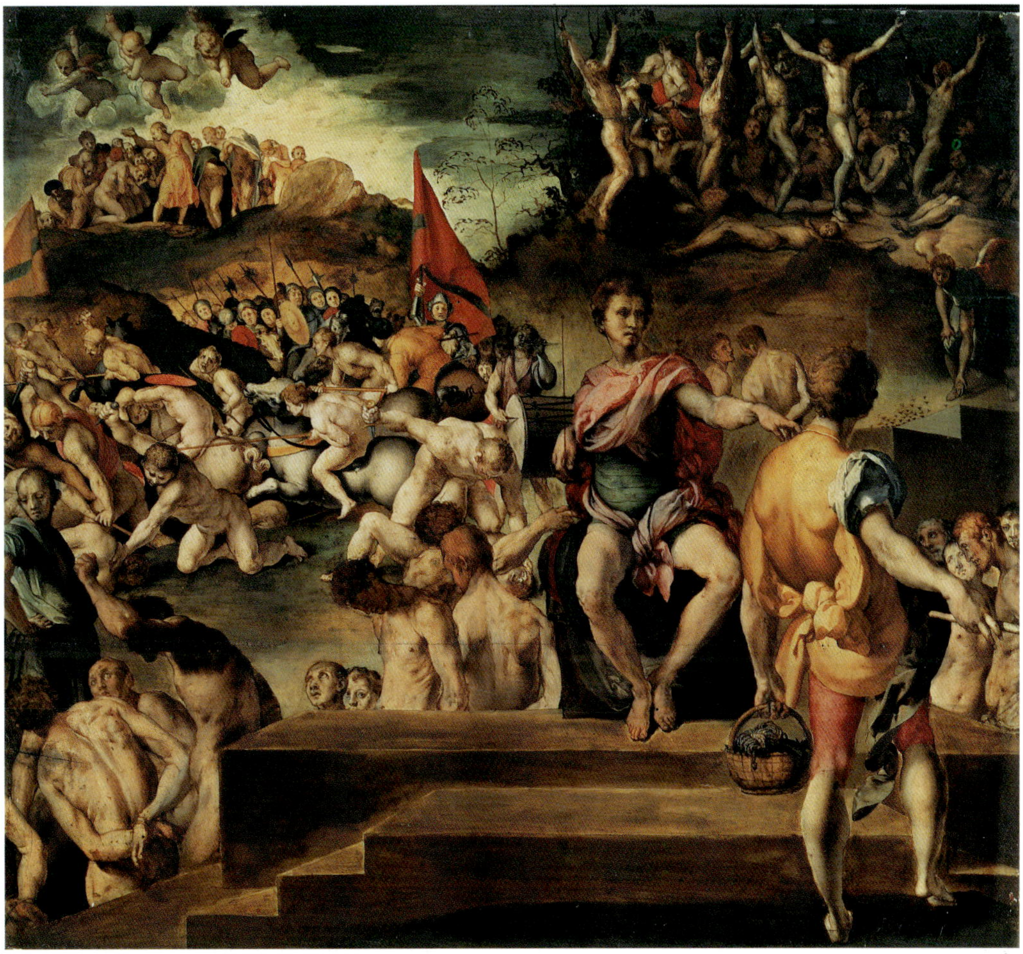

A valuable occasion for the study of and comparison with Michelangelo's style was offered to Pontormo between 1531 and 1532, when, according to Vasari, at the invitation of Buonarroti himself, he painted a cartoon portraying the episode of the *Noli me tangere*, the meeting of Mary Magdalene with the risen Christ, which the illustrious master had executed for Alfonso d'Avalos, a general of Charles V, then present in Florence for the military siege that had brought the Medici family back to power after the short republican period (1527-30). From an examination of various documents relative to this commission, it would seem that the translation of Michelangelo's design into finished painting was executed by Pontormo under the careful supervision of the older artist. Vasari recalls moreover that the finished work "was praised as an exceptional painting for the greatness of Michelangelo's drawing and for Jacopo's colours, so that, Signor Alessandro Vitelli having seen it, who was then captain of the guard of soldiers in Florence, ordered Jacopo to do a painting of the same cartoon which he sent to be hung in his houses at Città di Castello". Michelangelo's cartoon, which remained in Florence, was then used by the painter Battista Franco (1498-1561) to make a third painting of the same subject. The three painted versions, all of which survive, one in a private Milanese collection and the other two at Casa Buonarroti in Florence, have caused considerable problems for scholars of Pontormo who have debated at length on the identification of the original, i.e. the painting executed by the artist on a design by Michelangelo, and on the possible intervention of other artists in the pictorial translation of the cartoon. Until the end of the 1980s art critics considered Pontormo's original work to be the Milanese version, subjected to critical scrutiny for the first time in 1925 and exhibited together with one of the paintings from Casa Buonarroti — generally believed to be a late copy by Bronzino due to the distinctly plastic emphasis of the forms — in the "Exhibition of Pontormo and Early Florentine Mannerism", held in Florence in 1956. After a thorough analysis of the principal formal and compositional characteristics of these two paintings, scholars have recently reversed the attribution and identified the painting of Casa Buonarroti as the original by Pontormo, despite the obvious repainting of the central part of the work, finally assigning to Battista Franco the other ver-

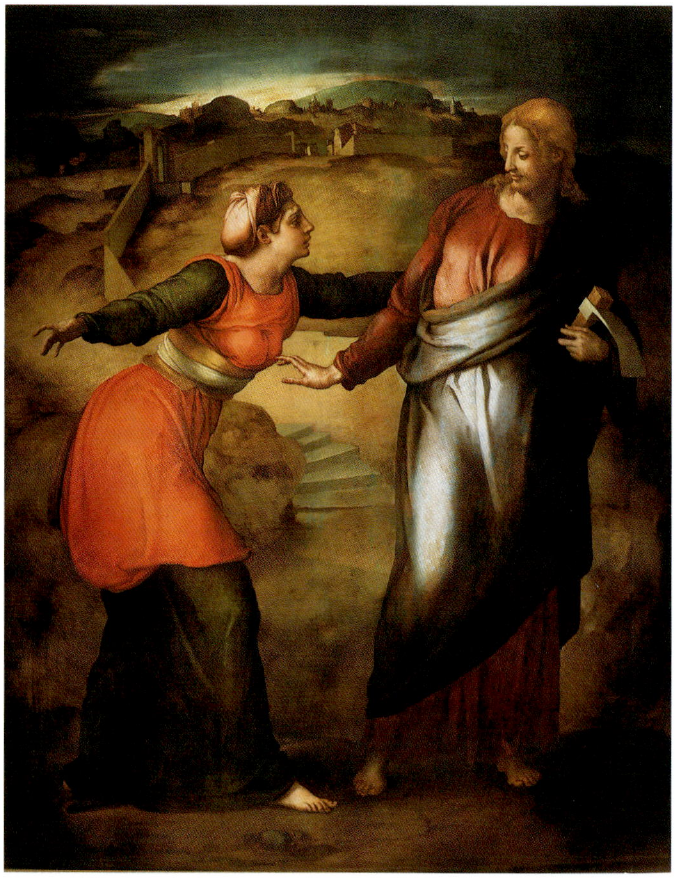

67. Pontormo
Noli me tangere
172x134 cm
Florence, Casa Buonarroti

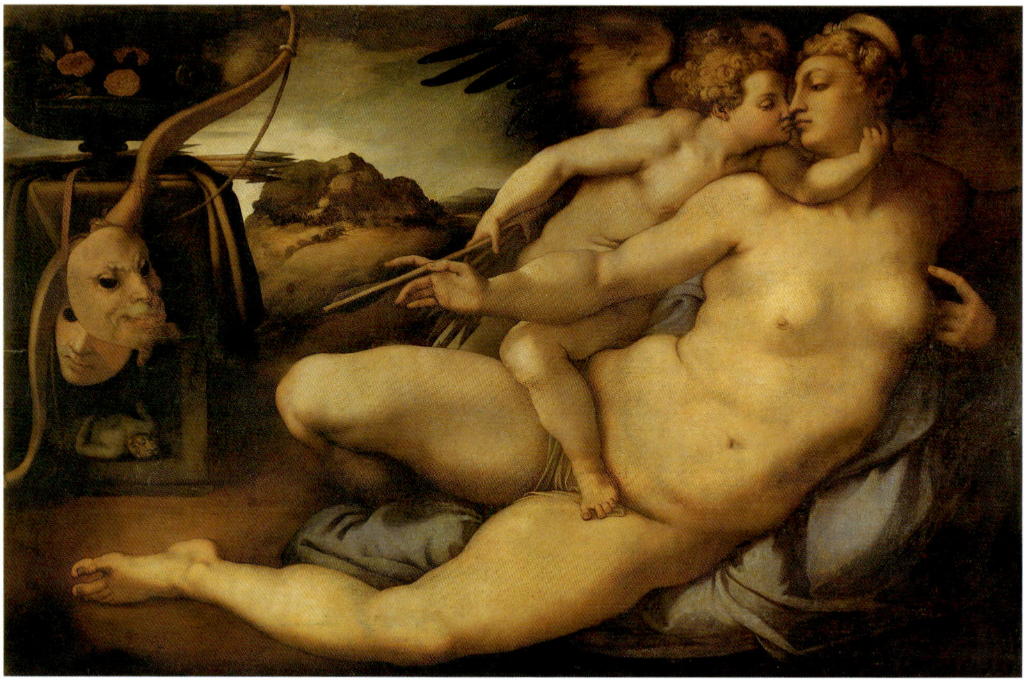

68. Pontormo (?)
Venus and Cupid
128x197 cm
Florence, Galleria dell'Accademia

sion conserved in the same Florentine collection and visibly different from the two paintings we have referred to, especially as regards the setting of the landscape. According to this same critical theory the Milanese version must be the copy for Vitelli (W. E. Wallace, 1988).

There is debate also over the authorship of *Venus and Cupid* (1532-34), now in the Galleria dell'Accademia in Florence, which some critics identify with the painting Pontormo executed for one of Michelangelo's friends, Bartolomeo Bettini, again from a cartoon by Buonarroti. Pontormo's works belonging to the period after the 1530s that refer to the figurative inventions of Buonarroti also include the painting with the *Madonna of the Book*. This work has been identified with the "painting of Our Lady", which according to Vasari was found in the Pontormo's house after the artist's death, together with numerous designs, cartoons and clay models, and was later donated to Piero Salviati by the artist's heirs. The original idea for this composition is known to us only through numerous copies, one of the best versions of these being the painting from a private collection dating to the years 1540-45, recently published (L. Berti, 1993).

The theme of the nude figure depicted anatomically and characterized by particular twists of the body, which forms the leit-motif of Michelangelo's figurative research, Pontormo addressed and reinterpreted in an entirely personal way in a series of extraordinary designs preparatory to the cartoons which the artist executed from the beginning of the 1530s for the decoration of various rooms in the Florentine Medicean villas. In 1532, on the orders of Clement VII, Ottaviano de' Medici commissioned Pontormo to complete the decoration of the salone of Poggio a Caiano, where the painter had already executed the fresco with *Vertumnus and Pomona*. According to Vasari, the artist prepared various cartoons intended for fresco paintings, depicting a "Hercules strangles Anthaeus", a "Venus and Adonis" and "a scene of ignudi playing football". The choice of the latter may have been influenced by a contemporary event, the game of football that took place in Piazza Santa Croce on 15 February 1530, a subject particularly well suited to the decoration of a Medicean villa since it is a known fact that both Alessandro de' Medici and Clement VII played football. Of the preparatory designs for the cartoon, the only surviving traces are the so-called *Kicking Player*, associated with the drawing of *Titius* which Michelangelo executed towards the end of 1532, and the remarkable red-ochre drawing with *Two Nudes Compared*, both in the Prints and Drawings Collection of the Uffizi. The theme of sexual ambiguity, on the other hand, is presented in the *Hermaphrodite Figure*, one of the most interesting among those associated with the decorations for the loggia of the Villa di Castello (1538-43).

The designs for the decorations of the Medicean villas involve the subversion of what may be called the unique characteristics of the Michelangiolesque nude: vigorous, energetic plasticism, solid monumentality and attentive anatomical representation. The same dialectical relationship with the theme dominating the rich artistic production of the illustrious Florentine master may be seen in the drawings which Pontormo executed in preparation for the frescoes of the choir, or great chapel of the Medici family, in the basilica of San Lorenzo in Florence, the artist's last commission (1546-56). These drawings are the only surviving evidence of the decorative cycle entrusted to Pontormo by Pier Francesco Ricci, the private secretary and major-domo of Cosimo I, which was irremediably destroyed in 1742 on the occasion of restoration work inside the church. The original layout of the frescoed scenes is still an open debate among art critics, despite the often convincing reconstructions advanced by authoritative scholars of Pontormo on the basis of indications supplied by Vasari and Francesco Bocchi in the *Bellezze della città di Fiorenza* (1591) and from what can be gleaned from a late 16th-century engraving, today conserved at the Albertina in Vienna. The content associated with the cycle's biblical scenes is not easy to interpret; indeed, Vasari declared that he was unable to understand its "doctrine" and asserted that taken as a whole the frescoes did not observe "the order of the scenes, measure, time, variety in the faces, or changes in the tones of the flesh, nor, in brief, any rules at all either of proportion or perspective". What resulted, in fact, and is clearly visible in the designs for San Lorenzo, is the total lack of any type of spatial or temporal support, the negation of the physicalness and sexual characterization of the individual figures, emphasis instead being placed

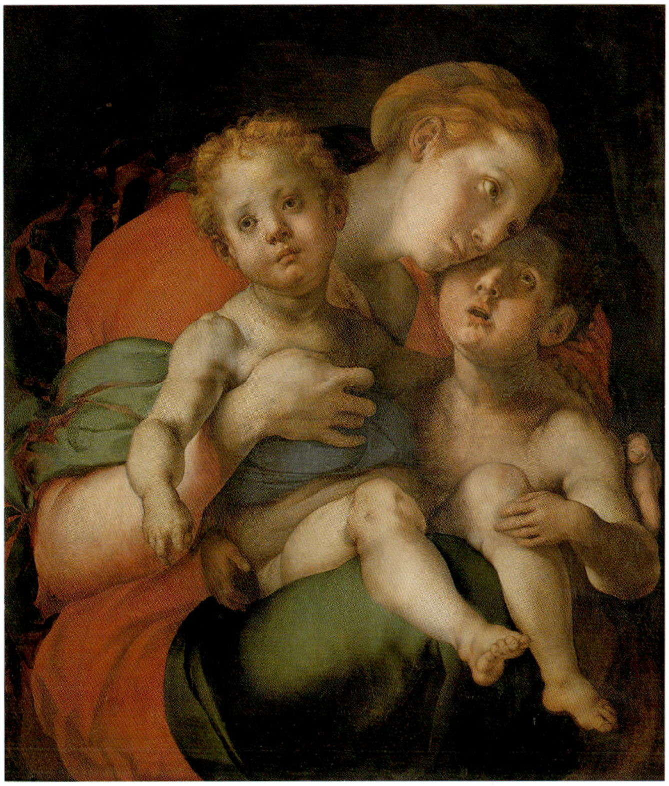

69. Pontormo
Madonna and Child with the Young St John
89x74 cm
Florence, Uffizi

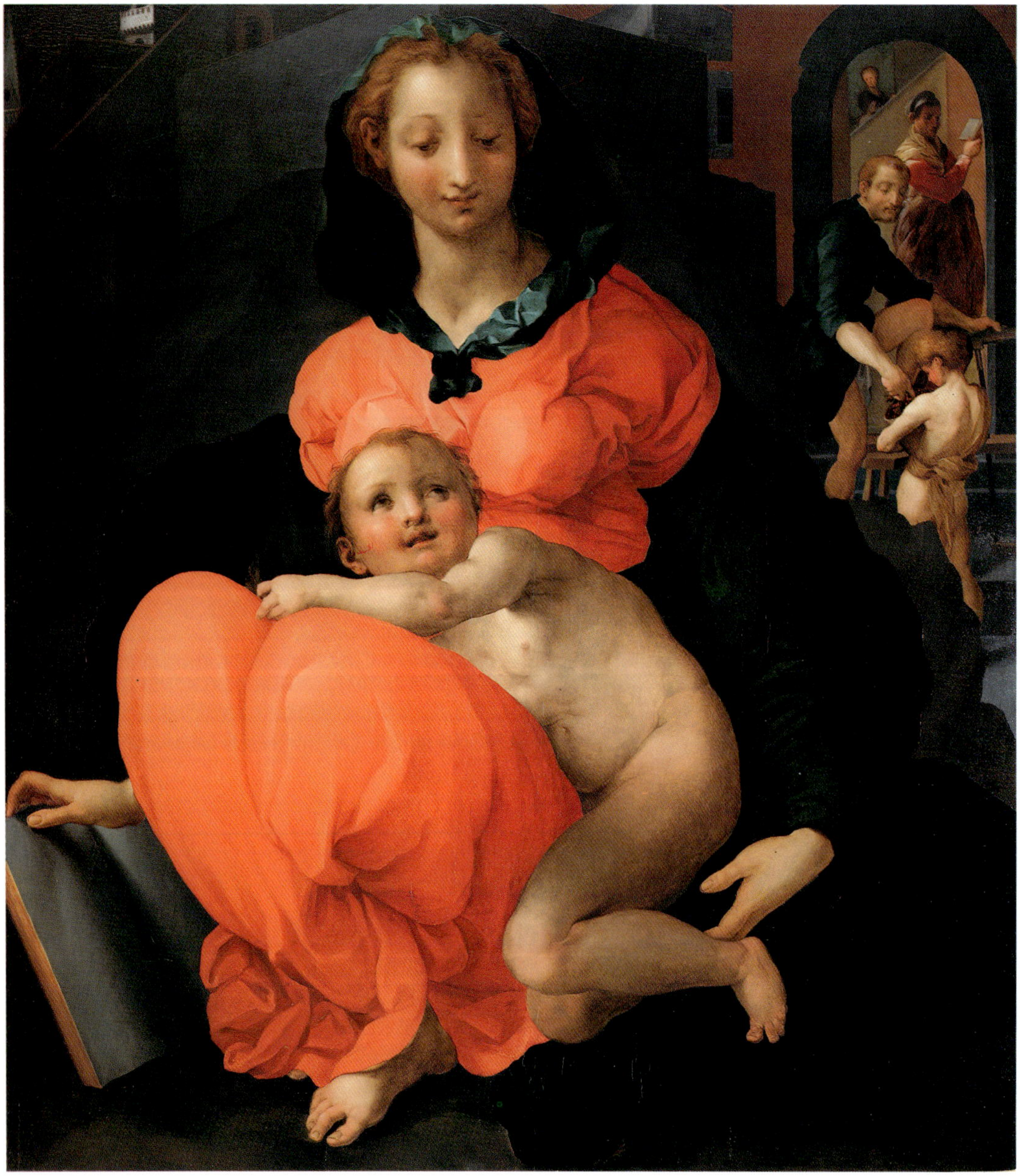

70. *After Pontormo*
Madonna of the Book
120x102 cm
Private collection

71. *Pontormo*
Kicking Player
Florence, Prints and Drawings Collection of the Uffizi, no. 6505 F

72. *Pontormo*
Two Nudes Compared
Florence, Prints and Drawings Collection of the Uffizi, no. 6738 F

73. *Pontormo*
Hermaphrodite Figure
Florence, Prints and Drawings Collection of the Uffizi, no. 6630 F

on the "inorganic aspects, the flaccidity of the flesh rather than the muscles, the absence of a precise individuality or any active or vital force" (R. Corti, 1977). This anticlassical and antinaturalistic choice represents a veritable reversal of the heroism and vigour of Michelangelo's anatomy and exalts the refined elaboration of the delineated forms, independently of any relationship with the reality of the senses and with the representative end. The twists characteristic of Michelangelo's figures in the Sistine Chapel, both those of the ceiling (1508-12) and especially those of the nudes of the *Last Judgement* on the end wall (1537-41) are taken to the extreme. The figures of the biblical stories of San Lorenzo assume a variety of highly precarious spiraliform and serpentine positions; frequently they intertwine and become entangled. Especially in the preparatory designs for the scenes of the *Judgement*, the *Ascension of Souls into Heaven*, and the *Deluge*, for example in the extraordinary *Group of the Dead* (Uffizi, Prints and Drawings Collection), which very probably occupied the lower part of the choir walls, the composition is reduced to an inextricable knot of chain-linked bodies, extending in width or projecting upwards within a space completely devoid of perspective laws. The 16th-century sources that were cited previously and the modern reconstructions of the original arrangement of the episodes in the cycle substantially agree on the exact position of the scene of *Christ the Judge with the Creation of Eve*, whose preparatory design is now in the Uffizi. The fresco was situated in the middle of the upper area of the wall behind the altar, between the two windows and the representations of *Original Sin* and the *Expulsion from Paradise*. The centrality given to the figure of Christ and to the redemption brought about by him after the initial ruinous victory of evil over mankind was one of the fundamental ideas of a particular type of religiousness, of reformist tendency, associated with the theory of the justification of faith alone, with a consequent belittlement of good works and a deepening of direct contact with God. According to one interpretation, it was precisely to this type of religious

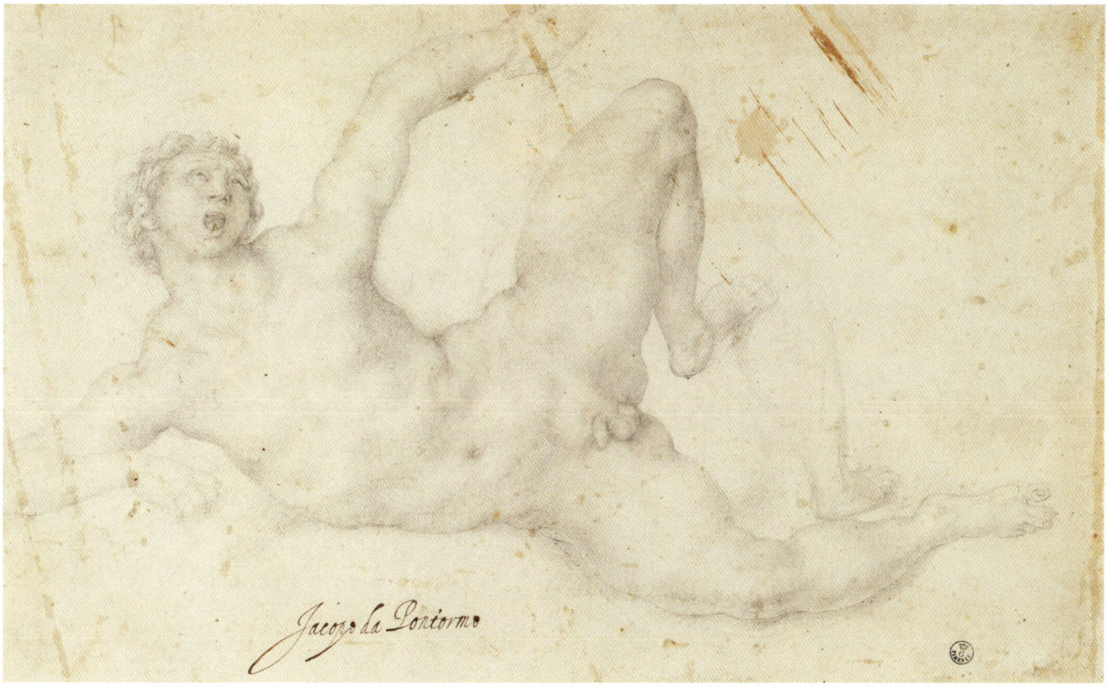
Jacopo da Pontormo

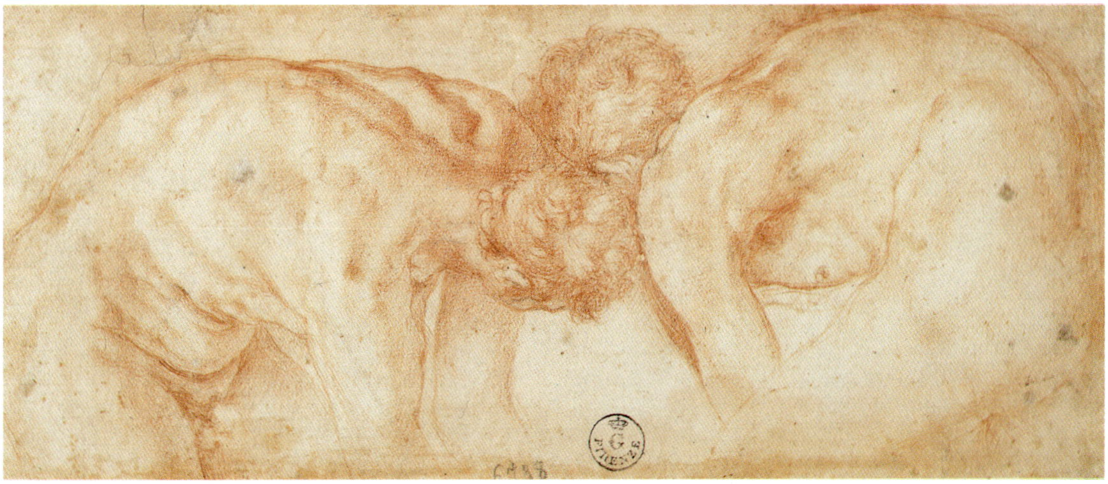

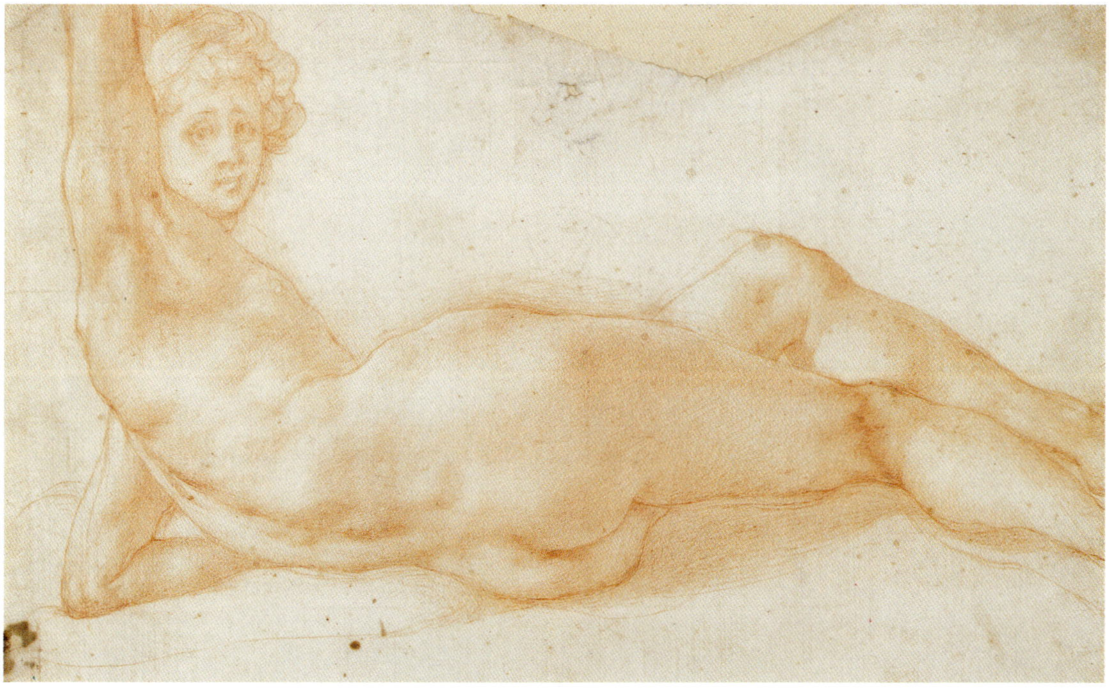

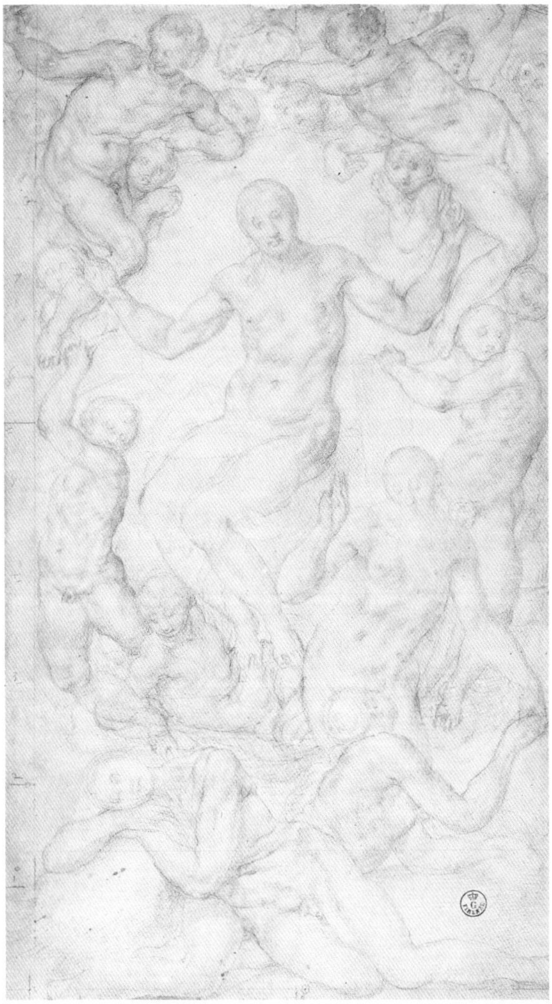
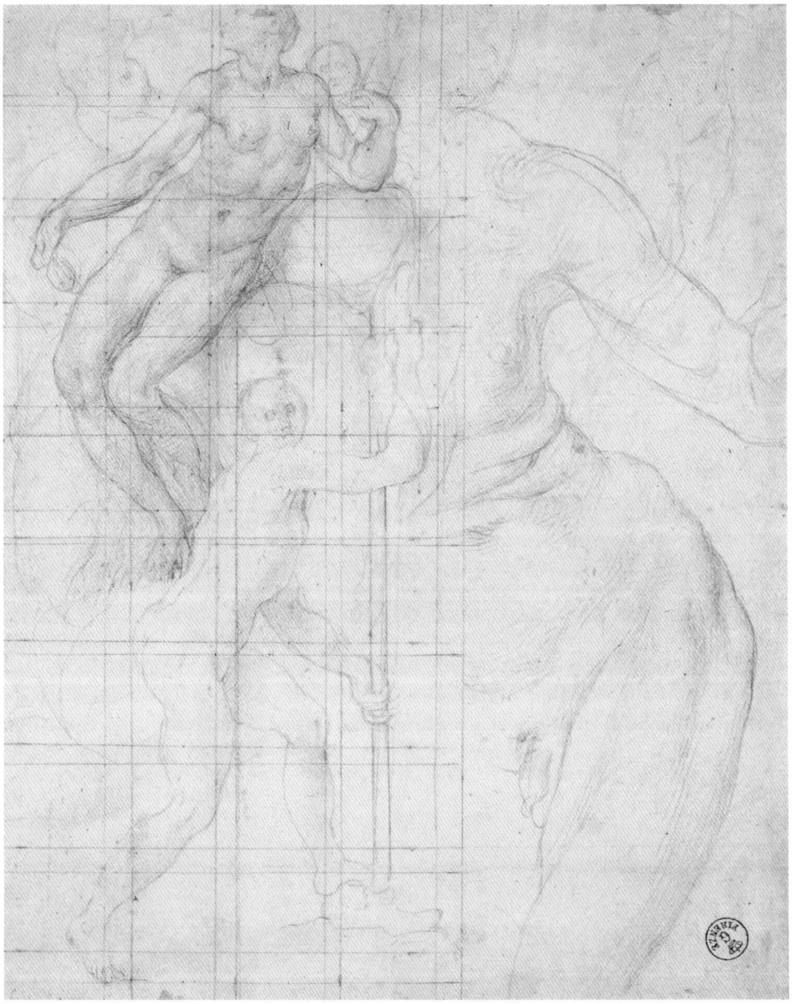
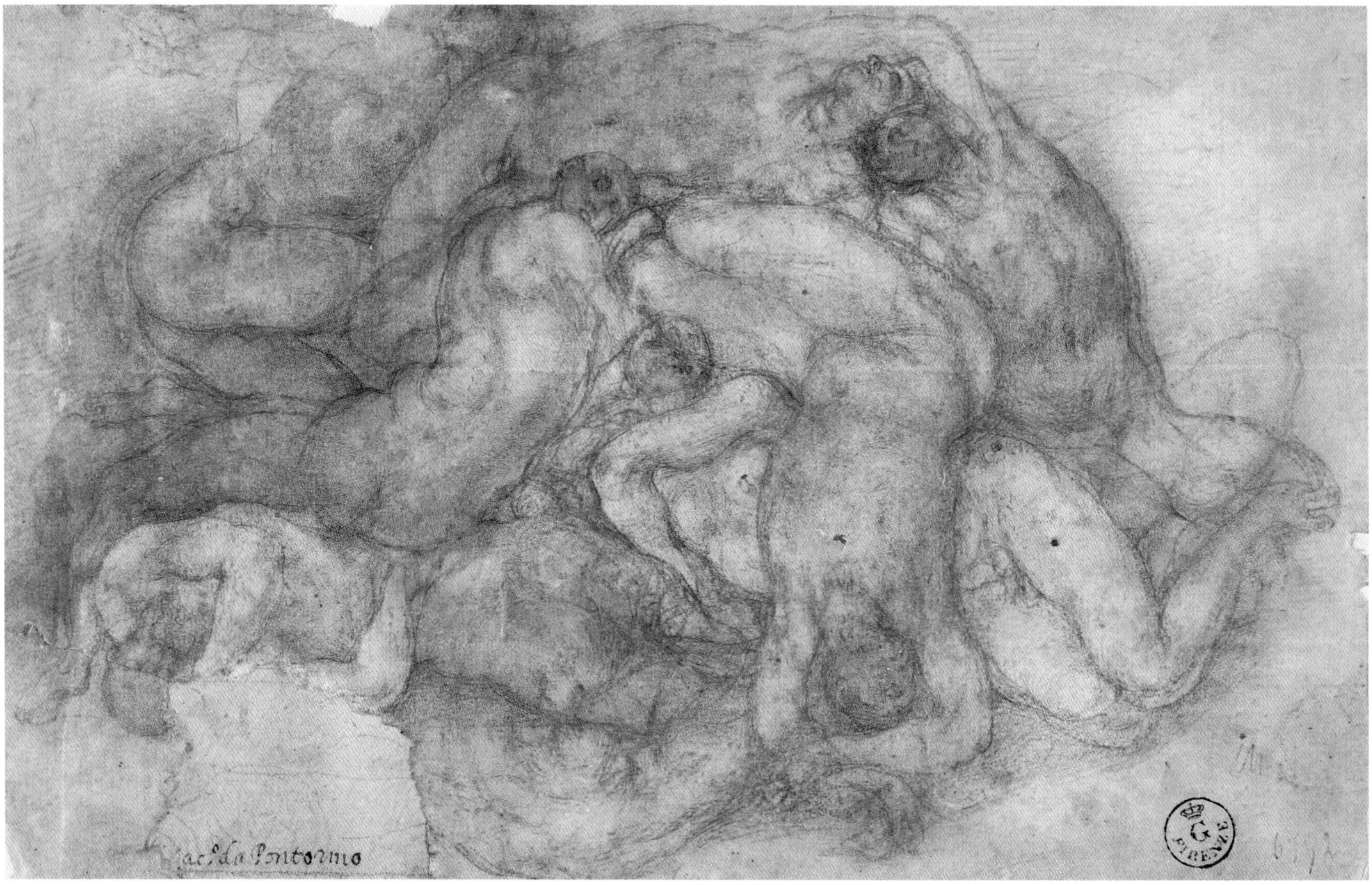

mentality that Pontormo must have referred in the nine scenes of the choir of San Lorenzo, which probably represented a reflection on the contrast between the world of law, error, and expiation on the one hand, and reality renewed by the grace of God through the sacrifice of Christ on the other. In this framework, the justifying value of his martyrdom and the new creation of man generated by his death, alluded to through reference to the first divine creation, is the idea behind the main scene we have just mentioned. Visibly evident in the preparatory design are the instruments of the Passion, the crown of thorns and the nails held up by the angel on the left of Christ. The scenes of *Cain and Abel* and *Adam and Eve at Work*, whose preparatory studies are both in the Prints and Drawings Collection of the Uffizi, probably refer to the disastrous effect of sin in the life of man. In the second of these, Adam drives a spade into the ground with his left foot while Eve holds in her hands implements for spinning. The hope of forgiveness was affirmed by the scene of *Noah*, the prefiguration of mankind's salvation by virtue of his being spared from the divine damnation of the Flood, and by that of the *Sacrifice of Isaac*. The portraits of the *Four Evangelists* and of *Moses receiving the Tables of the Law* refer to the new law of the love of Christ, who renews the ancient commandments. In the preparatory design (Uffizi), Moses, kneeling with his back to the observer, raises his arms aloft in the act of holding up the tablets which God's left forefinger points to. The end of the old world of law and punishment, and the last act in the story of mankind redeemed by Christ, were represented in the scenes of the *Deluge* and the *Judgement*, which prepared the way for the *Ascension of Souls into Heaven*, all depicted in the lower register of the walls.

74. Pontormo
Christ the Judge with the Creation of Eve
Florence, Prints and Drawings Collection of the Uffizi, no. 6609 F

75. Pontormo
Adam and Eve at Work
Florence, Prints and Drawings Collection of the Uffizi, no. 6536 F

76. Pontormo
Group of the Dead
Florence, Prints and Drawings Collection of the Uffizi, no. 6752 F

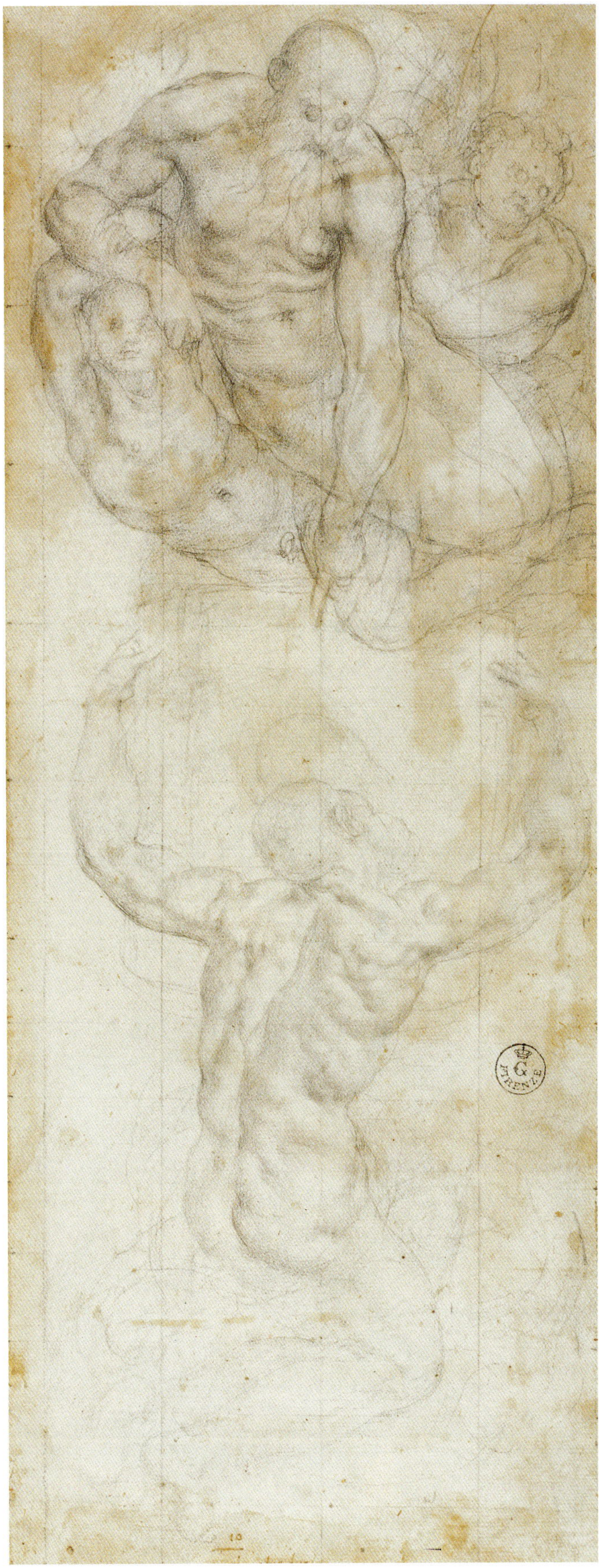

77. Pontormo
Moses receiving the Tables of the Law
Florence, Prints and Drawings Collection of the Uffizi, no. 6749 F r

Pontormo's portraits

Of the portraits attributed to Pontormo the *Lady with a Basket of Spindles* of the Uffizi, dated around 1516, has recently been assigned to Andrea del Sarto, although certain features of the lady's face reveal characteristics that are unquestionably Pontormesque, such as the deep eye-sockets and the full mouth with its slightly puckered upper lip, the ends of which, like the hairline, are marked by touches of Leonardesque *sfumato*. The slightly frowning expression, the reflection of a certain inner unease, recalls those of the saints portrayed in the *Pucci Altarpiece*. Raphael's "*Velata*", which Pontormo may have seen during his presumed visit to Rome of 1515, has been proposed as the figurative model for the painting. Indeed, Raphael's influence can be discerned in the intrusiveness of the ample right sleeve of the gold-highlighted red damask dress and the pleated blouse emerging from the cutting of the neckline.

The directional opposition of the arm and head of the *Jeweller* of the Louvre (1517-18), otherwise attributable to Domenico Puligo, appears to recall the arrangement of postures of the figures in the *Pucci Altarpiece*. As regards the identification of the person portrayed, the names of two Florentine engravers have been proposed: Michelino di Paolo Poggini and Domenico di Polo.

One of Pontormo's works that Vasari most admired is the *Portrait of Cosimo il Vecchio de' Medici*, which has recently been assigned to the end of the second decade of the century. The painting, as the Aretine biographer testifies, was executed for Goro Gheri da Pistoia, secretary and loyal counsellor of Lorenzo, Duke of Urbino. The work aimed to celebrate the *Pater Patriae*, the image of the Medici dynasty's founding father, some fifty years after his death. The painting, therefore, does not represent a figure portrayed from life, but evokes the per-

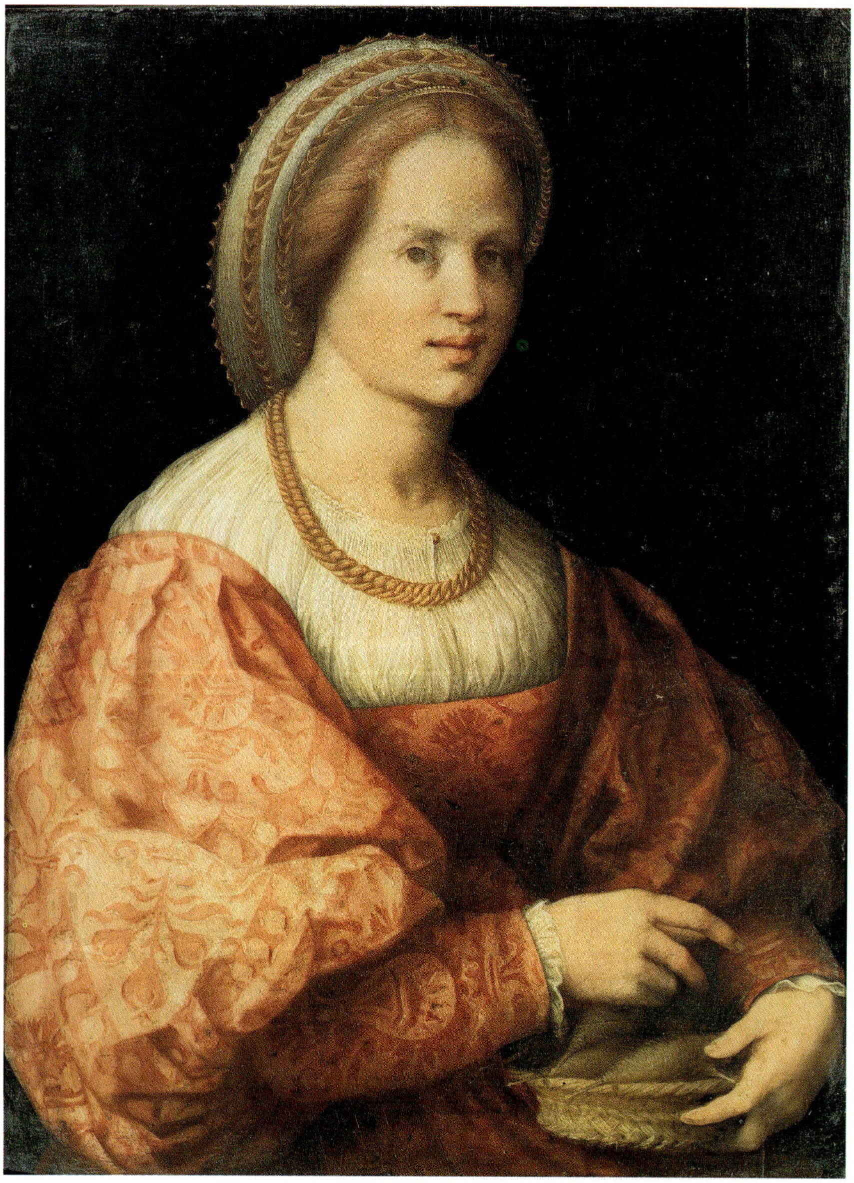

78. Pontormo
Lady with a Basket of Spindles
76x54 cm
Florence, Uffizi

79. Pontormo or Domenico Puligo
Jeweller
69x59 cm
Paris, Louvre

80. Pontormo (?)
Portrait of Maria Salviati
87x71 cm
Florence, Uffizi

81. Pontormo
Portrait of a Young Man
85x61 cm
Lucca, Museo Nazionale di Villa Guinigi

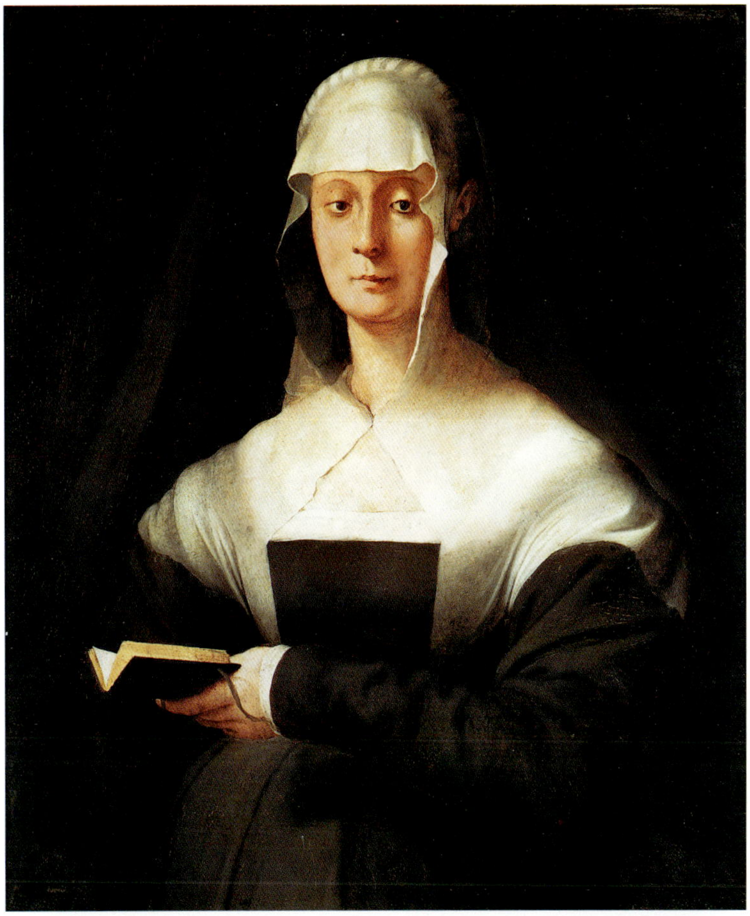

sonality of the illustrious statesman and humanist. The waxy, immobile face, rigorously represented in profile, reproposes the iconography of the 15th-century art of medal-making, which must have inspired the artist for this portrait. Standing out against the dark background of the painted composition is the bright red of the elegant velvet cape covering the skinny, almost insubstantial body of Cosimo, who is sitting on a chair with a high back and scroll-decorated armrests. The laurel sapling, depicted in the left of the painting, is the allegorical representation of the Medici dynasty, while its regeneration over the years is alluded to in the phrase from Virgil on the scroll wrapped round one of its branches: "UNO AVULSO NON DEFICIT ALTER" ("even though a member of the family may be snatched from this life, there will always be another to succeed him"). The motto was used by Cosimo I de' Medici when, between 1538 and 1539, he succeeded the first branch of the Medici family that had been violently cut short by the death of Duke Alessandro. The latter, born in 1511 by Lorenzo, Duke of Urbino, and assassinated in 1537, has been identified as the extraordinary *Portrait of a Young Man* of the Museo Nazionale di Villa Guinigi in Lucca, dating to 1525. There is great debate over the attribution of the *Portrait of Maria Salviati*, the mother of Cosimo I, presently conserved at the Uffizi.

It has recently been suggested that the celebrated *Halberdier* of the Paul Getty Museum of Malibu is a portrait of the young Duke Cosimo, who triumphed at Montemurlo over the last republican initiative led by Filippo

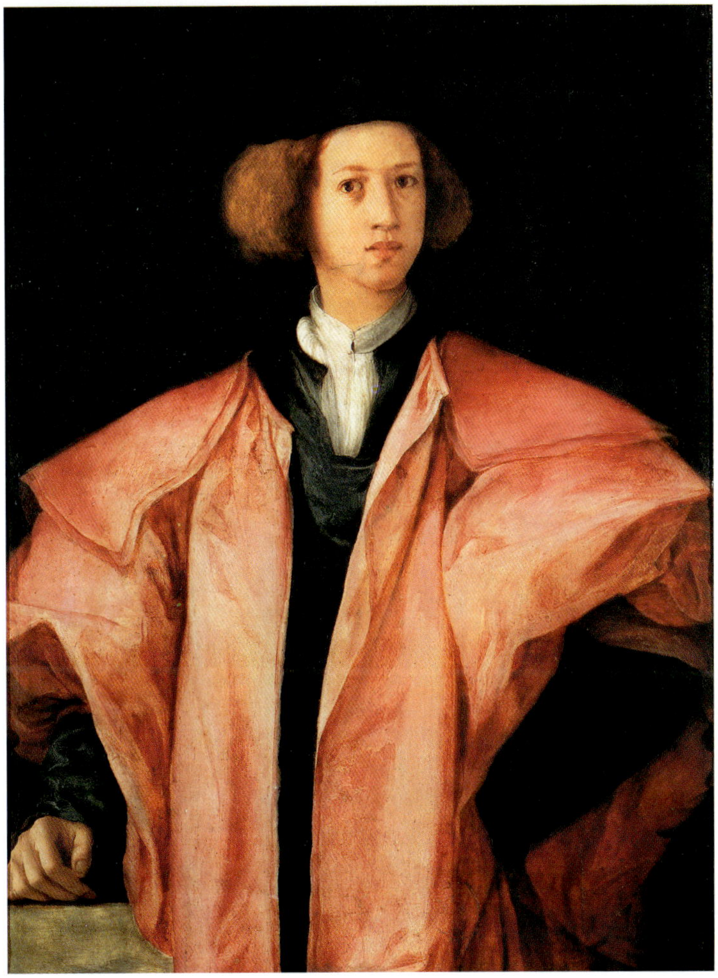

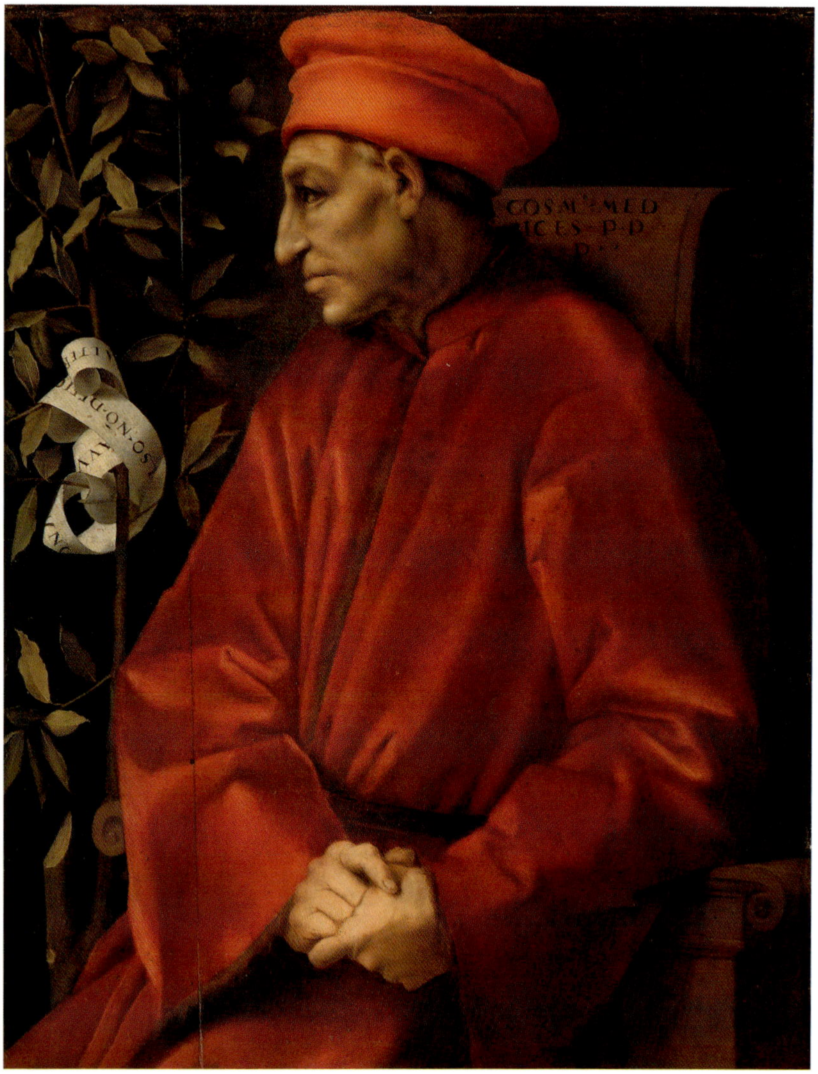

82. Pontormo
Portrait of Cosimo il Vecchio
86x65 cm
Florence, Uffizi

83. Pontormo
Study for the Halberdier
Florence, Prints and Drawings Collection of the Uffizi, no. 6701 F r

84. Pontormo
Halberdier
92x72 cm
Malibu, Paul Getty Museum

Strozzi and Baccio Valori (1537). Those, on the other hand, who identify the figure as Francesco di Giovanni di Gherardo Guardi, born in 1514 and resident in Florence in the district of Borgo la Croce, date the painting to the period of the siege of Florence (1529-30). The documentary evidence relative to this character attests to his active participation in Florentine public life: in 1550, for example, he belonged the Council of the Two Hundred. In Pontormo's painting the young halberdier is intent on guarding the defensive rampart painted in the background. A preparatory drawing of the painted version is today conserved at the Prints and Drawings Collection of the Uffizi. As in other works by Pontormo, the intense light that invests the foreground of the painting, contrasts strongly with the dark background and emphasizes the colours of the young man's clothing: the beige of the jacket, the white of the shirt, and the bright red of the pants and beret. A remarkable artistic skill is also discernible in the rendering of the various materials of the objects that distinguish the figure of this young soldier: the burnished metal of the hand-guard, the leather of the thick belt to which it is attached, the fine grain of the wooden halberd, the gold of the light chain hanging rounded the man's neck and the medallion with the relief of Hercules and Anthaeus on the cap.

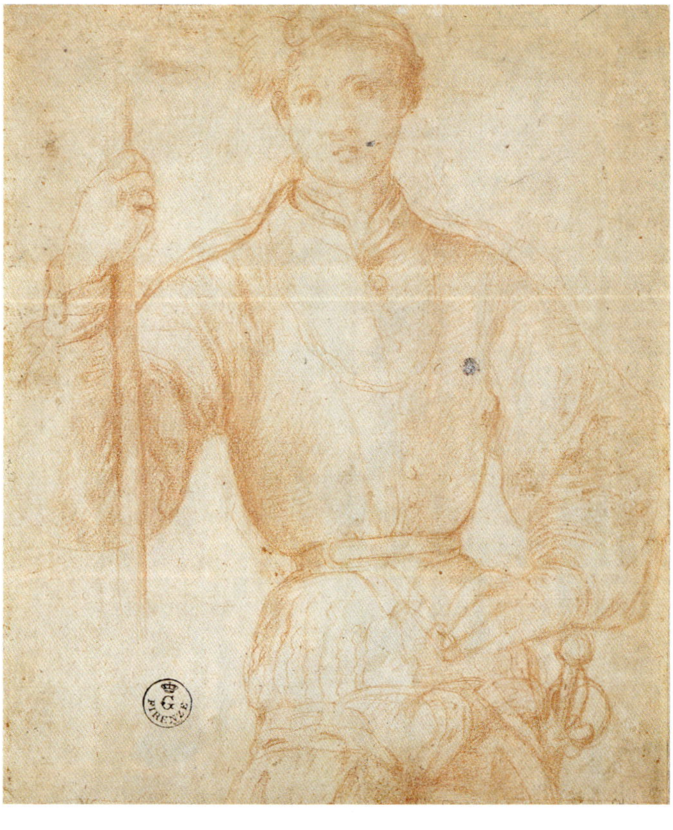

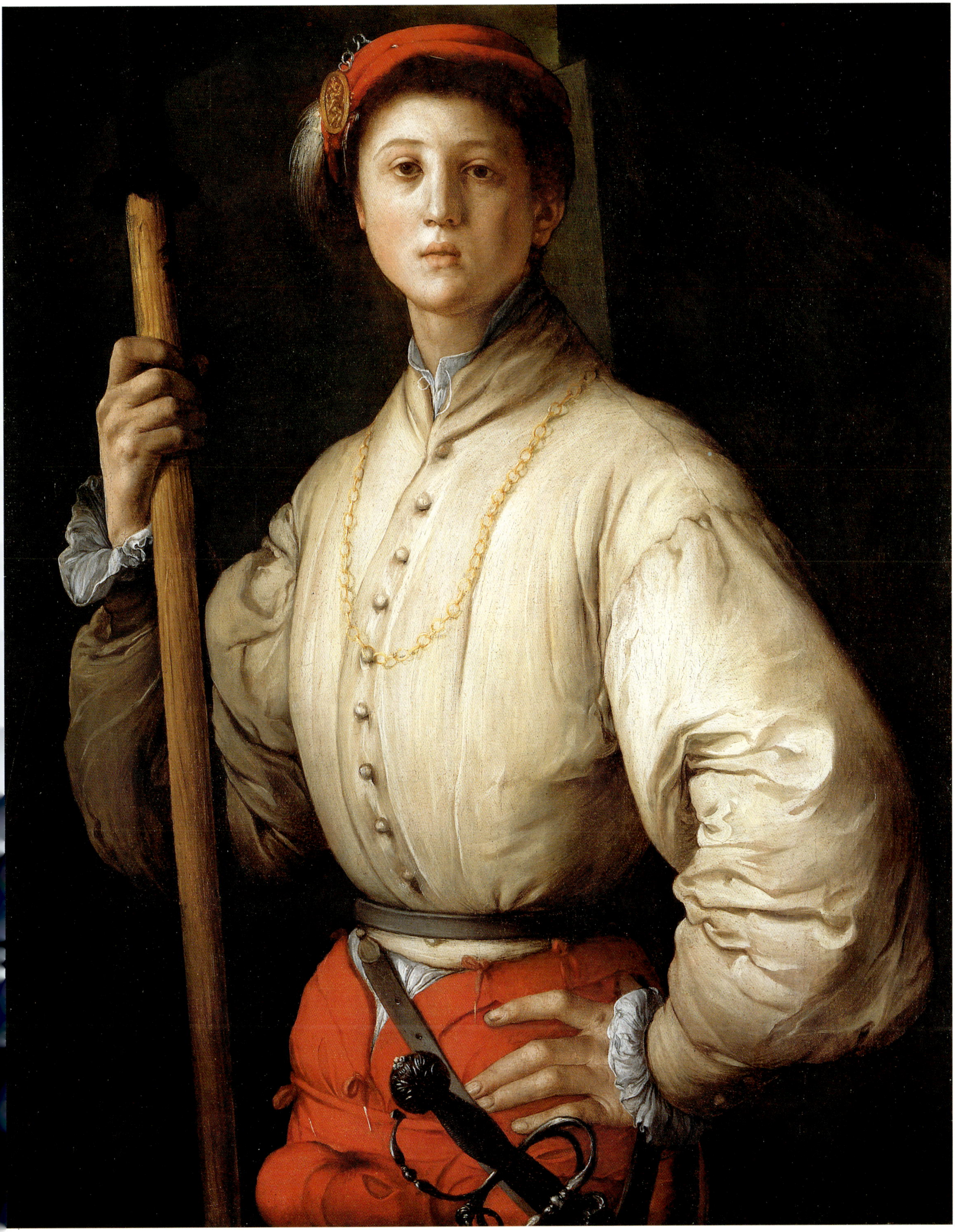

Rosso Fiorentino and the themes of the religious iconographical tradition

The theme of the deposition of Jesus from the cross, the dramatically conclusive moment of his sacrifice, sums up, and at the same time represents, all the phases of Christ's redeeming mission on Earth, which the Pauline scriptures describe as a gradual transition of the son of God from the divine to the human dimension. The subject, one of the most widely diffused by the religious iconographical tradition, was handled several times by Rosso Fiorentino during the course of his variegated and extraordinary artistic career. We may say, indeed, that the artist reflected intensely on the whole question of the dead Christ. Over the years, through a progressive reduction of the elements making up the composition, figures and objects, he concentrated increasingly specifically on the three figures that were the true protagonists of the event: the body of the dead Christ, the figure of the Virgin Mary, increasingly visibly wounded by the blade of that "sword" which, according to the terrible prophecy of the aged Simeon, would pierce her soul (cf. Luke 2, 25-35), and the figure of Mary Magdalene, reaching out to embrace the Virgin or delicately cover the lower part of Christ's limbs.

In the celebrated *Deposition* of Volterra, the body of Christ has just been freed from the nails that fastened him to the cross and is being lowered to the ground. The work, signed and dated in the lower right-hand corner on the lower end of the ladder behind the figure of St John (RVBEVS FLO. FAC. A. S. MDXXI), was executed in 1521 for the Compagnia della Croce and displayed in the Cappella della Croce di Giorno, adjacent to the church of San Francesco in Volterra. Rosso was probably influenced by his patrons in choosing to represent the moment of the deposition. The theme of the crucifixion was in fact better suited to the Compagnia della Croce di Notte which, together with the Croce di Giorno, used the church of San Francesco as a point of reference for their activities. According to the Gospel story at the moment of Christ's death darkness descended upon the Earth, similar to night, while the body of Christ was deposed at sunset (cf. Matthew 27, 45; 57).

The suffused glimmer of twilight is represented in the lower part of the sky, which forms the background of Rosso's pictorial representation. It is striking for the extraordinary rendering of the delicate fading of evening light on the horizon and its gradual merging into the darkness which dominates the upper part of the painting. From the time of his earliest works Rosso showed an unusual flare for experimenting with new forms and new ways of handling the composition, and here too he seized the opportunity to attempt a daring alternative to the traditional way of representing the religious subject. Indeed, he chose to characterize the act of deposition by portraying an aspect of it that the Gospels do not even mention: the body of Christ almost slipping from the grasp of the deposers, who are shown striving to prevent it from falling. But the uniqueness of this famous painting lies not so much in the iconographical peculiarity, but rather in the extraordinary and highly personal combination of incisive emotional force and intense spirituality, which are unleashed through the varied range of poses, the expressions of the figures, and the unprecedented formal innovations. The work has been widely acclaimed by art critics, who have called it the masterpiece of the Florentine painter. The painting is seen as highly representative of Rosso's particular predilection for experimenting with ever newer formal solutions, in which the various figurative ideas he knew and appreciated during the course of his artistic development are subjected to the transforming action of that "contrary opinion" which Vasari had identified as one of the most significant traits of his personality. The most immediately striking aspect of the Volterra *Deposition* is undoubtedly the originality of the complex range of colours and the juxtaposition of complementary tints, which under the influence of a powerful radiating light produce delicate *cangiante* effects with unprecedented touches of phosphorescence in the points of greatest brightness, and which stand out especially against the opaque background. In some areas of the composition, the thinness of the paint layer means that the ground and preparatory sketch underneath show through, proving how for Rosso the finished work is not "the realization of an idea already incorporated in the design, but rather the result of an uninterrupted and continually developing process right up until its final state, achieved after many modifications and changes of mind" (M. Burresi, A. Caleca, 1981). This fact is borne out by the curious autographed annotations indicating which tints should be used, clearly visible in some areas of the composition, indications which do not correspond with the colours used in the final version. Note the word "violoso" on the right shoulder of the woman in the left foreground, and the term "blue" between the folds of the loin-cloth worn by the lowest figure easing Christ down from the cross and in the high part of the ample *chignon* of Mary Magdalene. The juxtaposition of complementary co-

85-87. Rosso Fiorentino
Deposition from the Cross and details
341x201 cm
Volterra, Pinacoteca Civica

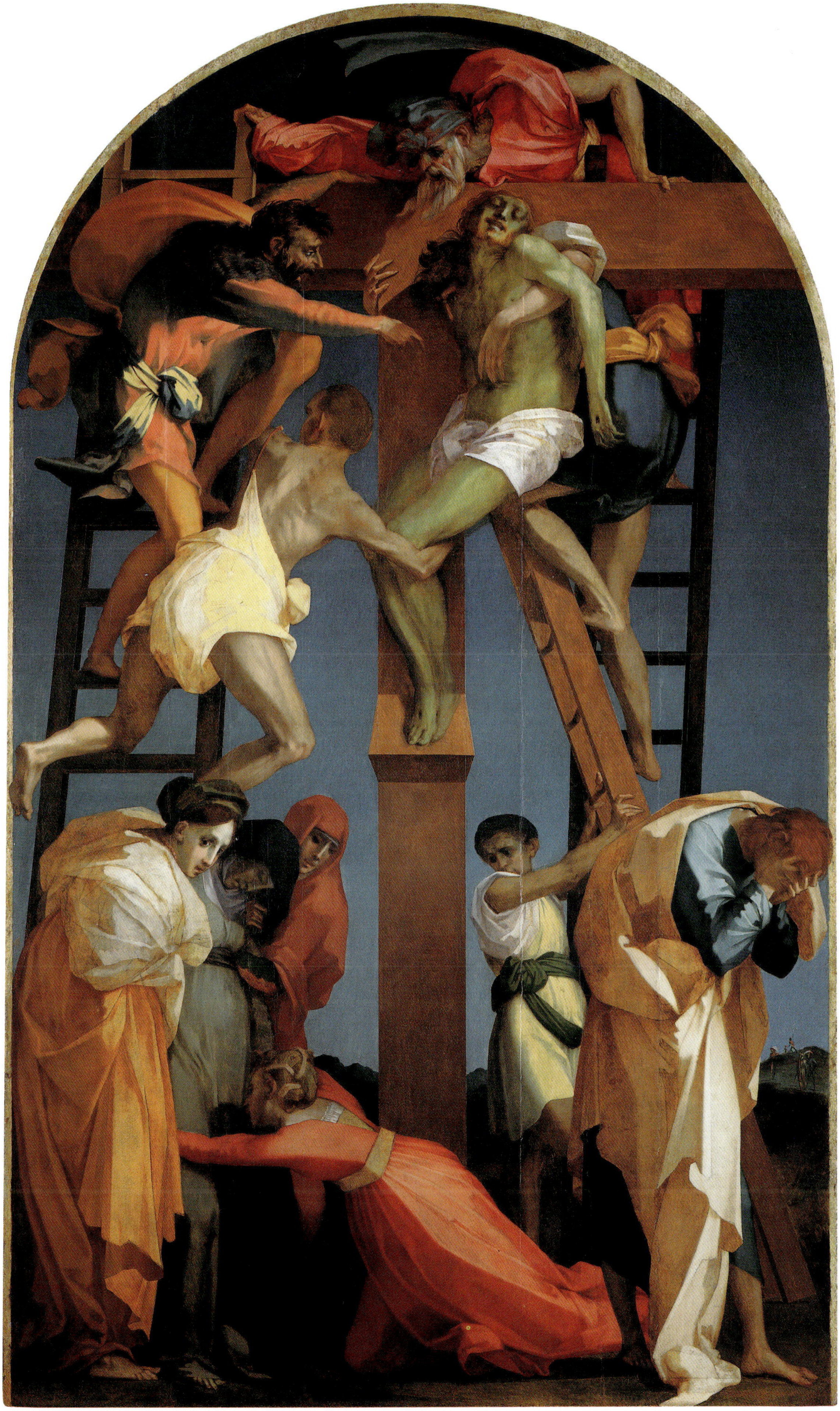

lours and the sharp contrasts of light and shadow put particular emphasis on the complex structure of lines, both the edges of the single painted surfaces and the lines within them, which together form a "web of tightly knit links" (K. Kusenberg, 1931). Lines and surfaces certainly reveal the artist's predilection for a geometric module comprising "a series of dihedral angles, used on a vast graduated scale of dimensions, which probe the space in every direction" (R. P. Ciardi, 1987). Great emphasis has been placed on a harsh angularity of pointed corners, described as "violentazione cubista" (G. Briganti, 1961), which forms a striking contrast with "the almost sensual ornamental effects that exist in Pontormo's line" (S. J. Freedberg, 1961). This geometrical arrangement of the pictorial space is most evident in the clothing; see for example the remarkable case of Mary Magdalene's red dress, tied at the waist by a yellow belt. The poses of the individual figures are also regulated by an angular module; that of the arms of Nicodemus, who peers down from the top of the cross, that of the head of the Virgin, her chin resting on the upper part of her chest, and that of the clutching arm of the person holding Christ by the knees, are all representative. An imaginary horizontal line, situated above the heads of the pious women and St John, separates the rectangle enclosing the lower part of the painting from the upper part; the only links between these two areas of the painting are the figures of Mary Magdalene, whose body cuts across the base of the cross, and the young attendant holding the ladder, seen sideways on. Above, the group of four figures deposing the body of Christ, arranged in a circle on the three ladders, follows the arch-like rhythm of the painting, which is completed by the ample curve of Nicodemus's cloak.

The identification of the possible figurative sources to which the artist may have referred in the execution of his *Deposition* remains a much-debated question. Opinions range from a vehement affirmation of the painting's absolute originality to the more or less recent theories concerning its connection with medieval art; the interesting suggestion that it may have been influenced by the 13th-century wooden *Deposition* of Volterra Cathedral enjoys some credibility.

The reference to the *Deposition* by Flippino Lippi, a work completed by Perugino at the beginning of the 16th century, cannot be denied. This painting, now at the Galleria dell'Accademia in Florence, has a similar cross with a short horizontal arm situated high up, as well as the two ladders seen face on. The question of links with Michelangelo is a complex one: the figure of the deposer on the left, wearing a yellow loin-cloth, draws on the cartoon of the *Battle of Cascina*, while the body of Christ is clearly inspired by the Vatican *Pietà*. Validating the theory that Rosso spent some time in Rome, presumably between 1518 and 1521 are clear references to the frescoes of the Sistine ceiling, in the "definition of colours, constructed with a plastic juxtaposition of complementary colours" (R. P. Ciardi, 1987) and in the use of the gesture of Eve expelled from Paradise for the posture of the figure of St John. This red-haired young man, who buries his head in his hands in an expression of intense anguish, has been interpreted as a "self-portrait denied" of Rosso (R. P. Ciardi, 1987), who by including this figure in the painting is thus personally involved in the event represented. Examples of this exist in more or less contemporary northern figurative art, in Dürer particularly, who has been identified as one of the most probable sources of inspiration for the painting and to whom some facial characterizations are referrable.

The reference to Dürer is also noticeable in the *Deposition from the Cross* of Sansepolcro, today conserved in the church of San Lorenzo. The work was commissioned in 1527 by the Confraternity of Santa Croce, and was probably finished before 1 July 1528, when Rosso signed the contract for the *Christ in Glory* of Città di Castello. Compared with the preceding Volterra *Deposition*, to which the painting refers in the

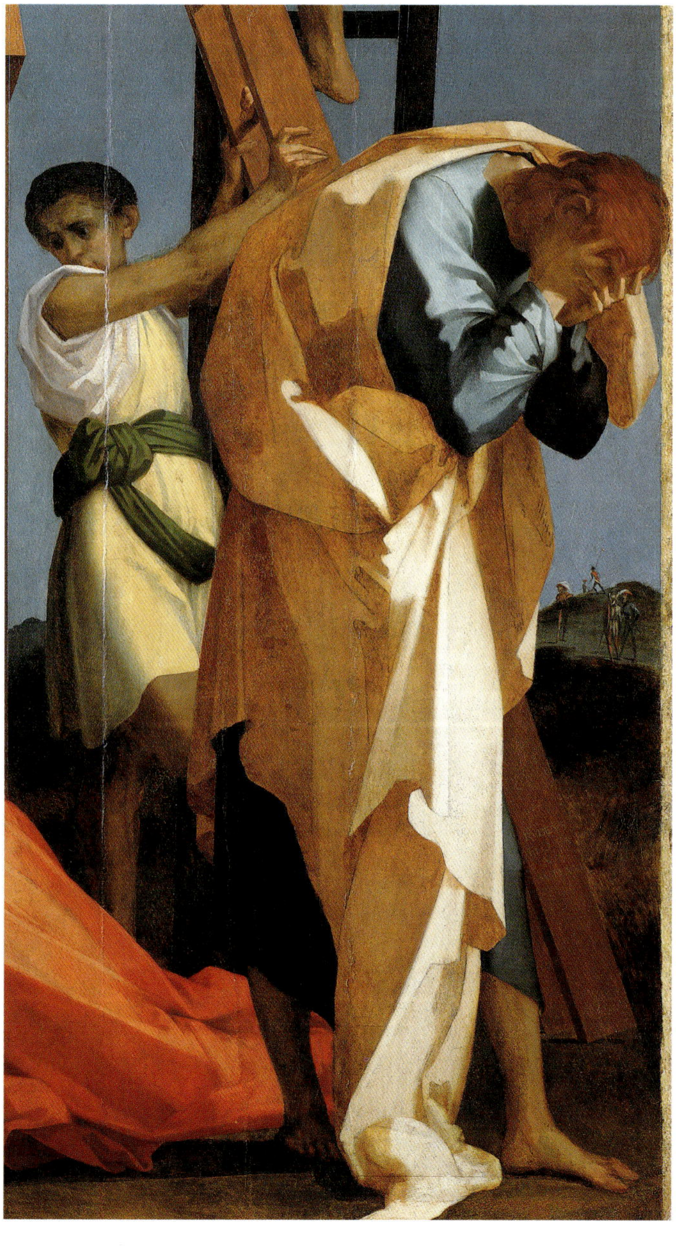

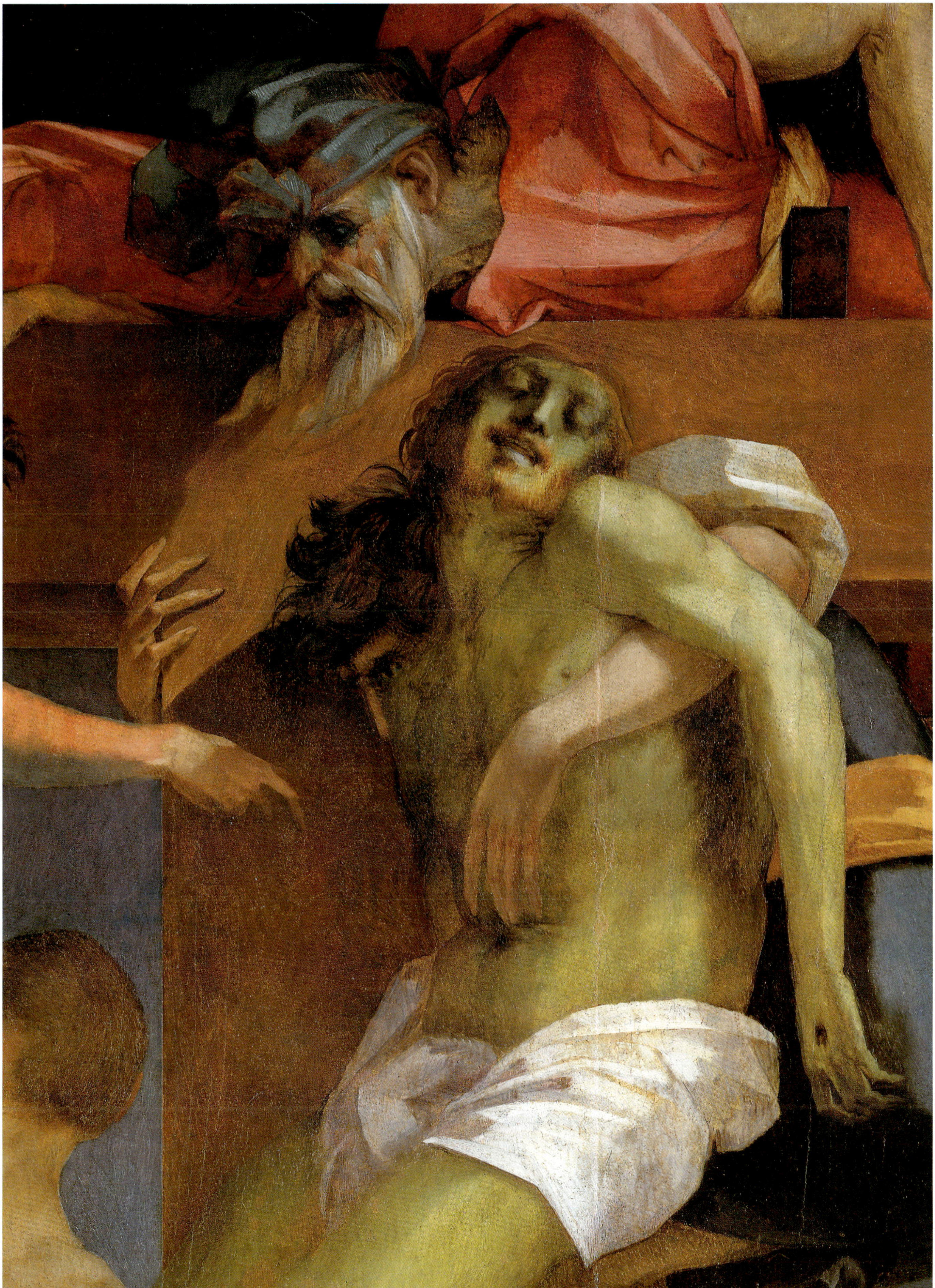

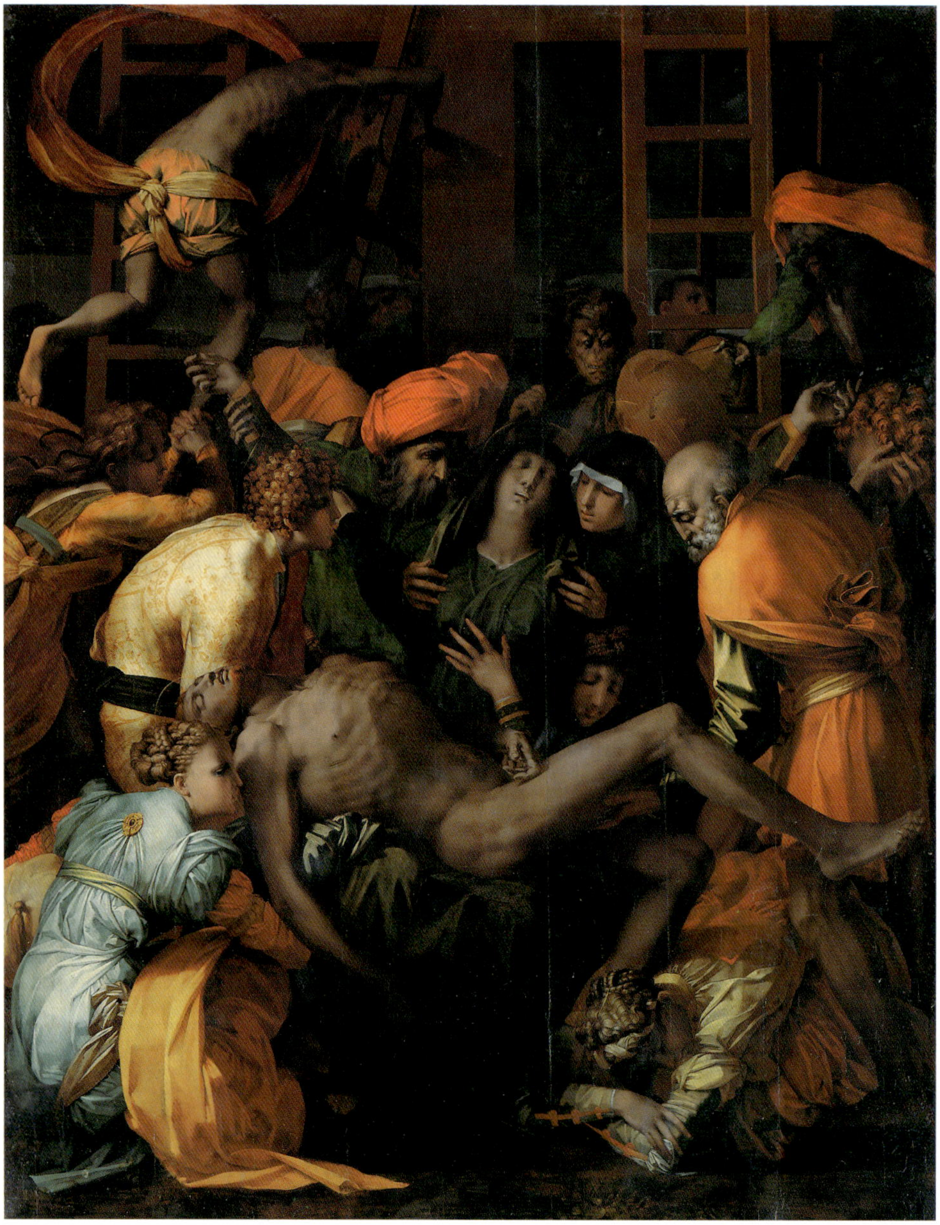

figure of the deposer on the left descending one of the three ladders resting against the cross, and in the curly-haired young St John, portrayed in the background burying his face in his hands, as in the Volterra altarpiece, the *Deposition* of Sansepolcro places a greater emphasis on the figure of Christ, who has been taken down from the cross and is now lying in the Virgin's lap in the foreground. The Confraternity who ordered the work strongly encouraged Rosso to make this iconographical choice in the act of commission, dating to 23 September 1527. A reference to the moulded characterization of Michelangelo's anatomies is visible in the bodies of Rosso's painting; observe, for example, the youth standing to the right of the Virgin bending slightly forward in the act of holding up Christ's back. The light which covers the foreground of the composition and contrasts with the dark background is brightest in the clothing of this figure, highlighting its refined golden-yellow floral motif, and produces the extraordinary changing colour effects of

88, 89. Rosso Fiorentino
Deposition from the Cross
270x201 cm
Sansepolcro, San Lorenzo

the dress of the bystander seated in the foreground to the left of Mary Magdalene. More than for the re-elaboration of elements associated with the art of Dürer and the great masters of classicism, the Sansepolcro *Deposition* is distinguished by a number of iconographical peculiarities. The most striking is the complete nudity of the body of Jesus, a clear break with tradition, emphasis being given to the ample volume of its swollen rib-cage. Transferring to the Virgin the iconography which from the 14th century in Italy was traditionally used to represent Mary Magdalene, Rosso portrays the mother of Christ with her arms splayed and held up, as if she herself was reliving the moment of crucifixion; the expression of the cruci-

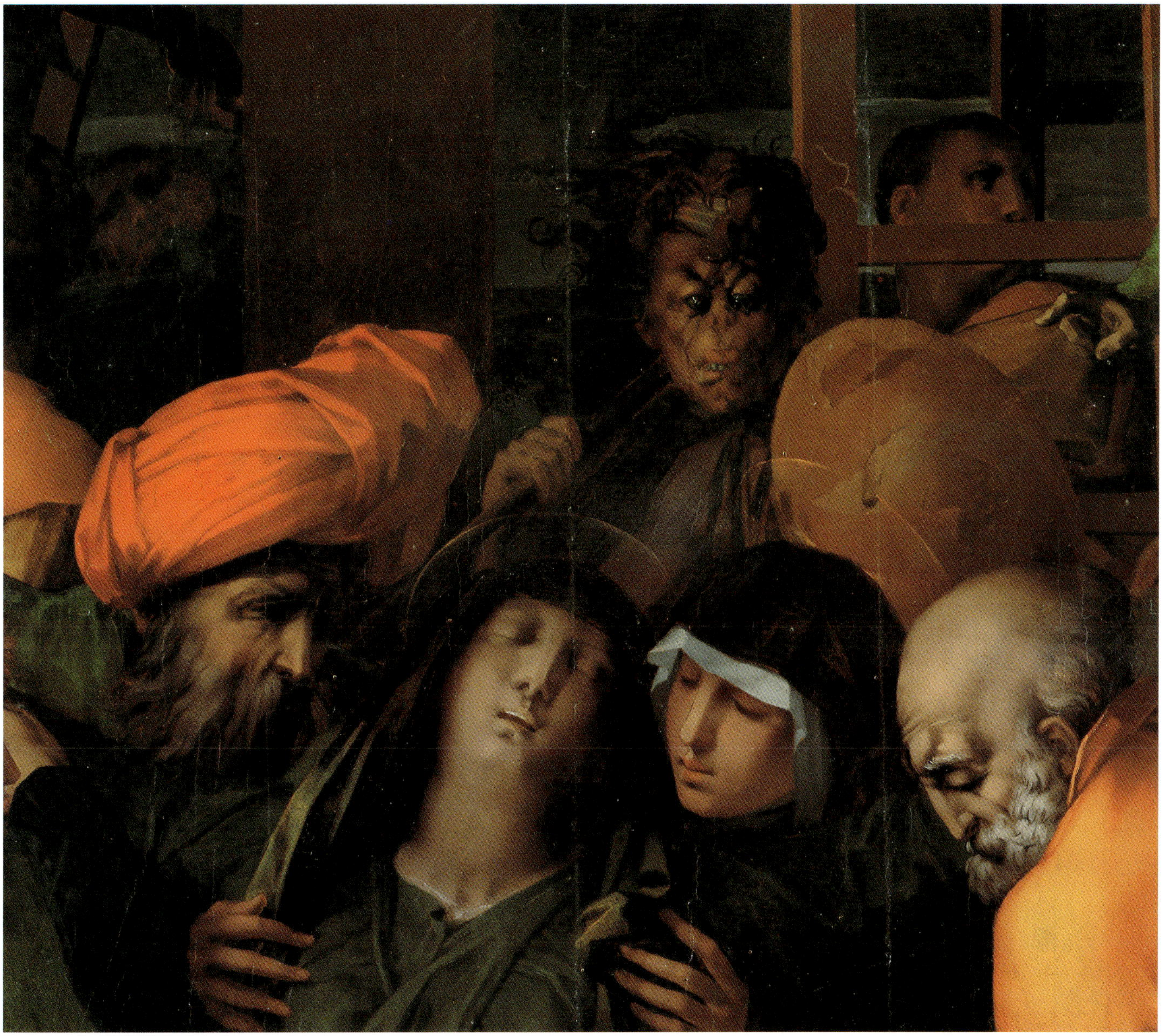

fied Jesus seems in fact to be impressed upon the face of Mary, who is now prostrate with grief. Behind her, the horrible animal-like figure directing his squint-eyed gaze away from the scene probably takes up the theme of the bodyguard, the symbol of the treachery and wickedness that determined the killing of Christ, and also present in the background of the Volterra *Deposition*.

Rosso addressed the theme of the dead Christ again towards the end of his artistic career (1537-40) when, after completing the decoration of the Gallery at Fontainebleau for Francis I, according to Vasari, "for the High Constable he painted a panel of the Dead Christ, an exceptional work located at one of his properties in Ecouen". The painting has been identified as the *Pietà* of the Louvre, which once hung above the door of the chapel of the High Constable Anne di Montmorency in the castle of Ecouen and which, of all the works executed by Rosso during his stay in France (1530-40), is the only surviving example that is certainly original. The painting is a "close-up" of the body of Christ, which extends across the whole width of the composition, literally filling the pictorial space. Christ's body, having been taken down from the cross, of which there is no trace in the composition, and from the maternal lap, is elegantly placed on a cushion lying on the ground. Behind the body of Jesus the Virgin opens her arms and collapses into the arms of one of the pious women. Light shines in the foreground of the composition, highlighting, compared with the dark background, the various shades of red in the clothing, which contrast with the white of the scarf surrounding the upper part of Mary's dress, and the delicate lace of Mary Magdalene dress, in which the golden yellow of the sleeve stands out.

The theme of the Madonna between saints, first portrayed in the famous painting for the church of Ognissanti in Florence (1518), was again handled by Rosso in 1521, when the artist executed the *Madonna enthroned between two saints* for the parish church of

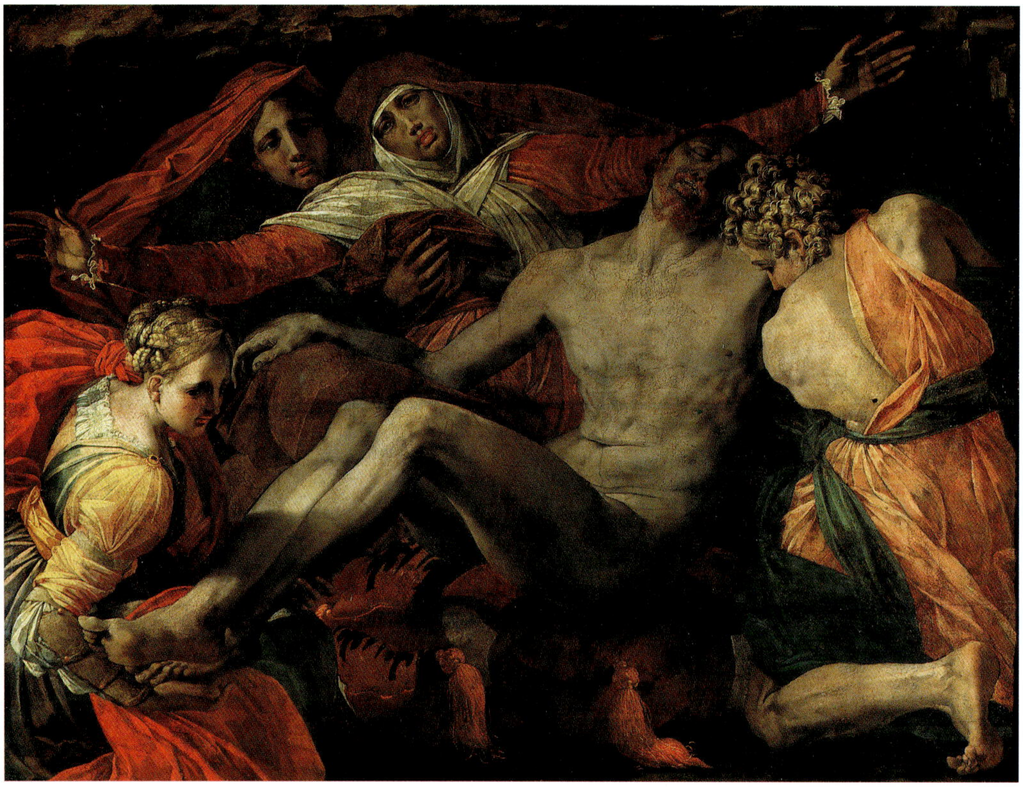

90. Rosso Fiorentino
Pietà
159x245 cm
Paris, Louvre

91. Rosso Fiorentino
Madonna enthroned between two saints
169x133 cm
Volterra, Museo Diocesano

Villamagna near Volterra. Compared to the complexity of the contemporary *Deposition*, and coming after the above-mentioned altarpiece of Santa Maria Nuova, the compositional solution of this painting, signed and dated in the lower left corner, at the foot of St John the Baptist, is regulated by a simpler scheme and a greater symmetry, an evident recall to classical tradition. Andrea del Sarto's *Madonna of the Harpies* is one of the most probable iconographical references for Rosso's painting as far as the general structure is concerned, and in the pose of the Virgin, who, firmly anchored to a supporting base, extends her knee forward and places her right arm around the Child clutching at her side. The figure of St Bartholomew with the book, who in Rosso's altarpiece looks towards the observer, recalls the St John the Baptist portrayed by Andrea del Sarto to the left of the Virgin and Child. In the framework of 15th-century revivals, which characterize numerous works by Rosso, an undeniable resemblance has recently been observed between the facial features of this saint and those of *St Paul* in the polyptych executed by Masaccio for the church of the Carmine in Pisa, where Rosso may have observed the painting personally during the time he spent in Volterra. Although the *Madonna enthroned and two saints* of the parish church of Villamagna reveals evident references to a more or less recent figurative tradition, the final result is totally original and clearly anticlassical. As in the previous painting of Santa Maria Nuova, the crowding together of the figures positioned in symmetrical poses, in a space with an extremely reduced depth, has a compositional scheme resembling bas-relief, in which, according to a now consolidated formal choice, the juxtaposition of complementary colours emphasizes the angularity of the linear structure. The various shades of yellow and green in the clothing of the figures, including the red of the Child's garments and the glow with green shadows of the Virgin's, tend towards a choice of declared formal austerity. In the *Villamagna Altarpiece* the paint layer thins considerably at the sides of the painting, so that the underlying preparatory design shows through, and gets gradually thicker towards the centre and in the upper area, revealing how much the "unfinished", characteristic of the works of this period, represents a precise formal choice, probably linked to a deliberate intention to place emphasis on the main figures of the scenes represented.

On his return to Florence, following the Volterra interlude, Rosso again turned his attention to the representation of the theme of the Madonna and saints. In 1522, on the commission of Ranieri, the son of Carlo Dei, the artist executed the *Madonna enthroned and ten saints* for the church of Santo Spirito, which was later transferred to Palazzo Pitti. The enlargement of the painting through the addition of broad wings at the sides, which have significantly altered its original proportions, may date to the time of its transferral. Following the restlessness of his youthful period, this painting, together with the *Ginori Altarpiece*, which we shall come to shortly, undoubtedly represents a moment of moderation, in which the references to the examples of Fra Bartolomeo and Andrea del Sarto appear more evident. The painting was much admired by Vasari, especially for the "vividness of the colours", which, with the greater regularity of

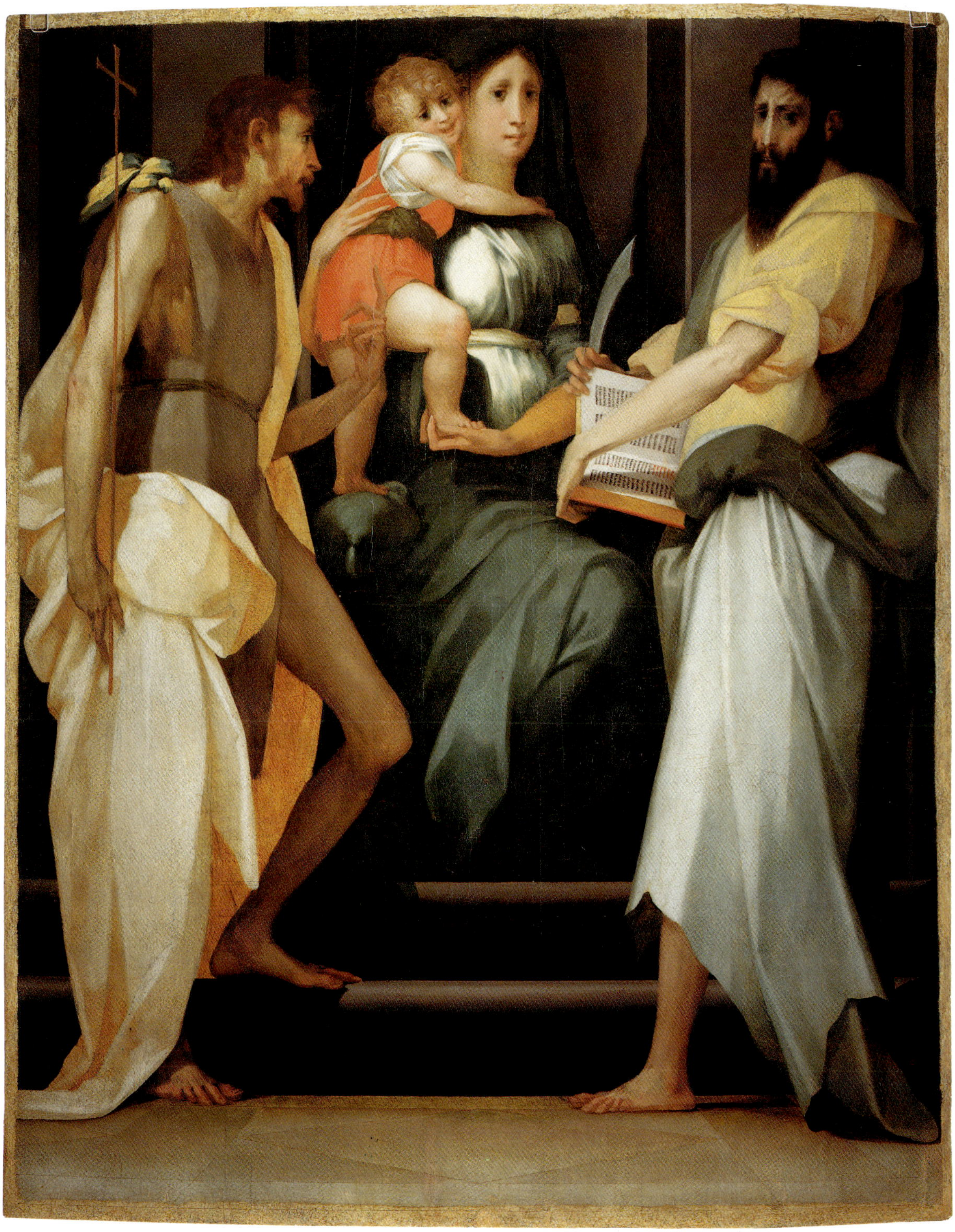

the composition and the poses of the single figures, reveal a more original quality and come closer to the eccentric use of colour in the previous works, especially in the St Catherine kneeling in the foreground.

An identical chromatic juxtaposition between the intense brightness of the green of the saint's dress, broken by dark areas of shadow in some parts of the pictorial surface, and the red of the cloth she is holding in her lap can be seen in the figure of St Apollonia, kneeling in the right foreground of the *Marriage of the Virgin*, executed by Rosso in 1523, on the commission of Carlo Ginori, for the chapel dedicated to Mary and Joseph in the church of San Lorenzo in Florence. The name of the artist, "Rubeus Florentino", is included among the letters of the first line of the second paragraph of text which the saint marks with her finger, and is also clearly written, together with the date of execution, on the step beneath the figure of the priest. Like the *Dei Altarpiece*, this painting is another example of moderation compared to the formal boldness of the works belonging to the early Florentine period and the sojourn in Volterra. The

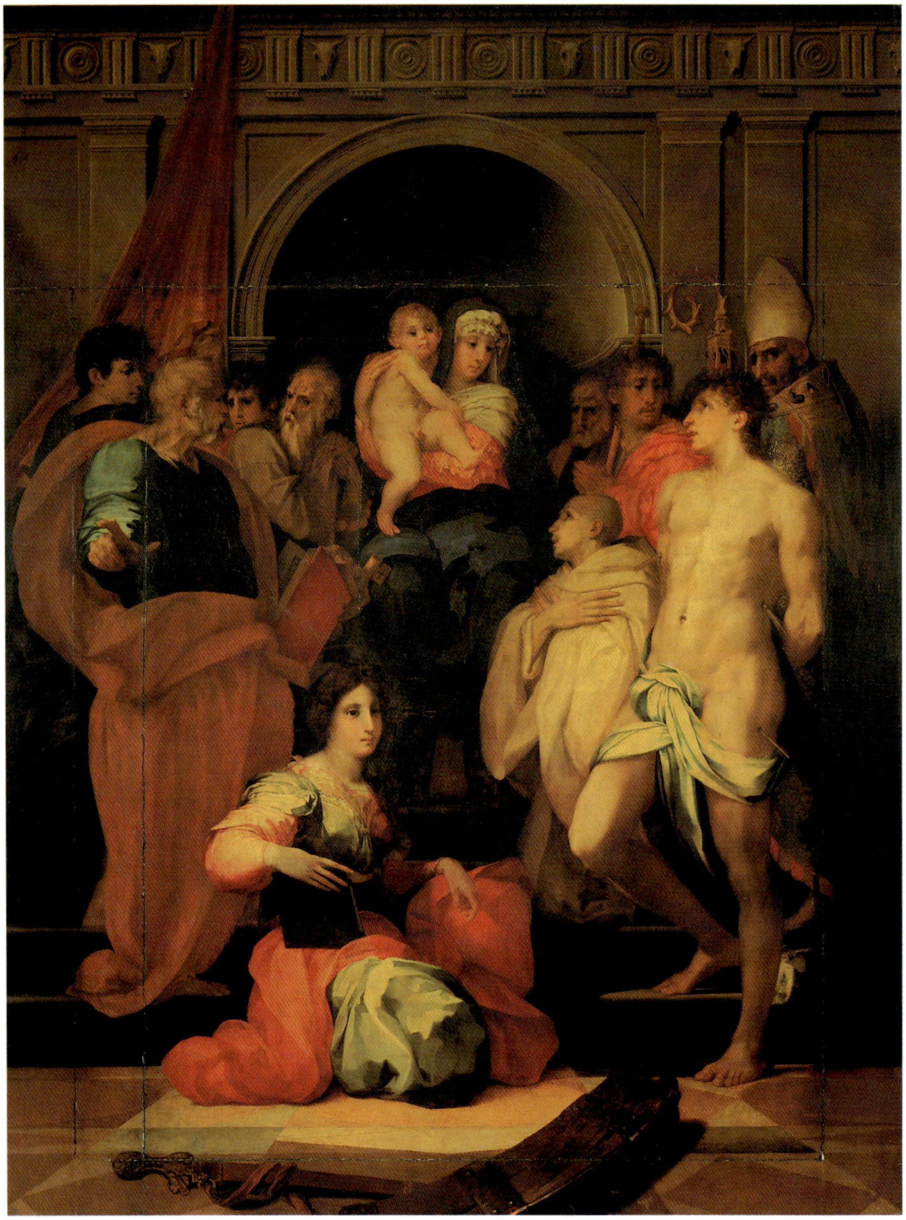

92, 93. Rosso Fiorentino
Madonna enthroned and ten saints
350x259 cm
Florence, Galleria Palatina

composition takes up some figurative ideas from the frescoes of Pontormo and Franciabigio in the Chiostrino dei Voti in Santissima Annunziata. From Pontormo's *Visitation* comes the idea of a group of figures, partly standing, partly seated or kneeling, arranged on the steps of the stairway in a circle that departs from the foreground and goes towards the centre of the composition. The latter is physically defined by the figure of the old priest, from whom a second group of bystanders departs, arranged in a semi-circle that moves towards the background. In this area of the painting, as in the *Marriage of the Virgin* by Franciabigio, there is an architectural structure. A reference to the Florentine figurative culture of the 15th century is discernible in the figure of St Joseph, whose profile and curly hair remind us of Donatello's marble *David* (1409, Florence, Bargello), a fact that might have justified the highly unusual choice of depicting the saint in his youth, thus infringing a consolidated iconographical tradition. The very young St Joseph is certainly one of the most striking iconographical peculiarities of the painting. Similarly unusual, as far as traditional representations of this theme are concerned, is the presence among the onlookers in the foreground of two people who certainly could not have witnessed the event: St Apollonia, whom we have already mentioned, and the figure behind her indicating the act of marriage with his right hand, identified as the Spanish St Vincenzo Ferrer. This figure has been seen as having a role of particular importance, since the facial features bear a striking resemblance to those of the person who commissioned the work, Carlo Ginori (G. Smith, 1976).

Among Rosso's paintings concerned with the representation of themes belonging to the religious iconographical tradition, the canvas of the Uffizi commonly known as *Moses defending the Daughters of Jethro* is a very special case, not least due to the rarity of the subject depicted. The title of the painting refers to an episode of Moses's youth narrated in the book

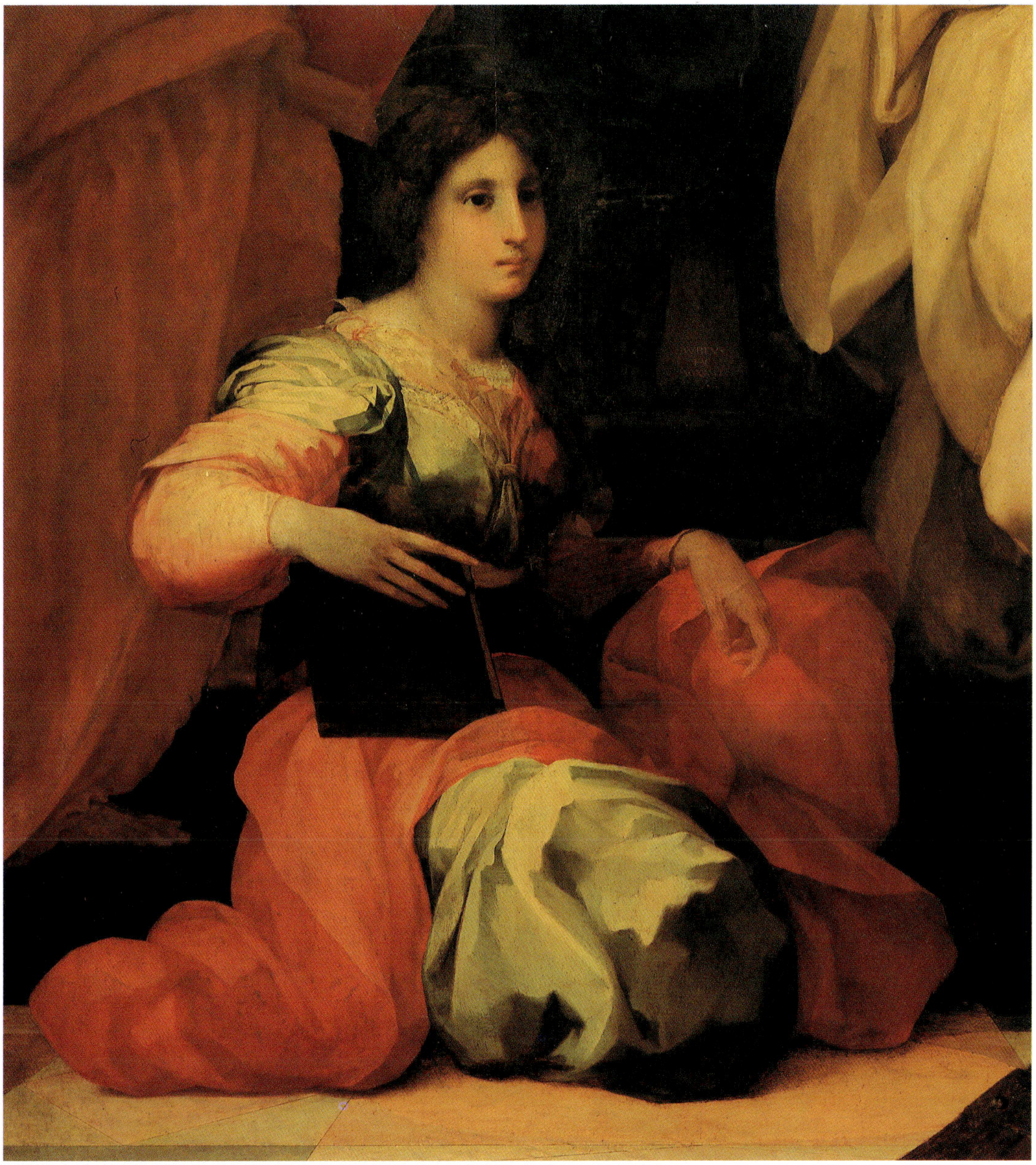

of *Exodus* (II, 16-22). The seven daughters of Jethro, priest of the land of Midian, while drawing water from a well and filling troughs to water their father's flock, are troubled by a group of Midianite shepherds who take advantage of the labours of the young women to water their own herds. Moses, sitting near the well, witnesses the scene; driving the Midianites away with threats he intervenes physically in defence of Jethro's daughters, who thanks to his help can finally water their flocks. In recognition of the meritorious action performed by the young Moses, Jethro gives him the hand of one of his daughters, Zipporah.

Interest in the events of Moses's life was very much alive in Florence from the beginning of the Quattrocento, due to the diffusion in humanistic circles of the *Life of Moses* written by the theologist and philosopher Filone Ebreo in the 1st century. Rosso must certainly have known of his writings if it is true he had "a sound grasp of philosophy", as Vasari testifies, and because in his pictorial representation he seems to have conserved the allegorical-moralizing connotation associated with the deeds of the young Hebrew, who is presented as the earthly dispenser of divine justice. Much more recently it has been noted how Rosso's extraordinary work represents one of the most significant expressions of the artist's broad reflection on the heroic theme of the triumphant victory of the moral force of virtue over the inexorably fickle action of fortune. The protagonist and at the same time principal emblem of this particular theme is the figure of Hercules, whose dynamic energy in facing adversity and danger is reproposed in the vigorous actions of Moses represented in the painting in question (A. Mugnaini, 1994). According to this recent theory, besides the episode that has traditionally given its name to the painting, two other events of Moses's youth are also shown in the painting, both of which took place in Egypt before he moved to the land of Midian and are often cited as magisterial examples of the young man's moral rectitude. In the centre of the scene Moses is

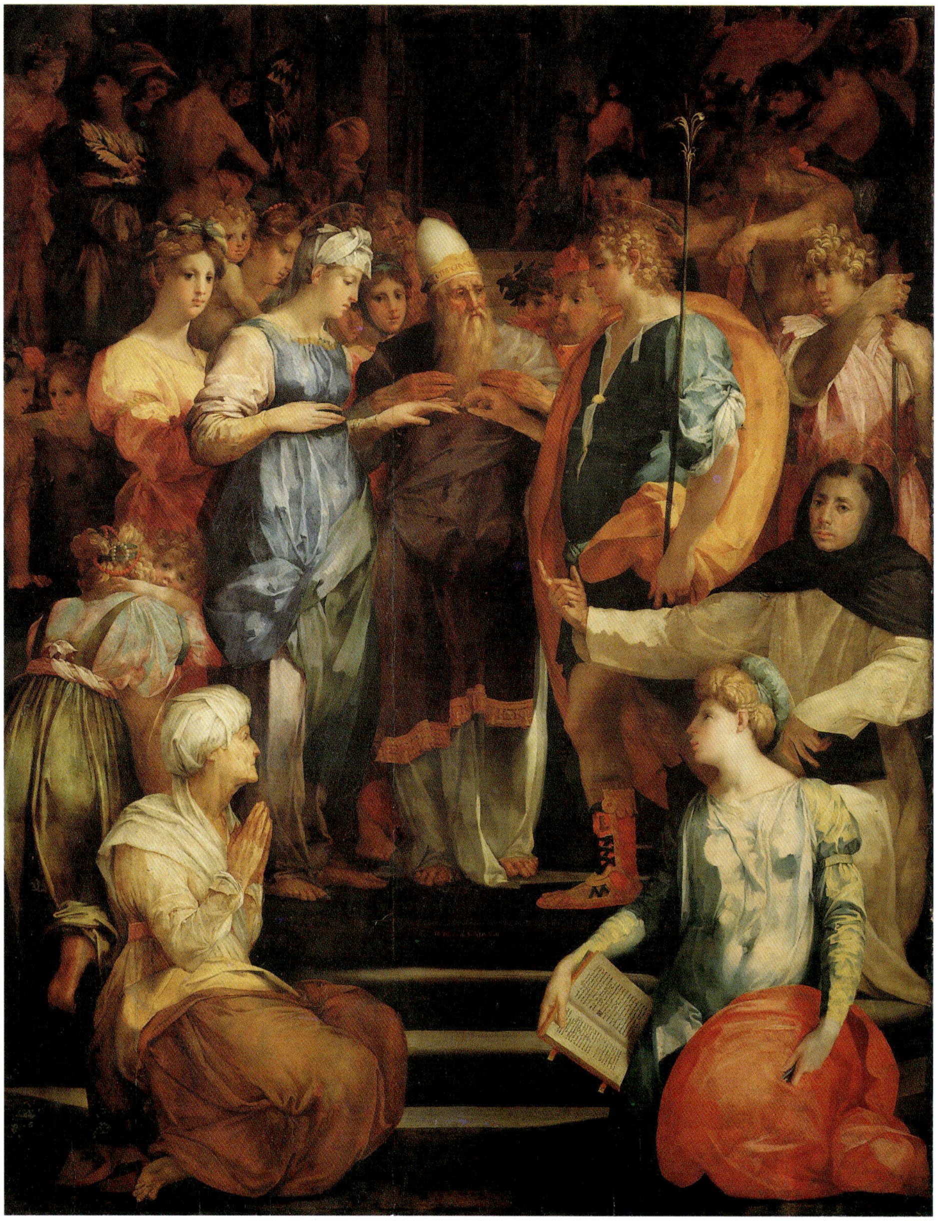

shown slaying an Egyptian who has attacked a Hebrew, one of his brethren; the latter is the person shouting to the right of the two figures engaged in combat (*Exodus*, II, 11-12). The episode of Moses who intervenes to stop a fight between two Hebrews (*Exodus*, II, 13-15) is suggested by the two bodies on the ground painted in the foreground. Behind the two scenes just described, the biblical hero is again seen running triumphantly towards Zipporah to tell her that the Midianite shepherds have been driven away from the well; in the background the sisters of Zipporah, not realizing what has happened, are still visibly frightened. The scene's division into three parts, comprising three main colour areas, is perfectly consistent with the complex arrangement of the painting's compositional structure, which overthrows the order reestablished after the eccentricity of Volterra. Here too the juxtaposition of complementary colours confers particular emphasis on the variety of geometrical forms in the single pictorial surfaces, helping to annul any effect of spatial depth and plastic modelling of the bodies. The deliberate overriding of perspective rules produces the effect of a crowding of people and objects in a single pictorial plane. In spite of the repaintings by one or more persons in addition to Rosso, clearly visible in certain areas of the painting (possibly those parts left unfinished by the artist), the most recent analyses have not doubted the authenticity of the work. It is certainly one of the works by Rosso most debated by contemporary critics, not only as regards the interpretation of the subject represented, but also as regards the definition of the place in which the work was executed.

A first orientation placed the painting between the end of 1523 and the beginning of 1524, assigning it therefore to the final phase of the second Florentine period, following which, as is known, Rosso took up residence in Rome. The unequivocal references to the two cartoons made by Michelangelo and Leonardo for the decoration of the Great Council Hall in Palazzo

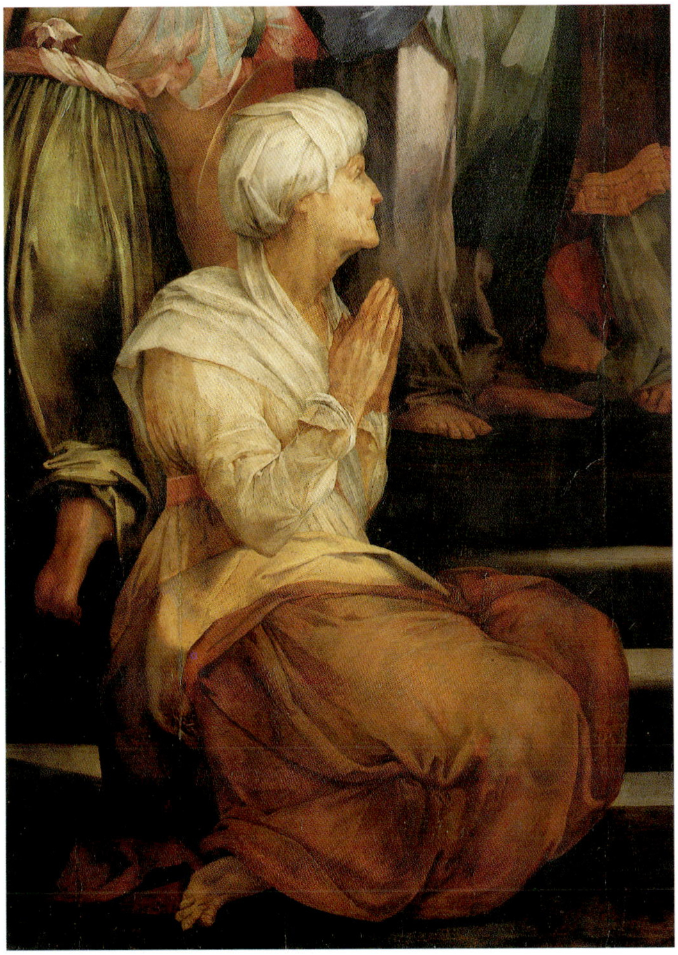

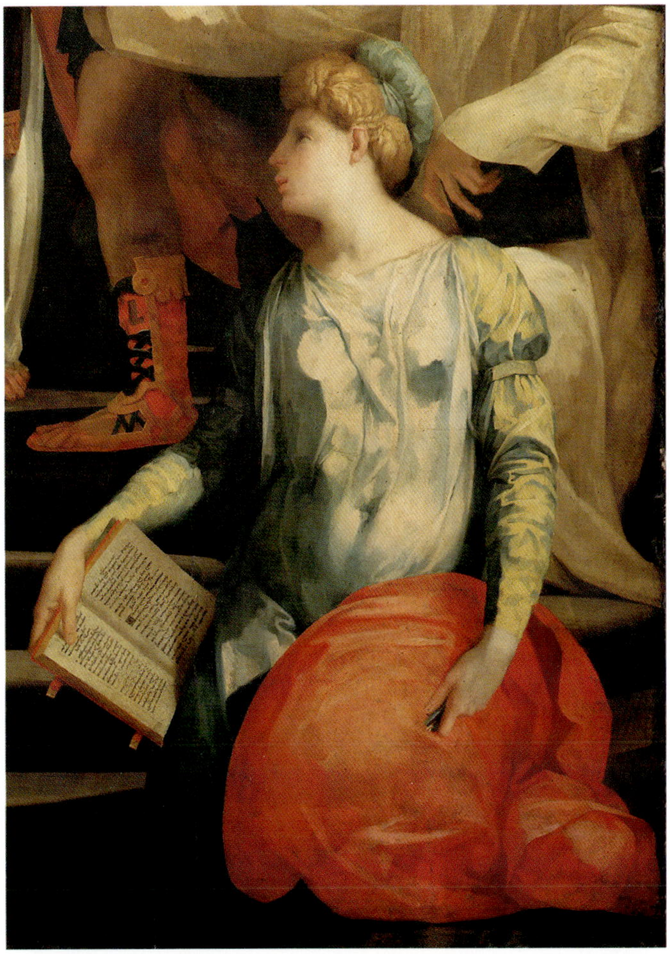

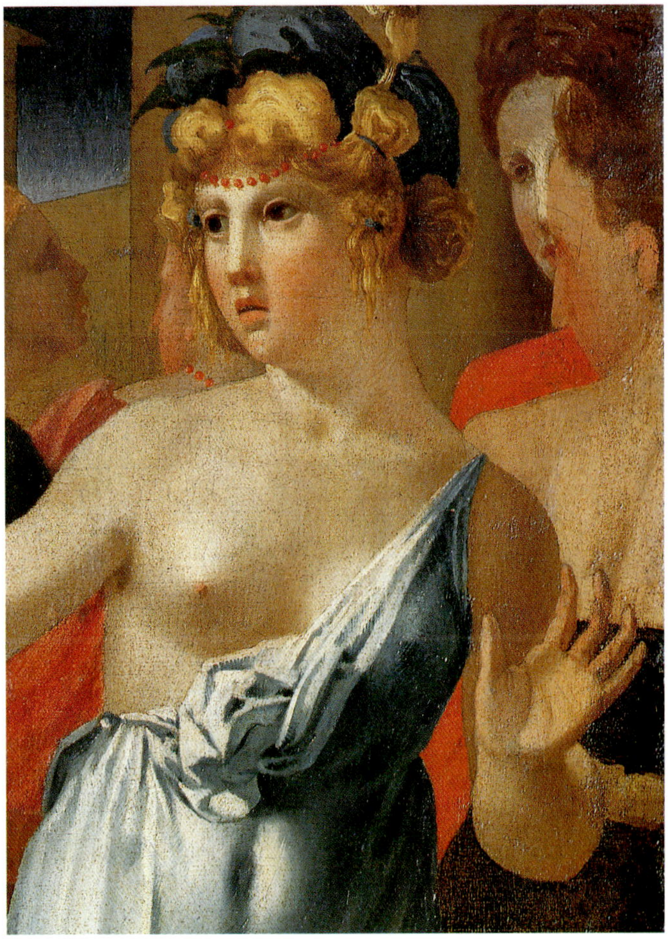

94-96. Rosso Fiorentino
Marriage of the Virgin
325x250 cm
Florence, San Lorenzo

97, 98. Rosso Fiorentino
Moses defending the Daughters of Jethro
160x117 cm
Florence, Uffizi

della Signoria are associated with Florentine artistic circles of the early 16th century. Rosso's canvas reproposes the extremely articulated compositional structure of Michelangelo's *Battle of Cascina*, displaying a broad range of nude figure poses which reflect the artist's predilection for counterpoise. The "emphasizing of gestures and clothing, and the impassioned savagery of the actions and expressions" (R. P. Ciardi), on the other hand, are associated with Leonardo's *Battle of Anghiari*. The Roman authorship of the painting and therefore a dating certainly after the years 1523-24 has been sustained by those who in the Uffizi canvas see references to classical works conserved in the great collections of Rome, to Michelangelo's Sistine Chapel, and to Constantine's Vatican Hall frescoed by pupils of Raphael under the direction of Giulio Romano (J. Peluso, 1976).

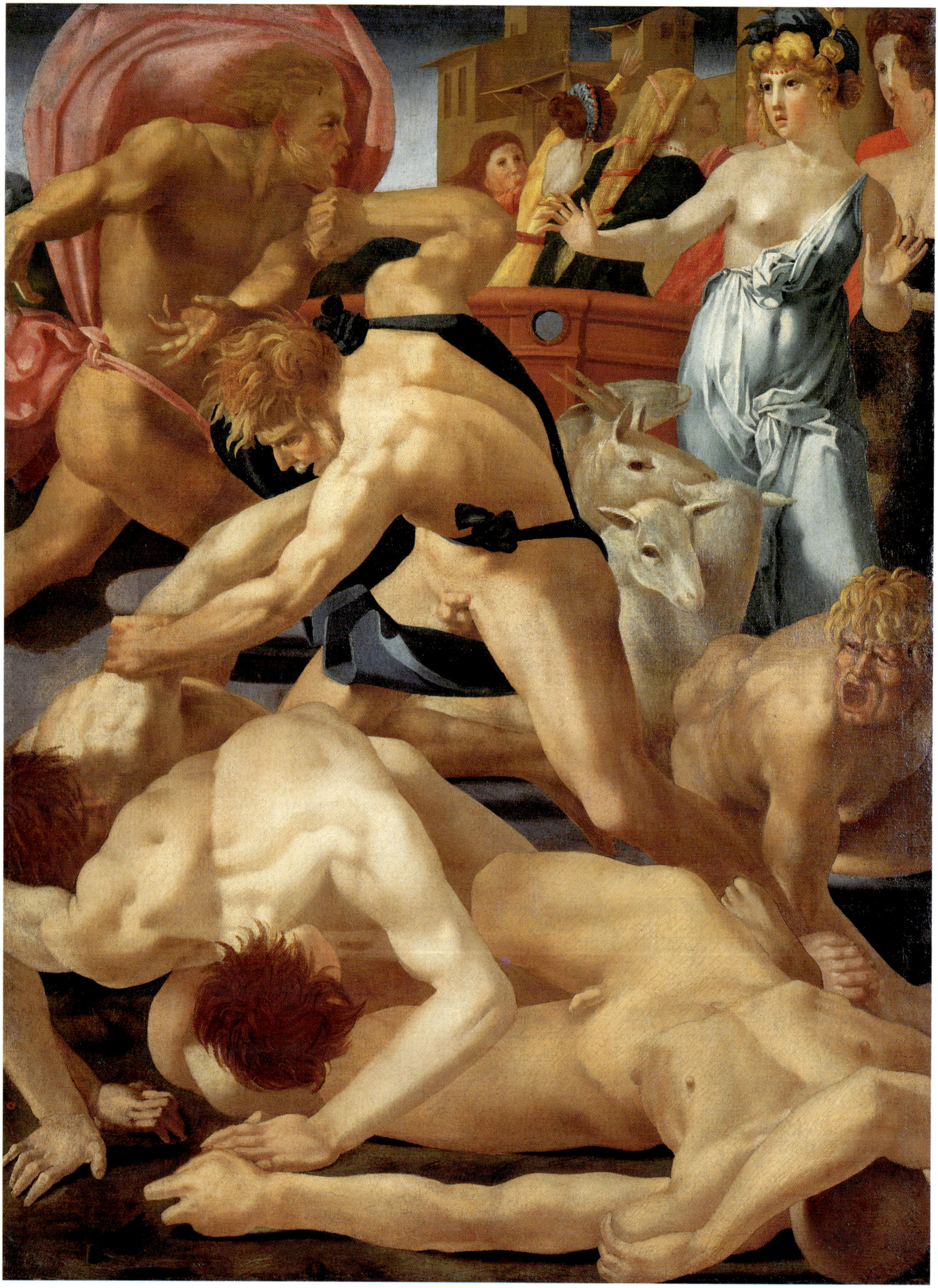

Rosso's final artistic period

From 1524 to 1527, the year of the sack, Rosso resided permanently in Rome, where the direct contact with the magisterial examples of Michelangelo's and Raphael's artistic maturity did not diminish his particular propensity for critical comparison with the fundamental precepts of the classical tradition. As the few surviving Roman works show, Rosso was perfectly familiar with the great artistic achievements of the two illustrious masters, yet he deliberately resolved to draw away from the figurative ideals of the Renaissance, arriving instead, as usual, at a type of pictorial representation that was wholly personal and independent.

On 26 April 1524, through the architect Antonio da Sangallo the Younger, Rosso received the commission to decorate the funerary chapel of Agnolo Cesi in the church of Santa Maria della Pace. The artist executed the frescoes with the *Creation of Eve* and *Original Sin*, but an argument with Sangallo prevented him from ever finishing the work.

Between 1525 and 1526 Rosso executed the remarkable painting of the *Dead Christ watched over by angels* for Bishop Leonardo Tornabuoni, a Florentine by birth, which is now in the Museum of Fine Arts in Boston. One of the striking formal characteristics of this painting is the highly refined modelling of the bodies, which become extraordinarily soft under the effect of a warm, intense light. The artist had clearly abandoned his taste for the sharp-cornered angularities that characterize the linear structure of his Florentine and Volterran works, which are, on the other hand, recalled in the varied range of complementary colours, with their delicate changing colour effects. Christ's naked body has undeniable similarities with works by Michelangelo: the Vatican *Pietà* and the *Risen Christ* from the church of Santa Maria sopra Minerva. What interested Rosso in this case, however, over and beyond the literal translation of Michelangelo's figurative ideas, was to exalt the beauty of the human body, which, following the example of the illustrious model, is accurately portrayed down to the very last detail. The total nakedness of Christ's body, not entirely free of a note of sexuality, forms part of this same tendency. The handsome young body, languidly and sensually slumped in a serene repose, and literally dominating the pictorial composition, retains little of the traditional iconography of the dead Christ, being closer to the pagan representation of the figure of Adonis. Indeed, the signs of Christ's martyrdom, which dramatically concluded the earthly existence of God's Son, are barely hinted at in the painting: the small wound in his side touched by the hand of an angel, the thin crown of thorns surrounding the head of the Redeemer, and the rod with the sponge soaked in vinegar and the nails, depicted along the lower edge of the painting.

Rosso's stay in Rome ended abruptly with the sack of 1527. Like many artists then present in the city, he was forced to move away. Initially he took refuge in Perugia, where he stayed with the painter Domenico Alfani; subsequently (1527-28), as we have seen, he painted the *Deposition* for the Confraternita di Santa Croce in Sansepolcro. On 1 July 1528 the Company of the Corpus Domini in Città di Castello commissioned him to do a painting of the *Christ in Glory*. As Vasari recounts, the sudden collapse of a wall in the room where Rosso was working seriously affected his health and caused work to be suspended. The work would be completed in around 1530 not in Città di Castello, where after the accident he had been involved in the artist refused to return, but in the nearby town of Sansepolcro, following the artist's participation in the decoration of the church of Madonna delle Lacrime in Arezzo. In the upper part of the painting, Christ stands out against the background between the figures of the Virgin and the three Maries; below, a crowd of common people are gathered. The unusual nature of this odd group of individuals which, as Vasari observed, included "Moors, gypsies and the strangest things in the world", failed to comply with the expectations of those who ordered the work and even in later times critical judgement has been far from positive. Today the painting is admired especially for the fine use of colours, typical of Rosso's artistic style, which have been brought to light following the recent providential restoration. The work is also seen as a masterly example of the artist's tendency to use iconologies that are particularly complex and difficult to interpret, in which much space is given over to the recovery of "archaic or archaizing ways of presentation" (R. P. Ciardi, 1994). The Gothic figurative typology of Christ in the mandorla, for example, reappears in the bright halo surrounding the Saviour, the edges of which are precisely marked by the profiles of the figures of the Virgin and St Anne. The lower area of the painting, both in its compositional structure and in some of the figures that populate the scene, has similarities with a 15th-century figurative model, the fresco of *The Tribute Money*, executed by Masaccio between 1424 and 1427 in the Cappella Brancacci of the church of Santa Maria del Carmine in Florence.

At the end of the 1520s, presumably following an appraisal of his own artistic fortune, Rosso nurtured the idea of leaving Italy for good. Indeed, the prestigious commissions for the Dei and Ginori families of Florence and the Cesi family of Rome, had been extremely successful. The works of the artist were more and more frequently commissioned in provincial centres and especially by confraternities. After a brief sojourn in Venice, probably with the help of Pietro Aretino, who Rosso had met in Rome between 1524 and 1525, in the autumn of 1530 the artist moved to France, where he soon succeeded in winning the favour of King Francis I. Here, having reached the height of his artistic career, he died prematurely in 1540. In the first two years of his stay in Paris

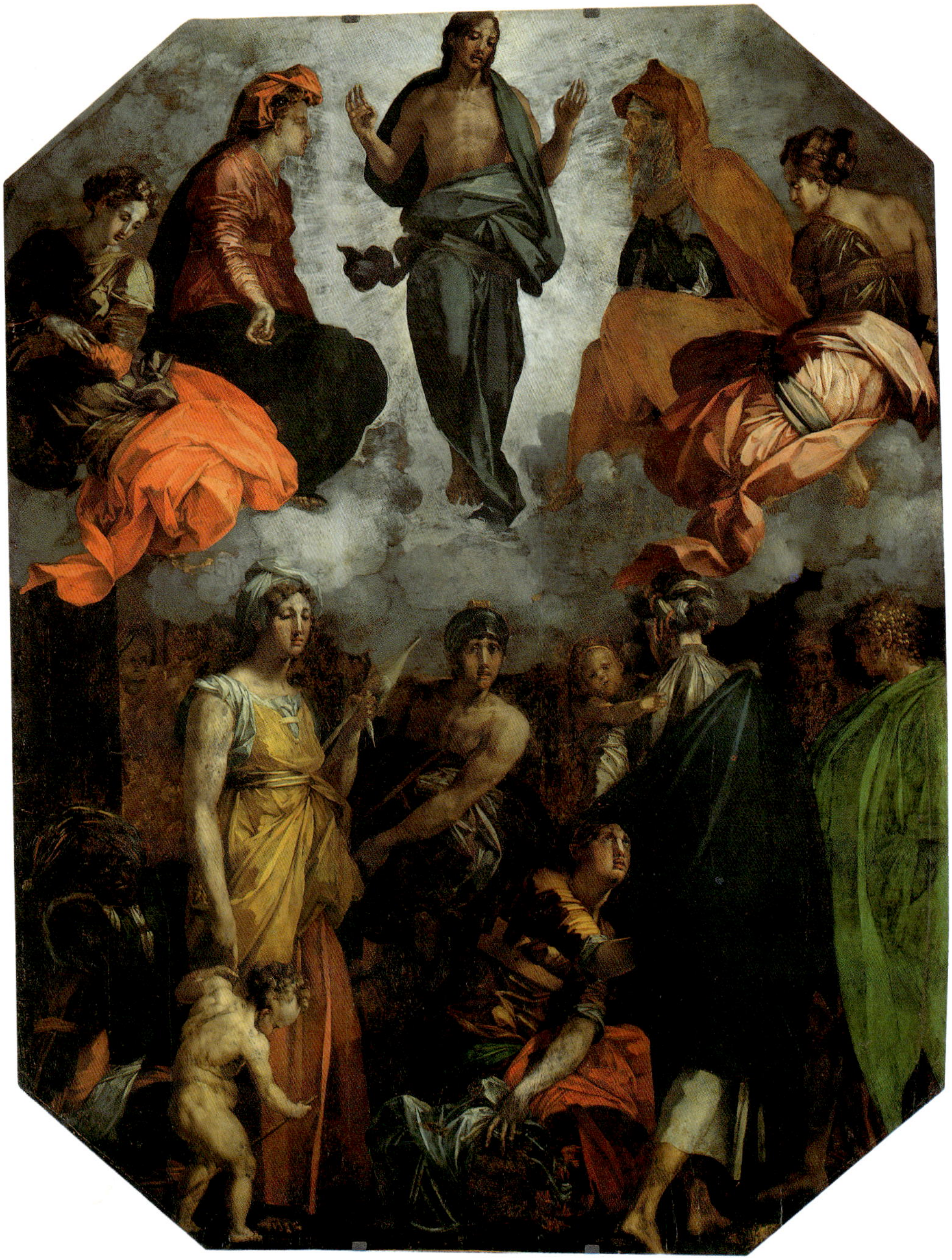

99. Rosso Fiorentino
Christ in Glory
345x258 cm
Città di Castello,
Cathedral

the king awarded him special honours and important commissions. From 1532 Rosso was involved in the decoration of Francis I's great gallery in the royal residence of Fontainebleau, which, according to the intentions of the king himself, was one of the most representative structures of the sumptuous architectural renovation of the old castle. Following the execution of the preparatory drawings, which the artist prepared while still in Paris, Rosso moved to Fontainebleau. Here, before dedicating himself entirely to the decoration of the gallery, he executed together with Primaticcio the two large frescoes with the *Loves of Vertumnus and Pomona* in a pavilion-shaped room, situated on the top floor of the building (1532-33). The work was destroyed when the pavilion was demolished in the 1760s. The registers of payments attest to the activity of Rosso at the gallery of Francis I from the July of 1533 until 1539; in 1536 the painter was referred to as director of all the works. A team of artists and skilled decorators assisted him in the execution of the frescoes and the elaborate stucco reliefs. Unfortunately, little is known of the cycle's original appearance, especially as far as the pictorial parts are concerned, owing to the modifications, radical repaintings and restorations that were made to the originals even quite soon after Rosso had begun this prestigious commission. However, much more faithful to the original works are the contemporary copies of the preparatory designs and the prints that show the main subjects of the whole decoration. The cycle seems to be an allegorical celebration of the life of Francis I, although a detailed understanding of the cycle's iconographical significance is still an open question.

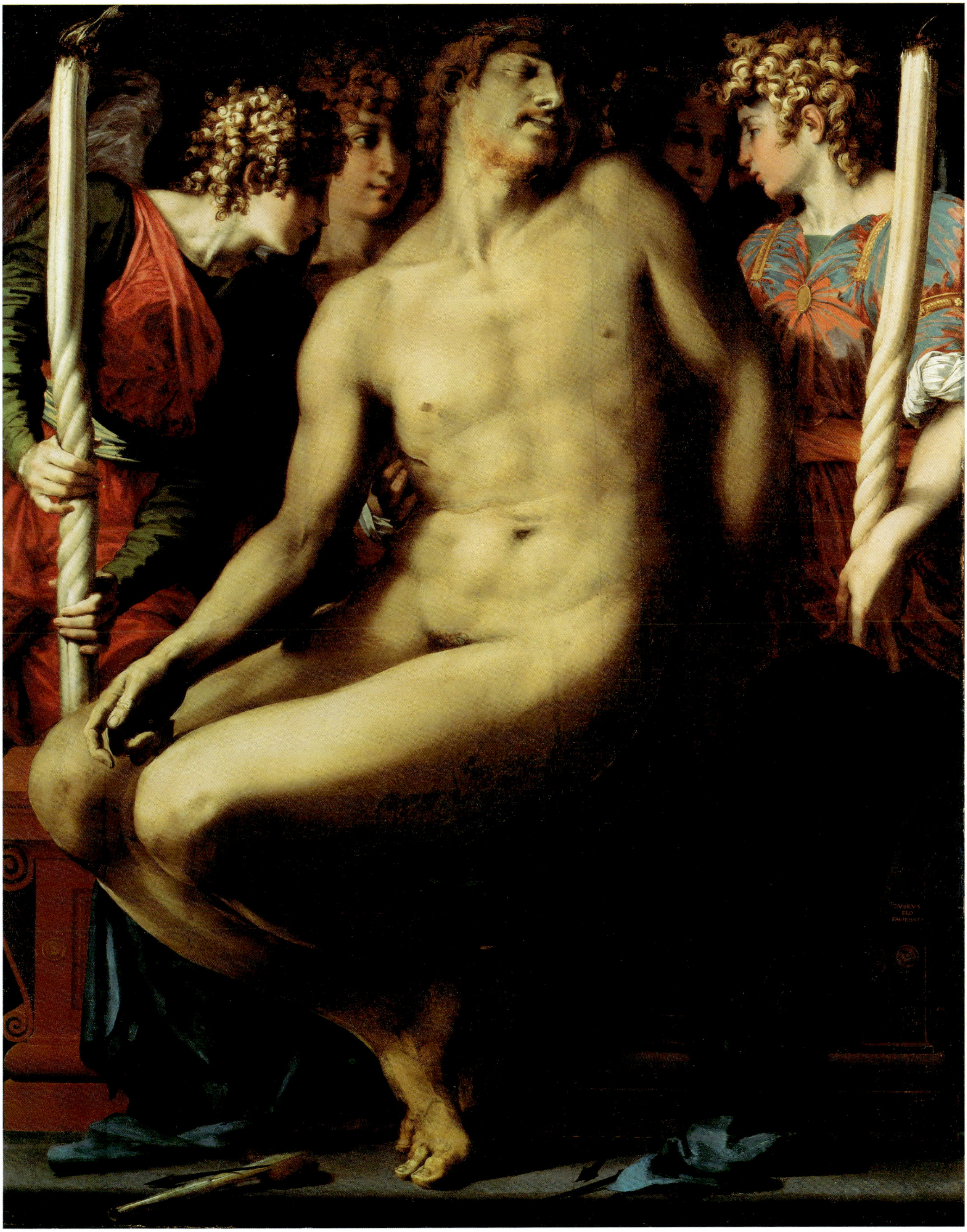

100. Rosso Fiorentino
Dead Christ watched over by angels
133.5x104 cm
Boston, Museum of Fine Arts

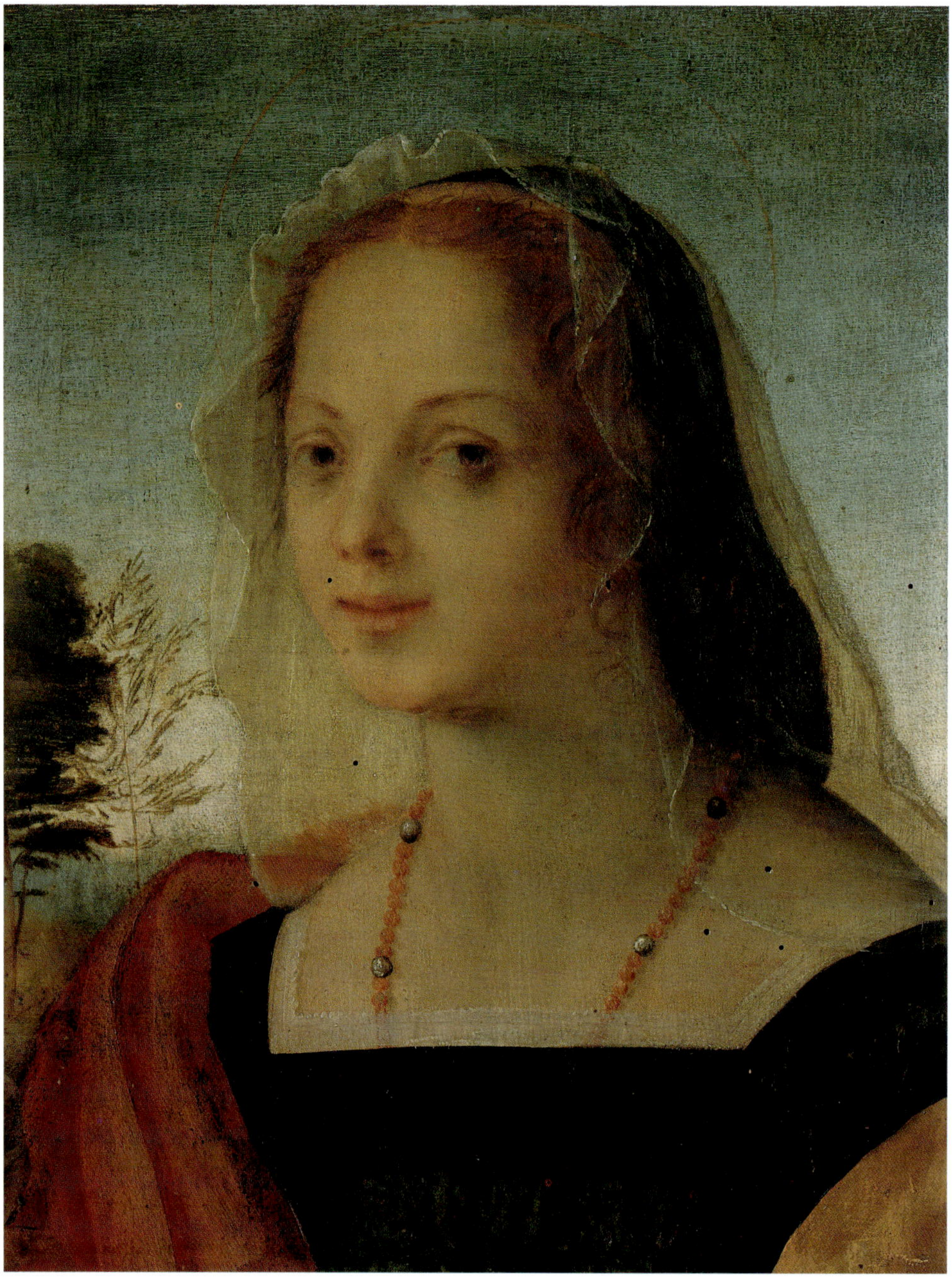

Three portraits by Rosso

In the series of extraordinary portraits that considerably enrich Rosso's pictorial production, the female portrait of the Uffizi undoubtedly belongs to the artist's youth. Some scholars have seen a reference to the Florentine works of Raphael in the delicate expression of this young woman, who is portrayed against the barely hinted background of an open landscape. Others have noted in the painting the influence of Andrea del Sarto and in particular his female figures in the *Birth of the Virgin* of Santissima Annunziata, thus placing Rosso's painting in the years 1514-15. This dating is also suggested by the evident resemblance of the young woman's facial features with those of the apostles of the *Annunciation of the Virgin*, executed by Rosso between 1513 and 1514 for the same decorative cycle of the above-mentioned work by Andrea del Sarto. The painting contains touches of surprising artistic skill, for example in the rendering of the delicate transparencies of the veil covering the woman's head, behind which a slight golden aureola is just noticeable. Another touch of refinement can also be seen in the details of the dress: the white lace-

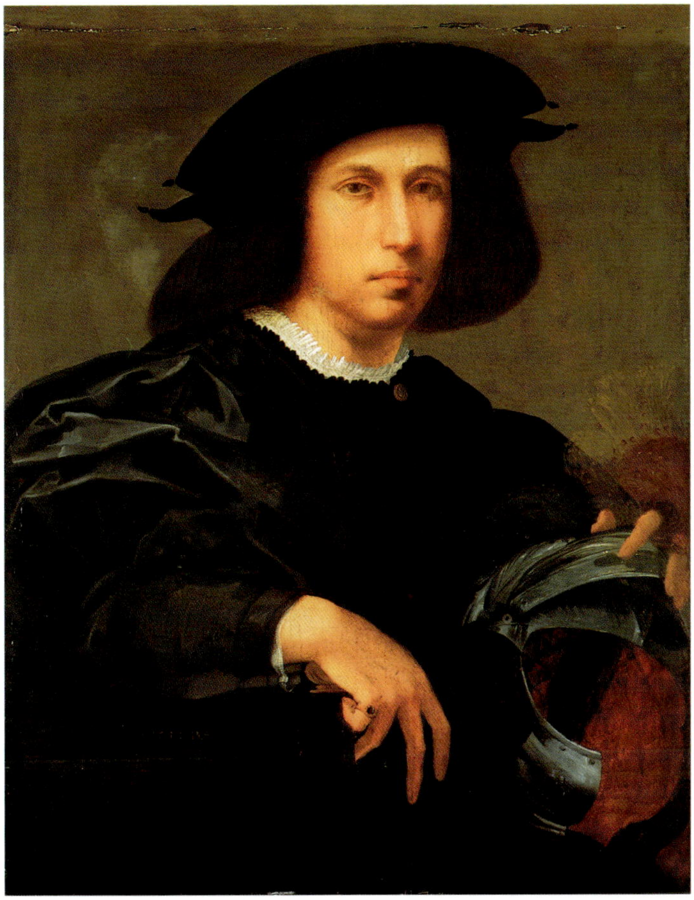

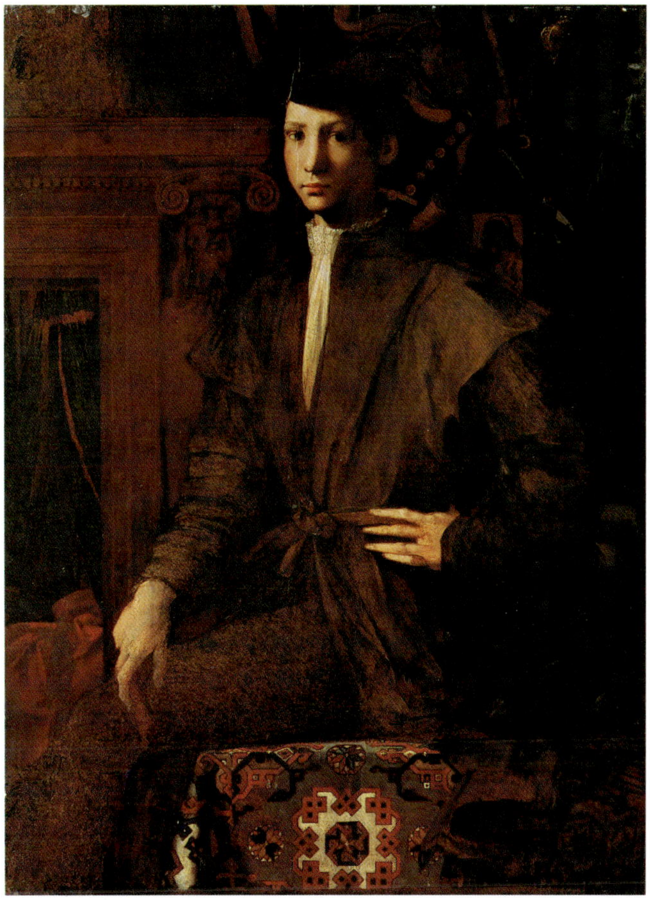

101. Rosso Fiorentino
Portrait of a Young Woman
45x33 cm
Florence, Uffizi

102. Rosso Fiorentino
Portrait of a Man with a Helmet
88.6x67.3 cm
Liverpool, Walker Art Gallery

103. Rosso Fiorentino
Portrait of a Young Man
120x86 cm
Naples, Gallerie Nazionali di Capodimonte

work that decorates the edge of the neckline and the delicate frieze beneath it. The same skill in the rendering of material qualities is seen in the *Portrait of a Man with a Helmet* of the Walker Art Gallery of Liverpool, in which emphasis is given to the silky sheen of the full right-hand sleeve and the metallic reflections on the helmet on which this enigmatic character rests his left hand. The Liverpool painting is the only signed portrait by Rosso: the inscription RUBEVS FACIEBAT on the arm of the chair on which the noble warrior is sitting was brought to light during the restoration of 1950, although even today it is difficult to decipher due to a heavy cancellation made possibly in the 17th century. The painting is usually dated to between the end of the second and the beginning of the third decade of the 16th century.

The *Portrait of a Young Man*, presently conserved at the Museo di Capodimonte in Naples, is believed to be the latest of the portraits attributed to Rosso. Its compositional structure, compared to the others, is in fact more complex, and is associated with the artist's Roman period. The painting has therefore been placed between the end of the Roman sojourn (1527) and the year 1529. In 1957, following the removal of the dark patina that covered the background of the painting, there emerged the fine objects that fill the room in which the young man is standing upright, proud and resolute: the red and green-striped curtain on the right, at whose upper edge a pomegranate is attached, the tapestry hanging on the rear wall, where a knight is portrayed with an old image of the Virgin and Child hanging from the bridle of his steed, and lastly the rich marble cornice with herma to the left of the young man, inside which hangs a baldachin. Another refined detail is the carpet in the foreground, whose rich geometrical design incorporates the colours used in the rest of the painting. Particularly striking among them is the ivory of the left side of the young man's face, the point of greatest brightness, and the white of his shirt puff.

Essential Bibliography

G. MAGHERINI GRAZIANI, *L'arte a Città di Castello*, Città di Castello 1897

G. VASARI, *Le Vite...*, ed. by G. Milanesi, Florence 1906

F. GOLDSCHMIDT, *Pontormo, Rosso und Bronzino. Ein Versuch zur Geschichte der Raumdarstellung*, Leipzig 1911

F. MORTIMER CLAPP, *Jacopo Carrucci da Pontormo*, New York-London 1916

C. GAMBA, *Il Pontormo*, Florence 1921

K. KUSENBERG, *Le Rosso*, Paris 1931

A. VENTURI, *Storia dell'Arte Italiana*, IX, 5, Milan 1932

B. BERENSON, *Pitture italiane del Rinascimento*, Milan 1936

C. GAMBA, "Rosso Fiorentino" in *Enciclopedia Italiana*, 1936

L. BECHERUCCI, *Manieristi Toscani*, Bergamo 1944

G. NICCO-FASOLA, *Pontormo o del Cinquecento*, 1947

P. BAROCCHI, *Il Rosso Fiorentino*, Rome 1950

L. BERTI (ed. by), "Il Pontormo" in *Mostra del Pontormo e del Primo Manierismo Fiorentino* (catalogue), Florence 1956

J. SHEARMAN, "Rosso, Pontormo, Bandinelli and others at SS. Annunziata" in "The Burlington Magazine", 1960, pp. 152 ff.

G. BRIGANTI, *La Maniera Italiana*, Rome 1961

S.J. FREEDBERG, *Painting of the High Renaissance in Rome and Florence*, Cambridge (Massachusetts) 1961

L. BECHERUCCI, "Manierismo" in *Enciclopedia Universale dell'Arte*, 1962

F. ZERI, "Eccentrici fiorentini" in "Bollettino d'Arte", 1962, 47, pp. 216-236

E. BOREA, *Rosso Fiorentino*, Milan 1965

A. HAUSER, *Il Manierismo*, Turin 1965

J. SHEARMAN, "The Dead Christ by Rosso Fiorentino" in "Boston Museum Bulletin", 1966, 64, 338, pp. 148-172

J. SPARROW, "Pontormo's Cosimo il Vecchio: A New Dating" in "Journal of the Warburg and Courtauld Institutes", 1967, 30, pp. 163-175

A. CHASTEL, "La Galerie François Ier à Fontainebleau" in "Bulletin de la Société Nationale des Antiquaires de France", 1968, pp. 186-188

VARIOUS AUTHORS, "La Galerie François Ier au Château de Fontainebleau" in "Revue de l'Art", 1972, 16-17

J. KLIEMANN, "Vertumnus und Pomona: Zum Programm von Pontormos Fresko in Poggio a Caiano" in "Mitteilungen des Kunsthistorischen Institutes in Florenz", 1972, 16, pp. 293-328

L. BERTI, *L'opera completa del Pontormo*, Milan 1973

L. STEINBERG, "Pontormo's Capponi Chapel" in "The Art Bullettin", 1974, 56, pp. 385-399

J. F. PELUSO, "Rosso Fiorentino's *Moses defending the daughters of Jethro and its pendant*" in "Mitteilungen des Kunsthistorischen Institutes in Florenz", 1976, 20, 1, pp. 87-106

G. SMITH, "Rosso Fiorentino's *Sposalizio* in San Lorenzo" in "Pantheon", 1976, 34, 1, pp. 24-30

R. CORTI, "Pontormo a San Lorenzo: un episodio figurativo dello *spiritualismo italiano*" in "Ricerche di Storia dell'Arte", 1977, 6, pp. 5-47

G. SMITH, "*Moses and the Daughters of Jethro* by Rosso Fiorentino" in "Pantheon", 1977, 35, pp. 198-204

A. BRAHAM, "The bed of Pierfrancesco Borgherini" in "The Burlington Magazine", 1979, 121, pp. 754-765

M. G. BURRESI - A. CALECA, *Momenti dell'Arte a Volterra*, Pisa 1981

L. BERTI, "Per gli inizi del Rosso Fiorentino" in "Bollettino d'Arte", 1983, 68, pp. 45-60

E. DARRAGON, *Maniérisme en crise. Le Christ en gloire de Rosso Fiorentino à Città di Castello* (1528-'30), Rome 1983

J. COX-REARICK, *Dynasty and Destiny in Medici Art. Pontormo, Leo X and the two Cosimos*, Princeton 1984.

M. APA, *Pontormo. "La Visitazione" a Carmignano*, Albano Laziale 1984

S. NIGRO (ed. by), *Pontormo. Il libro mio*, Genoa 1984

D. TRENTO, *Pontormo: il Diario alla prova della filologia*, Bologna 1984

E. J. OLSZEWSKI, "The subject of Rosso's painting of Moses in the Uffizi" in "Source", 1984, IV, 1, pp. 1-6

F. GALLUZZI, "...veddi la bagatella. Su Pontormo a Poggio a Caiano" in "Bullettino storico empolese", 1985, 29, pp. 279-282

W. SIMEONI, "Il tabernacolo del SS. Crocifisso in San Michele a Pontorme" in "Bullettino storico empolese", 1985, 29, 5-6, pp. 273-277

T. LEONI ZANOBINI, "Cangiante del Rosso Fiorentino" in "Critica d'arte", 1986, LI, 10, pp. 92-96

E. A. CARROLL, *Rosso Fiorentino. Drawings, Prints and Decorative Arts*, Washington D.C. 1987

R. P. CIARDI - M. BOCCI - F. A. LESSI, *Il Rosso Fiorentino. Realtà e Visione*, Volterra 1987

V. GASTON, "The Prophet Armed. Machiavelli, Savonarola and Rosso Fiorentino's *Moses defending the daughters of Jethro*" in "Journal of the Warburg and Courtauld Institutes", 1988, 51, 88, pp. 220-225

W. E. WALLACE, "Il *Noli me tangere* di Michelangelo: tra sacro e profano" in "Arte Cristiana", 1988, 76, pp. 443-450

D. HAITOVSKY, "Pontormo's *Eleven Thousand Martyrs* and Leonardo's *Adoration of the Magi*" in "Source. Notes in the History of Art", 1990, 9, 3, pp. 11-18

J. WASSERMAN, "La Vergine e Cristo con Sant'Anna del Pontormo" in *Kunst des Cinquecento in der Toskana* Florence 1992

L. BERTI, *Pontormo e il suo tempo*, Florence 1993

R. P. CIARDI - A. MUGNAINI, *Il Rosso e Volterra*, Venice 1994

Index of Illustrations

Pontormo

Rosso Fiorentino

Other artists

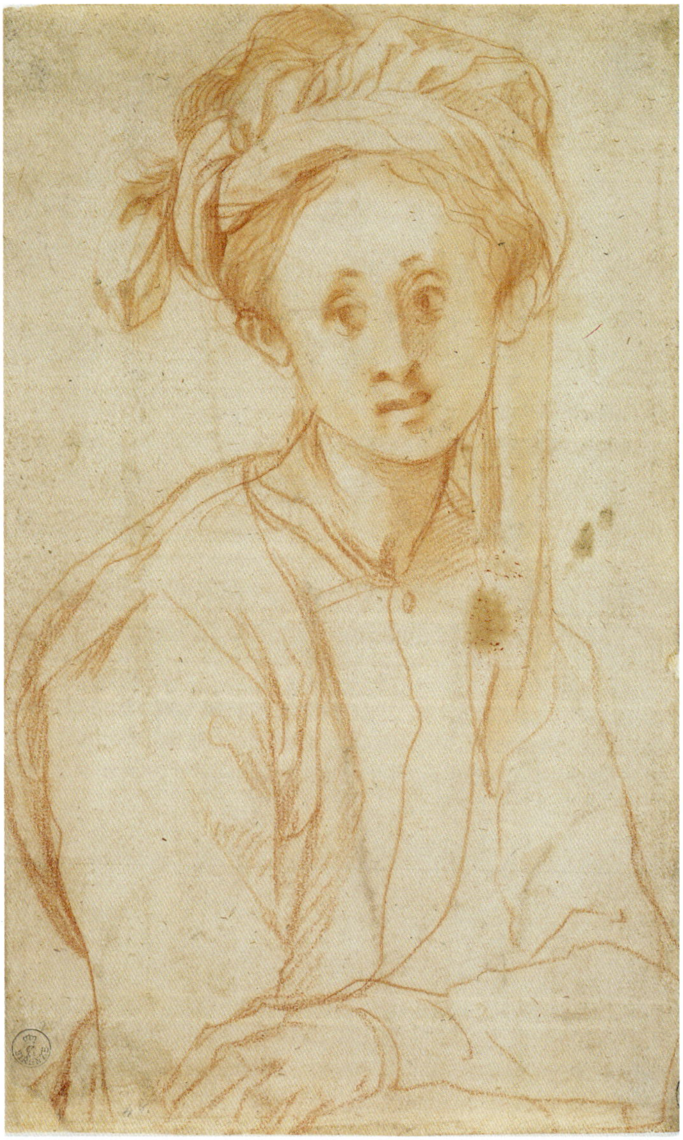

THE GREAT MASTERS OF ART

Andrea del Sarto
Benozzo Gozzoli
Bernini
Botticelli
Brunelleschi
Caravaggio
Carpaccio
Cimabue
Correggio
Della Robbia
Domenico Ghirlandaio
Donatello
Duccio
Filippo Lippi
Fra Angelico
Giotto
Giovanni Bellini
Leonardo da Vinci
Luca Signorelli
Mantegna
Masaccio
Michelangelo
Piero della Francesca
P. and A. Lorenzetti
Pontormo/ Rosso Fiorentino
P. Uccello/ D. Veneziano/ A. del Castagno
Raphael
Simone Martini
Titian

Forthcoming monographies:

Bronzino
Canaletto
Cellini
Perugino